GW00374092

Microsoft

PowerPoint 2000

At a Glance

Microsoft Press

Microsoft PowerPoint 2000 At a Glance

PUBLISHED by **Microsoft Press**
A Division of Microsoft Corporation
One Microsoft Way
Redmond, Washington 98052-6399

Library of Congress Cataloging-in-Publication Data
Microsoft PowerPoint 2000 At a Glance. Perspection, Inc.
    p.   cm.
   Includes index.
   ISBN 1-57231-944-5
   1. Microsoft PowerPoint (Computer file)   2. Computer graphics.   I. Perspection, Inc.
T385.M52225   1999
006.6'869—dc21   98-48186
                                              CIP

Printed and bound in the United States of America.

1 2 3 4 5 6 7 8 9   WCWC   4 3 2 1 0 9

Distributed in Canada by ITP Nelson, a division of Thomson Canada limited.

A CIP catalog record for this book is available from the British Library.

Microsoft Press books are available through booksellers and distributors worldwide. For further information about international editions, contact your local Microsoft Corporation office. Or contact Microsoft Press International directly at fax (425) 936-7329. Visit our Web site at mspress.microsoft.com.

For Perspection, Inc.
Writer: Nicole Jones Pinard
Managing Editor: Steven M. Johnson
Series Editor: Jane E. Pedicini
Production Editor: David W. Beskeen
Developmental Editor: Lisa Ruffolo
Technical Editors: Nicholas Chu; Craig Fernandez

For Microsoft Press
Acquisitions Editors: Kim Fryer; Susanne Forderer
Project Editor: Jenny Moss Benson

Contents

Start PowerPoint.
See page 6

Get Help with the
Office Assistant.
See page 17

Create consistent sides.
See page 24

*"How do I correct
mistakes?"*

See page 48

Change colors in a
color scheme.
See page 62

Modify a drawing object.
See page 80

Crop a picture.
See page 110

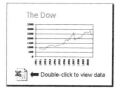

Embed an object.
See page 122

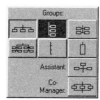

Structure an organization chart.
See page 136

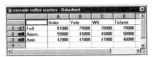

Import data into a datasheet.
See page 144

Select a chart type.
See page 150

Export slides to Word.
See page 176

"How do I add hyperlinks to objects?"

See page 184

Create slide transitions.
See page 204

Emphasize points in your presentation.
See page 220

Acknowledgments

The task of creating any book requires the talents of many hardworking people pulling together to meet almost impossible demands. For their effort and commitment, we'd like to thank the outstanding team responsible for making this book possible: the writer, Nicole Pinard; the developmental editor, Lisa Ruffolo of The Software Resource; the technical editors, Nicholas Chu and Craig Fernandez; the production team, Gary Bellig and Tracy Teyler; and the indexer, Michael Brackney.

At Microsoft Press, we'd like to thank Kim Fryer and Susanne Forderer for the opportunity to undertake this project, and Jenny Benson for project editing and overall help when needed most.

Perspection

Perspection

Perspection, Inc., is a software training company committed to providing information to help people communicate, make decisions, and solve problems. Perspection writes and produces software training books, and develops interactive multimedia applications for Windows-based and Macintosh personal computers.

Microsoft PowerPoint 2000 At a Glance incorporates Perspection's training expertise to ensure that you'll receive the maximum return on your time. With this staightforward, easy-to-read reference tool, you'll get the information you need when you need it. You'll focus on the skills that increase productivity while working at your own pace and convenience.

We invite you to visit the Perspection World Wide Web site. You can visit us at:

http://www.perspection.com

You'll find descriptions of all of our books, additional content for our books, information about Perspection, and much more.

About This Book

Microsoft PowerPoint 2000 At a Glance is for anyone who wants to get the most from their software with the least amount of time and effort. We think you'll find this book to be a straightforward, easy-to-read, and easy-to-use reference tool. With the premise that your computer should work for you, not you for it, this book's purpose is to help you get your work done quickly and efficiently so that you take advantage of Microsoft PowerPoint 2000 while using your computer and its software to the max.

No Computerese!

Let's face it—when there's a task you don't know how to do but you need to get it done in a hurry, or when you're stuck in the middle of a task and can't figure out what to do next, there's nothing more frustrating than having to read page after page of technical background material. You want the information you need—nothing more, nothing less—and you want it now! And the information should be easy to find and understand.

That's what this book is all about. It's written in plain English—no technical jargon and no computerese. There's no single task in the book that takes more than two pages. Just look up the task in the index or the table of contents, turn to the page, and there it is. Each task introduction gives you information that is essential to performing the task, suggesting situations in which you can use the task, or providing examples of the benefit you gain from completing the procedure. The task itself is laid out step by step and accompanied by a graphic that adds visual clarity. Just read the introduction, follow the steps, look at the illustrations, and get your work done with a minimum of hassle.

You may want to turn to another task if the one you're working on has a "See Also" in the left column. Because there's a lot of overlap among tasks, we didn't want to keep repeating ourselves; you might find more elementary or more advanced tasks laid out on the pages referenced. We wanted to bring you through the tasks in such a way that they would make sense to you. We've also added some useful tips here and there and offered a "Try This" once in a while to give you a context in which to use the task. But, by and large, we've tried to remain true to the heart and soul of the book, which is that information you need should be available to you *at a glance*.

What's New

If you're looking for what's new in PowerPoint 2000, just look for our new icon: **New** 2000. We've inserted it throughout this book. You will find the new icon in the table of contents so you can quickly and easily identify new or improved features in PowerPoint. You will also find the new icon on the first page of each section. There it will serve as a handy reminder of the latest improvements in PowerPoint as you move from one task to another.

Useful Tasks...

Whether you use PowerPoint for work, play, or some of each, we've tried to pack this book with procedures for everything we could think of that you might want to do, from the simplest tasks to some of the more esoteric ones.

...And the Easiest Way to Do Them

Another thing we've tried to do in *Microsoft PowerPoint 2000 At a Glance* is to find and document the easiest way to accomplish a task. PowerPoint often provides many ways to accomplish a single result, which can be daunting or delightful, depending on the way you like to work. If you tend to stick with one favorite and familiar approach, we think the methods described in this book are the way to go. If you prefer to try out alternative techniques, go ahead! The intuitiveness of PowerPoint invites exploration, and you're likely to discover ways of doing things that you think are easier or that you like better. If you do, that's great! It's exactly what the creators of PowerPoint had in mind when they provided so many alternatives.

A Quick Overview

You don't have to read this book in any particular order. The book is designed so that you can jump in, get the information you need, and then close the book, keeping it near your computer until the next time you need it. But that doesn't mean we scattered the information about with wild abandon. If you were to read the book from front to back, you'd find a logical progression from the simple tasks to the more complex ones. Here's a quick overview.

First, we assume that PowerPoint 2000 is already installed on your computer. If it's not, the setup wizard makes installation so simple that you won't need our help anyway.

So, unlike most computer books, this one doesn't start out with installation instructions and a list of system requirements. You've already got that under control.

Sections 2 through 5 of the book cover the basics: starting Microsoft PowerPoint; working with menus, toolbars, and dialog boxes; entering text and modifying text; rearranging and modifying slides; adding color and special effects to slides; drawing and modifying objects; and saving presentations.

Sections 6 through 8 describe tasks for enhancing the look of a presentation: inserting multimedia objects (clip art, pictures, sounds, and videos); playing sounds and videos; and inserting Microsoft Excel charts, Microsoft Word tables, organization charts, stylized WordArt text, and Microsoft Graph charts.

Section 9 describes tasks essential to completing a presentation and creating supplements for the speaker and the audience.

Sections 10 describes tasks for creating a Web presentation for use on the World Wide Web: creating hyperlinks to other slides and programs; creating a Web page; viewing presentations in a Web browser; and accessing Microsoft Office information on the Web.

Sections 11 and 12 describe tasks for preparing and presenting a slide show live and over the Web: setting up slide shows; creating custom slide shows; adding slide transitions and animations; setting up timing for a self-running slide show; recording a voice or music narration; and broadcasting and collaborating on a presentation over the Web.

Section 13 covers information that isn't vital to using PowerPoint, but will help you work more efficiently, such as setting PowerPoint options, recording and running macros, and customizing toolbars and toolbar buttons.

A Final Word (or Two)

We had three goals in writing this book. We want our book to help you:

◆ Do all the things you want to do with PowerPoint 2000.

◆ Discover how to do things you didn't know you wanted to do with PowerPoint 2000.

◆ Enjoy doing your work with PowerPoint 2000.

Our "thank you" for buying this book is the achievement of those goals. We hope you'll have as much fun using *Microsoft PowerPoint 2000 At a Glance* as we've had writing it. The best way to learn is by doing, and that's what we hope you'll get from this book.

Jump right in!

2

Getting Started with PowerPoint

Whether you need to put together a quick presentation of sales figures for your management team or create a polished slide show for your company's stockholders, Microsoft PowerPoint 2000 can help you present your information efficiently and professionally.

PowerPoint is a *presentation graphics program*: software that helps you create a slide show presentation. A slide show presentation is made up of a series of slides that can contain charts, graphs, bulleted lists, eye-catching text, multimedia video and sound clips, and more. PowerPoint makes it easy to generate and organize ideas, and it provides tools for creating the parts of an effective slide show. PowerPoint also makes it easy to create slide show supplements, such as handouts, speaker's notes, and transparencies.

When you're ready, you can share your presentation with others, even if they haven't installed PowerPoint. Show your presentation to people in your office or on the Internet. You can take advantage of the power of the World Wide Web from your planning stages, using the Web to gather information and download graphics, right up to showing your presentation and participating in online meetings. PowerPoint also includes powerful slide show management tools that give you complete control over your presentation.

Starting PowerPoint

Because PowerPoint is an integrated part of Microsoft Office 2000, you start and quit it the same way you would any Office program. You can use the Start menu, or, if you have installed PowerPoint as part of the Microsoft Office 2000 suite of programs, you can start PowerPoint from the New Office Document dialog box.

Start PowerPoint from the Start Menu

1. Click the Start button on the taskbar.

2. Point to Programs.

3. Click Microsoft PowerPoint.

TIP

Add a shortcut to the desktop. *Right-click the desktop, point to New, and then click Shortcut. Click the Browse button, locate and double-click the PowerPoint program file, click Next, and then click Finish. You can now double-click the shortcut on the desktop to start PowerPoint.*

Start PowerPoint as a New Office Document

1. Click the Start button on the taskbar, and then click New Office Document.

2. Click the General tab.

3. Click Blank Presentation.

4. Click OK.

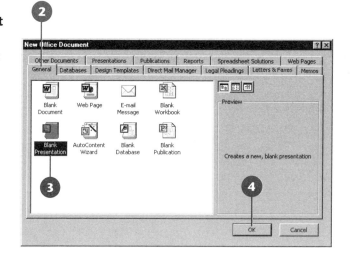

Creating a New Presentation

When you start PowerPoint, you see a dialog box listing your options for creating a presentation. You can use a *wizard* to guide you through the steps of creating a presentation. Using a wizard is the quickest way to create a presentation. You can also select a design *template*—a special document with predefined formatting and placeholder text—to give you a head start in creating a presentation. If you want to start from scratch, you can start with a blank presentation. You can also create a new presentation while working within PowerPoint.

Start a New Presentation

1. Start PowerPoint.

2. Click the option button you want to use to begin your presentation.

3. Click OK.

4. Follow the instructions that appear. These vary depending on the presentation option you chose.

Start a New Presentation Within PowerPoint

1. Click the File menu, and then click New.

2. Click the tab corresponding to the way you want to begin your presentation.

3. Click the icon you want to use as the basis of your presentation.

4. Click OK.

Helps you generate presentation content

Opens a list of templates that you can preview before selecting one

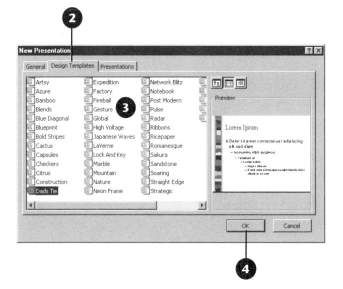

Creating a Presentation Using the AutoContent Wizard

Often the most difficult part of creating a presentation is knowing where to start. PowerPoint solves this problem for you. Use the AutoContent Wizard to help you develop presentation content on a variety of business and personal topics. An AutoContent presentation usually contains 5 to 10 logically organized slides. Edit the text as necessary to meet your needs. Many AutoContent presentations are available in Standard and Online formats.

Create a Presentation Using the AutoContent Wizard

1 Start PowerPoint, click the AutoContent Wizard option button, and then click OK.

2 Read the first wizard dialog box. Click Next to continue.

3 Click the presentation type you want to use. If you want to focus on one set of presentations, such as sales presentations, click the appropriate category button, and then click the presentation type you want.

4 Click Next to continue.

5 Click the presentation style you want to use. Click Next to continue.

6 Enter a presentation title and any items you want to include on each slide. Click Next to continue.

7 Read the last wizard dialog box, and then click Finish.

Presentation categories

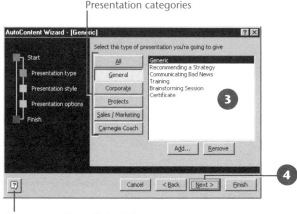

Click to open PowerPoint Help.

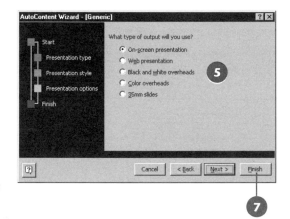

Choosing a Template

PowerPoint provides a collection of professionally designed templates that you can use to create effective presentations. Start with a template when you have a good idea of your content but want to take advantage of a template's professional design and formatting. Each template provides a format and color scheme so you only need to add text. You can choose a new template for your presentation at any point: when you first start your presentation or after you've developed the content.

TIP

Create a new presentation with a template anytime.
Click the File menu, and then click New. Click the Design Templates tab, click the template you want to use, and then click OK.

Create a Presentation with a Template

1. Start PowerPoint, click the Design Template option button, and then click OK.

2. Click the Design Templates tab.

3. Click the type of presentation design you want to create.

4. Click OK.

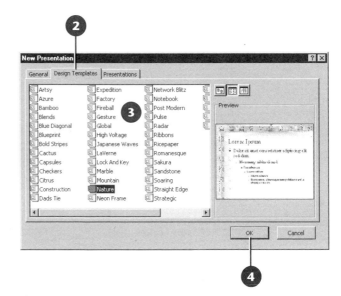

Apply a Template to an Existing Presentation

1. Click the Format menu or click the Common Tasks button on the Formatting toolbar, and then click Apply Design Template.

2. Click the template you want to apply to your slides.

3. Click Apply.

Viewing the PowerPoint Window

Title bar
The *title bar* displays the program name: Microsoft PowerPoint. If you have a presentation open and maximized, the name of the presentation appears, too.

Minimize button
The *Minimize button* shrinks the program window to a button on the taskbar.

Maximize button
The *Maximize button* expands the program window so it fills the entire screen. When you click this button, a Restore button replaces it. Click the Restore button to restore the window to its original size.

Menu bar
The *menu bar* contains the names of the available PowerPoint menus. The menus change depending on the task at hand.

Close button
The *Close button* closes the program window and quits the program.

Toolbars
The *toolbars* contain buttons you click to carry out commands. You can display additional toolbars as you need them.

Presentation window
The *presentation window* displays the presentation you are currently working on. It has its own Minimize, Maximize, and Close buttons.

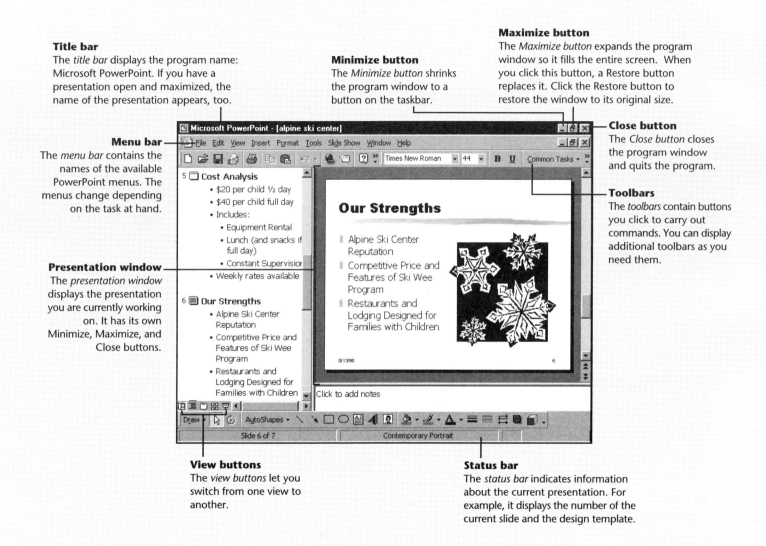

View buttons
The *view buttons* let you switch from one view to another.

Status bar
The *status bar* indicates information about the current presentation. For example, it displays the number of the current slide and the design template.

Opening a Presentation

You can open an existing presentation from the first PowerPoint dialog box you see when you start the program. You can also open an existing presentation after you have started PowerPoint using the Open dialog box. If you are not sure where a file is stored, you can search for it.

TIP

Open a presentation from the Startup dialog box. *Start PowerPoint, click the Open An Existing Presentation option button, select the presentation you want to open, and then click OK.*

TIP

Switch to another open presentation. *You can have more than one presentation open at a time—a useful feature when you want to copy slides from one presentation to another. To switch between open presentations, click the Window menu, and then click the presentation name you want or click the open presentation button on the taskbar.*

Open a Presentation

1. Click the Open button on the Standard toolbar.

2. Click one of the icons on the Places bar for quick access to an often-used folder.

3. If the file is located in another folder, click the Look In drop-down arrow, and then select the drive or folder containing the file you want to open.

4. If necessary, double-click the folder containing your presentation file.

5. Double-click the file you want to open.

Find a Presentation

1. Click the Open button on the Standard toolbar.

2. Type as much of the filename as you know. PowerPoint tries to match those characters.

3. Click the Tools drop-down arrow, and then click Find.

4. If necessary, click to select the Search Subfolders check box.

5. Click Find Now.

6. Double-click the file you want to open.

Preview of selected file

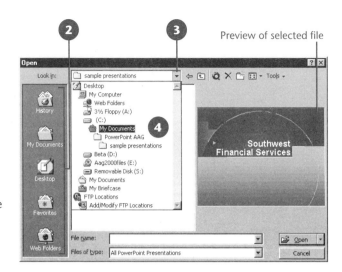

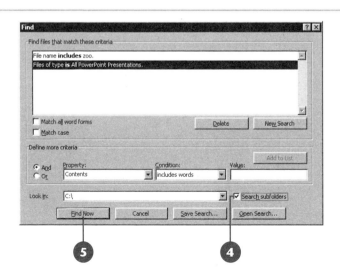

The PowerPoint Views

To help you during all phases of developing a presentation, PowerPoint provides five different views: Normal, Outline, Slide, Slide Sorter, and Slide Show. You can switch from one view to another by clicking a view button located next to the horizontal scroll bar.

Normal View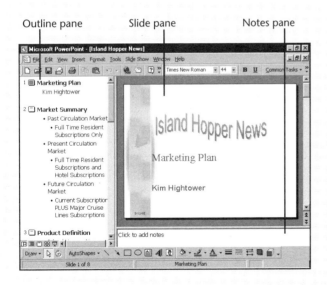

Use the Normal view to work with the three primary elements of a presentation—the outline, slide, and notes—each in their own pane. These panes provide an overview of your presentation and let you work on all of its parts. You can adjust the size of the panes by dragging

the pane borders. You can use the outline pane to develop and organize your presentation's content; the slide pane to add text, graphics, movies, sounds, and hyperlinks to individual slides; and the notes pane to add speaker notes or notes you want to share with your audience.

Outline View

Use the Outline view to develop your presentation's content. Click a topic with a slide icon to see a *thumbnail*, or miniature illustration, of the slide. Individual slides are numbered. A slide icon appears for each slide. You can add notes for the active slide if you want.

Outline pane   Slide pane   Notes pane

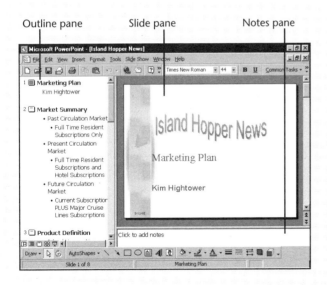

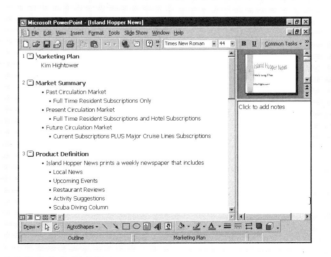

Slide View

Use the Slide view to preview each slide. Click the number of the slide you want to view in the outline pane. You can also move through your slides using the scroll bars or the Previous and Next Slide buttons. When you drag the scroll box up or down on the vertical scroll bar, a label appears that indicates which slide will be displayed if you release the mouse button.

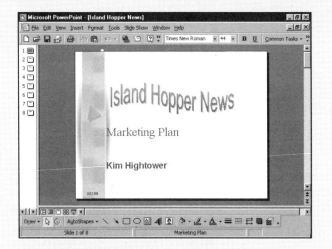

Slide Sorter View

Use the Slide Sorter view to organize your slides, add actions between slides—called *slide transitions*—and apply other effects to your slide show. The Slide Sorter toolbar helps you to add slide transitions and to control your presentation. When you add a slide transition, you see an icon that indicates an action will take place as one slide replaces another during a show. If you hide a slide, you see an icon that indicates the slide will not be shown during the presentation.

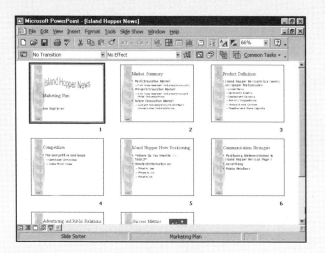

Slide Show View

Slide Show view presents your slides one at a time. Use this view when you're ready to rehearse or give your presentation. To move through the slides, click the screen or press the Enter key to move through the show.

Choosing Menu Commands

The PowerPoint commands are organized in menus on the menu bar. The menus are personalized as you work—when you click a menu name, you first see the commands you use most frequently. After a few moments, you see the entire list of commands. You can also open a *shortcut menu*—a group of related commands—by right-clicking a PowerPoint element.

TIP

Use a shortcut key to choose a command. *Press and hold down the first key and then press the second key. For example, press and hold the Ctrl key and then press S to select the Save command.*

SEE ALSO

See "Working with Toolbars" on page 16 for more information about using toolbar buttons.

Choose a Command from a Menu

1. Click a menu name on the menu bar.

2. If necessary, click the double-headed arrow to expand the menu, or wait until the expanded list of commands appears.

3. Click the command you want. If the command is followed by an arrow, point to the command to see a list of related options, and then click the option you want.

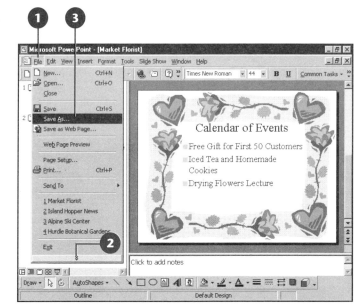

Choose a Command from a Shortcut Menu

1. Right-click an object (a text or graphic element).

2. Click a command on the shortcut menu. If the command is followed by an arrow, point to the command to see a list of related options, and then click the option you want.

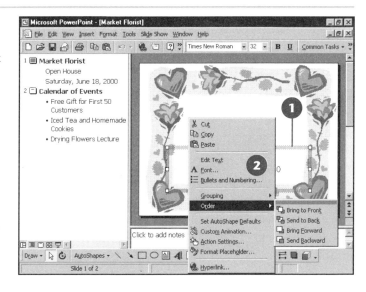

Choosing Dialog Box Options

A *dialog box* is a special window in which you provide additional information to complete a task. A dialog box opens when you click a menu command or button name followed by an ellipsis (...). A dialog box may contain one or more of the following components:

◆ Tabs. *Tabs* organize items into categories for easy access. Click a tab to display its contents.

◆ Option buttons. Click an *option button* to select that option. You can select only one option button in a group of related option buttons.

◆ Drop-down lists. A *drop-down list* provides available choices. Click the drop-down arrow to display the list, and then click the option you want. A scroll bar appears if the list is longer than the box.

◆ Text boxes. You type information directly into a *text box*.

◆ Check boxes. A *check box* precedes an option that can be on or off. Click a check box to turn the option on or off. A check in the box means the option is on; a clear box means it's off.

◆ Command buttons. A *command button* carries out an action. If the button name is followed by an ellipsis, another dialog box opens when you click the button.

◆ Preview area. The *preview area* allows you to preview your selections before closing the dialog box.

After you enter information or make selections in a dialog box, click the OK button to complete the command. Click the Cancel button to close the dialog box without issuing the command. In many dialog boxes, you can also click an Apply button to apply your changes without closing the dialog box.

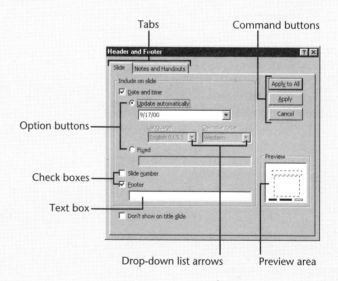

Working with Toolbars

PowerPoint includes its most common commands on toolbars. Click a toolbar button to choose a command. When PowerPoint starts, the Standard and Formatting toolbars are at the top of the window aligned on a single bar, and the Drawing toolbar is at the bottom, unless you've changed your settings. The toolbars are personalized as you work, showing only the buttons you use most often. Additional toolbar buttons are available by clicking the More Buttons drop-down arrow at the end of the toolbar. You can hide or display any toolbar, and you can move a toolbar around the screen so it's right where you need it.

TIP

Choose a toolbar quickly.
To quickly display the list of available toolbars, right-click a toolbar and then click the toolbar you want to use.

Choose a Command Using a Toolbar Button

1. If you are not sure what a toolbar button does, point to it to display a ScreenTip.

2. To choose a command, click the button or click the More Buttons drop-down arrow, and then click the button.

When you select a button from the More Buttons drop-down list, the button appears on the toolbar, which shows only the buttons you use most often.

Display or Hide a Toolbar

1. Click the View menu, and then point to Toolbars.

2. Click the toolbar you want to display or hide.

A check mark next to the toolbar name indicates that it is currently displayed on the screen.

The Standard and Formatting toolbars are displayed within a single bar.

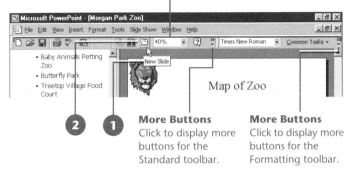

More Buttons
Click to display more buttons for the Standard toolbar.

More Buttons
Click to display more buttons for the Formatting toolbar.

Getting Help from the Office Assistant

One way to get helpful information about PowerPoint is to ask the Office Assistant questions. The *Office Assistant* is an animated Help feature that you can use to access information that is directly related to the task you need help with. You can turn this feature on and off whenever you need to. And to enhance its task-oriented capabilities, the Office Assistant will display its Presentation Assistant (via a light bulb icon). The *Presentation Assistant* extends the functionality of the Office Assistant by activating the *StyleChecker*, which provides tips on creating, publishing, and delivering your presentation.

Help button

Show the Office Assistant and Ask for Help

1. Click the Help menu, and then click Show The Office Assistant to display the Office Assistant.

2. Click the Office Assistant or click the Help button on the Standard toolbar.

3. Type a question.

4. Click Search.

5. Click a topic you want help with.

6. When you're done, click the Close button on the Help window.

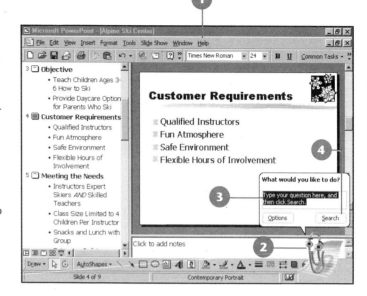

Hide the Office Assistant

1. Right-click the Office Assistant.

2. Click Hide.

TIP

Change the Assistant character. *You can change your Assistant. Right-click the Assistant and then click Choose Assistant. Click the Next and Back buttons to view the available Assistants. Click OK when you've found one you like. You might be asked to insert the original installation CD.*

TRY THIS

Animate the Assistant. *Right-click the Assistant, and then click Animate!*

SEE ALSO

See "Correcting Mistakes" on page 48 for information on specifying the style options the Presentation Assistant checks.

SEE ALSO

See "Accessing Office Information on the Web" on page 196 for information on getting help from the Microsoft Office Web site.

Get Help from the Presentation Assistant

1. Click the light bulb icon on the presentation window.

2. Click the option you want to apply to the slide.

   If necessary, select additional options.

3. If you don't want this tip in the future, click to select the Don't Show Me This Tip Again check box.

4. Click OK to cancel the Presentation Assistant.

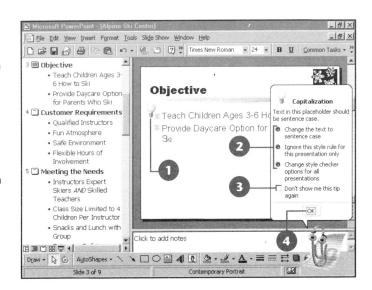

Turn Off the Office Assistant

1. Right-click the Office Assistant, and then click Options.

2. Click to clear the Use The Office Assistant check box.

3. Click OK.

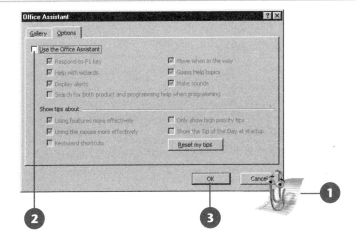

Getting Help by Topic

PowerPoint provides several ways to get instantaneous help. You can search for information on a particular topic using PowerPoint's Help topics, or you can use the Help pointer to get information on any PowerPoint object.

SEE ALSO

See "Getting Help from the Office Assistant" on page 17 for information on turning off the Office Assistant.

TIP

The Help button opens the Assistant or Help window. *Click the Help button on the Standard toolbar. You see the Assistant if it is turned on. If the Assistant is turned off, the Help window appears.*

TIP

Use the Help button. *Click the Help button on the title bar of a dialog box to get help with that dialog box.*

Get Help on a Particular Topic

1. Turn off the Office Assistant.

2. Click the Help button on the Standard toolbar.

3. Click the Answer Wizard tab.

4. Type what you would like to do, and then click Search. In the Topic list, double-click the topic you want to read about.

5. To see a table of contents, click the Contents tab. Double-click a Help book icon to open it, and then click a question mark icon to open that topic.

6. Click the Close button.

Get Help on a PowerPoint Object

1. Click the Help menu, and then click What's This?

2. Click the object about which you want more information.

3. Click anywhere on the screen to close the Help information box.

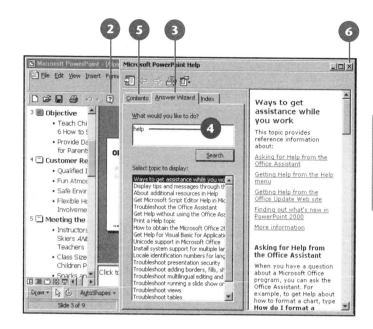

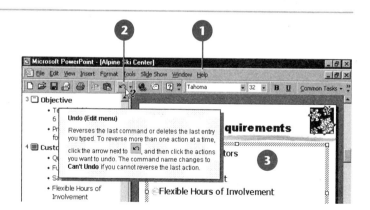

Saving a Presentation

When you create a PowerPoint presentation, save it as a file on a disk so you can work with it later. When you save a presentation for the first time or if you want to save the file with a new name, use the Save As command. When you want to save your changes to an open presentation, use the Save button on the Standard toolbar.

Save a Presentation for the First Time

1 Click the File menu, and then click Save As.

2 Click one of the icons on the Places bar to select a location to save the presentation file.

3 If necessary, click the Save In drop-down arrow, and then select the drive and folder where you want to save the presentation file.

4 Type the new presentation name.

5 Click Save.

The new filename appears in the title bar.

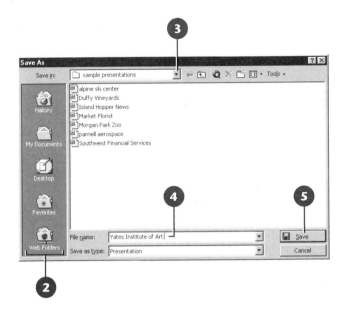

Save Changes to a Previously Saved Presentation

1 Click the Save button on the Standard toolbar.

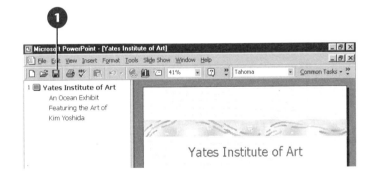

Detecting and Repairing Problems

At times you may determine that PowerPoint is not working as efficiently as it once did. This sometimes happens when you install new software or move files into new folders. Use the *Detect And Repair* command to improve performance by repairing problems such as missing files from setup and registry settings. Note that this feature does not repair personal files such as your presentations. If you try to access a feature or file, such as a template, not currently installed, PowerPoint will install the feature or file on first use.

TIP

Troubleshooting problems.
If the Detect And Repair command does not fix the problem, you might have to reinstall PowerPoint.

Detect and Repair Problems

1. Click the Help menu, and then click Detect And Repair.

2. Click Start.

    Insert the PowerPoint or Office CD in your drive.

3. If necessary, click Repair Office, and then click the Reinstall Office or Repair Errors In Your Office Installation option button.

4. Click Finish.

Perform Maintenance on Office Programs

1. In Windows Explorer, double-click the Setup icon on the PowerPoint or Office CD.

2. Click one of the following maintenance buttons.

    ◆ Repair Office to repair or reinstall Office

    ◆ Add Or Remove Features to determine which and when features are installed or removed

    ◆ Remove Office to uninstall Office

3. Follow the wizard instructions to complete the maintenance.

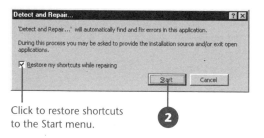

Click to restore shortcuts to the Start menu.

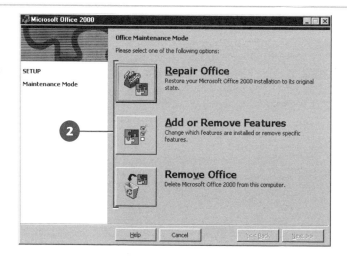

Closing a Presentation and Quitting PowerPoint

After you finish working on a presentation, you can close it. Closing a file makes more computer memory available for other activities. Closing a presentation is different from quitting PowerPoint: after you close a presentation, PowerPoint is still running. When you're finished using PowerPoint, you can quit the program. To protect your files, always quit PowerPoint before turning off the computer.

Close button

SEE ALSO

See "Saving a Presentation" on page 20 for more information about saving your presentation.

Close a Presentation

1. Click the Close button on the presentation window, or click the File menu, and then click Close.

2. If you have made changes to any open files since last saving them, a dialog box opens, asking if you want to save changes. Click Yes to save any changes, or click No to ignore your changes.

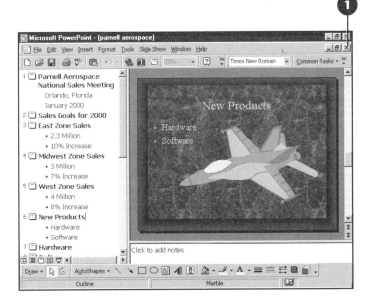

Quit PowerPoint

1. Click the Close button on the PowerPoint window, or click the File menu, and then click Exit.

2. If you have made changes to any open files since last saving them, a dialog box opens asking if you want to save changes. Click Yes to save any changes, or click No to ignore your changes.

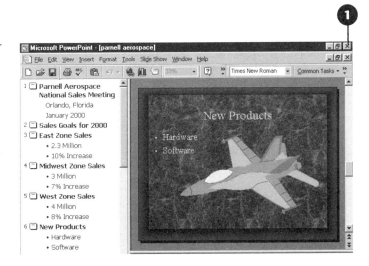

3

Developing a Presentation

Before you can create a slide presentation that includes text, charts, graphs, and pictures, you need to learn a few fundamentals about working with objects in Microsoft PowerPoint 2000.

Building a Presentation with Objects

Objects are the building blocks of a slide. Almost everything that you place on a slide is an *object*—any item with characteristics that you can resize, move, modify, and format. Whether the object is text, a picture, or an animated effect, you can create your slides by manipulating each of these objects with the same basic set of skills.

- ◆ Select an object so that you can work with it.

- ◆ Resize and move an object.

- ◆ Format an object.

- ◆ Delete an object.

Creating Consistent Slides

You need to arrange the objects on your slides in a visually meaningful way so that others can understand your presentation. PowerPoint's *AutoLayout* feature helps you arrange objects on your slide in a consistent manner. Choose from the 24 AutoLayouts designed to accommodate the most common slide arrangements. When you create a new slide, you apply an AutoLayout to it. You see design elements and place-holders for text and other objects. You can also apply an AutoLayout to an existing slide at any time. When you change a slide's AutoLayout, you keep existing information. PowerPoint applies the new AutoLayout, and you can arrange the placeholders the way you want them.

Insert a New Slide

1. Click the New Slide button on the Standard toolbar.

2. Click the AutoLayout you want to use.

3. Click OK.

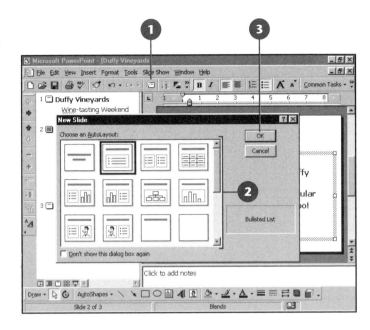

Apply an AutoLayout to an Existing Slide

1. In Normal or Slide view, display the slide you want to change.

2. Click the Common Tasks button on the Formatting toolbar, and then click Slide Layout.

3. Click the AutoLayout you want.

4. Click Apply.

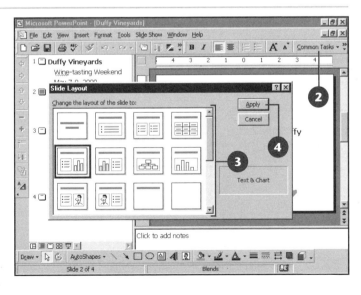

TIP

Use placeholders to enter information efficiently.

When you apply an AutoLayout to a slide, an arranged group of placeholders appears—one placeholder for each object on the slide. The placeholders include instructions for entering object contents.

SEE ALSO

See "Modifying a Bulleted List" on page 44 for more information on bulleted lists.

SEE ALSO

See Section 6, "Adding Multimedia Clips," for more information on clip art, media clips, and objects.

SEE ALSO

See Section 7, "Inserting Linked and Embedded Objects," for more information on tables and organization charts.

SEE ALSO

See Section 8, "Inserting Charts with Microsoft Graph," for more information on charts.

Enter Information in a Placeholder

◆ For text placeholders, click the placeholder and then type the text.

◆ For other objects, double-click the placeholder and then work with the accessory PowerPoint starts.

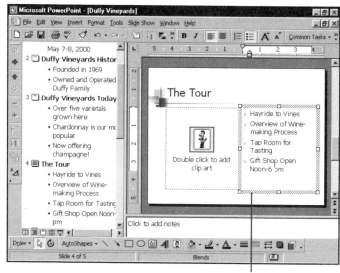

A placeholder is a border that defines the size and location of an object.

AUTOLAYOUT PLACEHOLDERS	
Placeholder	**Description**
Bulleted List	Displays a short list of related items
Clip Art	Inserts a picture
Chart	Inserts a chart
Organization Chart	Inserts an organizational chart
Table	Inserts a table from Microsoft Word
Media Clip	Inserts a music, sound, or video clip
Object	Inserts an object created in another program, such as an Excel spreadsheet or a WordArt object

Working with Objects

Once you create a slide, you can modify any of its objects, even those added by an AutoLayout. To manipulate objects, use Normal or Slide view. To perform any action on an object, you first need to select it. When you select a text object, the text is surrounded by a rectangle of gray dots called a *selection box*. When you select a graphic object, the graphic is surrounded by *sizing handles* (small white squares). You can resize, move, delete, and format selected objects.

TIP

Use the mouse button to select multiple objects. *To select objects in the same area, drag to enclose the objects you want to select in the selection box.*

Select and Deselect an Object

◆ To select an object, move the pointer (which changes to a four-headed arrow) over the object, and then click.

◆ To select multiple objects, press and hold Shift as you click each object.

◆ To deselect an object, click outside its border.

◆ To deselect one of a group of objects, press and hold Shift and then click the object you want to deselect.

Selection box   Four-header arrow pointer

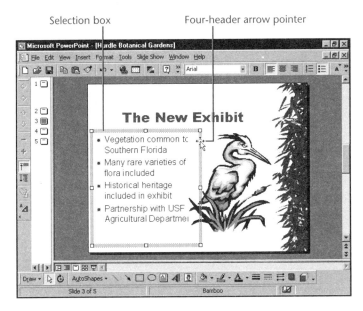

Resize an Object

① Move the pointer over a sizing handle.

② Drag the sizing handle until the object is the size you want.

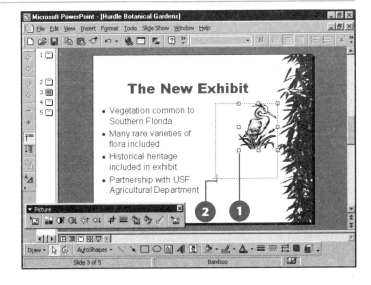

TIP

Select all objects on a slide. *Click the Edit menu, and then click Select All.*

TIP

Use the Tab key to select hard-to-click objects. *If you are having trouble selecting an object that is close to other objects, click a different object and then press Tab until you select the object you want.*

TIP

Use a corner sizing handle to create proportional objects. *To resize the object using the same proportions, press and hold Shift as you drag a corner sizing handle in a diagonal direction. This is especially useful when you are resizing a picture or clip art where changing the proportions might make the picture look distorted.*

TIP

Use keyboard shortcuts to cut, copy, and paste objects. *To cut an object from a slide, select the object and then press Ctrl+X. To copy an object, select the object and then press Ctrl+C. To paste an object on a slide, press Ctrl+V.*

Move an Object

◆ Using the mouse: Move the pointer (which changes to a four-headed arrow) over the object, and then drag it to the new location. To move unfilled objects, drag the border. You can move an object in a straight line by pressing Shift as you drag the object.

◆ Using the keyboard: Click the object, and then press the arrow keys to move the object in the direction you want.

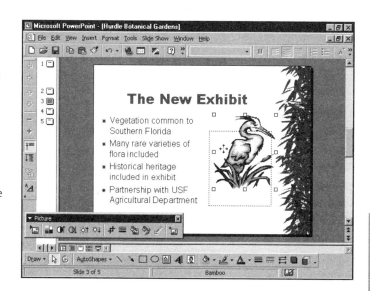

Delete an Object

1 Click the object you want to delete.

2 Press Delete.

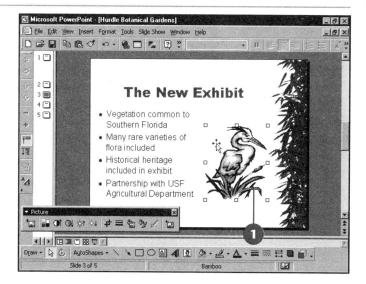

Developing Text

Your presentation's text lays the foundation for the presentation. Keep these basic presentation rules in mind when developing your text.

◆ Keep it simple.

◆ If you plan to present your slides to a large group, think about the people at the back of the room and what they can see.

◆ Keep the text to a minimum with no more than five bullets per slide and no more than five words per bullet.

◆ If you find a graphic that illustrates your point in a memorable way, use it instead of a lot of text.

PowerPoint provides several views that help you organize your text. You can work with text and other objects one slide at a time in Normal view or Slide view. You can work with all the presentation text on all slides at once in Normal view or Outline view.

PowerPoint also offers many text formatting features traditionally associated with word processing software. You can apply fonts and text attributes to create the look you want. You can set tabs, indents, and alignment. Finally, you can edit and correct your text using several handy tools, including style, grammar, and spelling checkers.

PowerPoint includes three types of text objects.

◆ *Title text objects*. Presized rectangular boxes that appear at the top of each slide—used for slide titles and, if appropriate, subtitles

◆ *Bulleted list objects*. Boxes that accommodate bulleted or numbered lists

◆ *Text box objects*. Boxes that contain non-title text that you don't want to format in bulleted or numbered lists—often used for captions

The first slide in a presentation typically contains title and text and a subtitle. Other slides often start with a title and then list major points in a bulleted list. Use text boxes only occasionally—when you need to include annotations or minor points that don't belong in a list, for example.

When to Enter Text on the Slide

Use the slide pane of Normal view or Slide view to enter text when you are focusing on the text or objects of one slide at a time.

Title text object

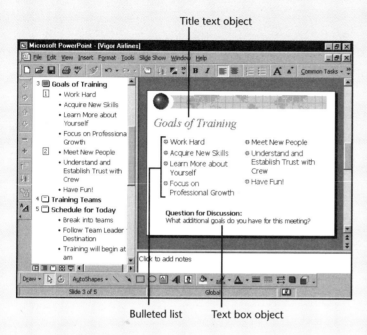

Bulleted list   Text box object

When to Enter Text in an Outline

When you are concentrating on developing presentation content, but not on how the text looks or interacts with other objects on the slide, use the outline pane of Normal

view or Outline view. These views let you see the titles, subtitles, and bulleted text on all your slides at a single glance.

The outline panes of Normal view and Outline view are particularly useful for reorganizing the content of your presentation and ensuring that topics flow well from one to the next. You can easily move presentation topics up and down the outline.

Title text in Outline view appears next to the slide number and slide icon.

Text boxes do not appear in Outline view.

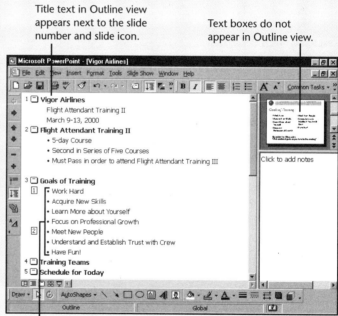

Bulleted lists appear in list format with different levels indented.

Entering Text

In Normal or Slide view, you type text directly into the text placeholders. A *text placeholder* is an empty text box. If you type more text than fits in the placeholder, the text is automatically resized to fit on the slide. The *AutoFit Text* feature changes the line spacing—or *paragraph spacing*—between lines of text and then changes the font size to make the text fit. You can also manually increase or decrease the line spacing or font size of the text. The *insertion point* (the blinking vertical line) indicates where text will appear when you type. To place the insertion point into your text, move the pointer over the text. The pointer changes to an I-beam to indicate that you can click and then type.

SEE ALSO

See "Editing Text" on page 32 for information on selecting text.

Enter Text into a Placeholder

1. In Normal or Slide view, click the text placeholder if it isn't already selected.

2. Type the text you want to enter.

3. Click outside the text object to deselect it.

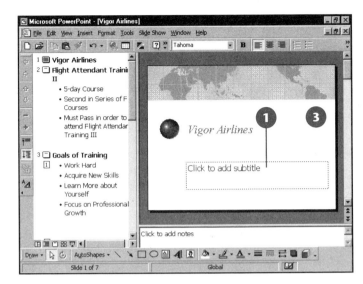

Insert Text

1. Click to place the insertion point where you want to insert the text.

2. Type the text.

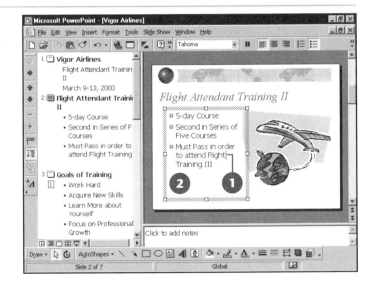

Use the insertion point to determine text location. *When entering bulleted text, be sure the insertion point is at the beginning of the line, and then press Tab to indent a level or press Shift+Tab to move back out a level.*

Insert symbols. *You can enter symbols in your text, such as © and ®, or accented characters, such as Ô, depending on the fonts installed on your computer. Click the Insert menu, click Symbol, click the Font drop-down arrow, click the font that contains the symbol you want, click the symbol, and then click Insert. Click Close when you're done.*

Use caution when you adjust line spacing. *When you decrease paragraph spacing, make sure you leave enough space for the height of each entire letter, including extenders such as the bottom of "p" and the top of "b."*

Enter Text in a Bulleted List

1 In Normal or Slide view, click the bulleted text placeholder.

2 Type the first bulleted item.

3 Press Enter.

4 Type the next bulleted item.

5 Repeat steps 3 and 4 until you complete the list.

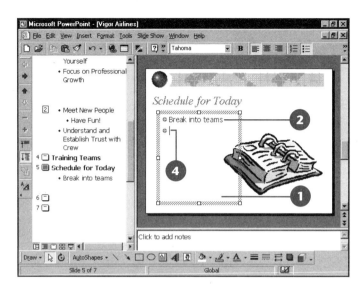

Adjust Paragraph Line Spacing

1 Click anywhere in the paragraph you want to adjust.

2 Click the Format menu, and then click Line Spacing.

3 Set the spacing options that you want.

4 Click OK.

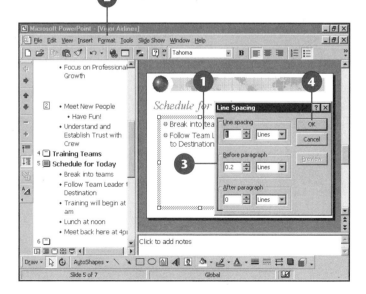

Editing Text

If you are familiar with word processing programs, you probably already know how to perform most text editing tasks in PowerPoint. You can move, copy, or delete existing text; replace it with new text; and undo any changes you just made. Some of the editing methods require that you select the text first. When you select text, the text is surrounded by a rectangle of gray slanted lines, which indicates that you can now edit the text.

TIP

Different ways to select text. *To select a single word, double-click the word. To select a paragraph, triple-click a word in the paragraph.*

TIP

Select bulleted text. *Position the mouse pointer over the bullet next to the text you want to select; when the pointer changes to ✛, click the bullet.*

Select Text

1. Position the mouse pointer to the left of text you want to highlight.

2. Drag the pointer over the text—just a few words, a few lines, or entire paragraphs.

3. Release the mouse button when you have selected all the text you want.

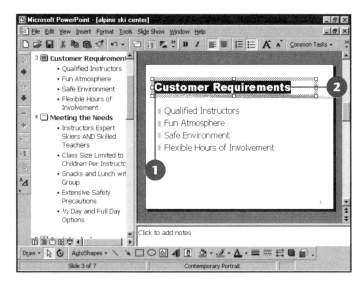

Move or Copy Text

1. Select the text you want to move or copy.

2. Move or copy the text the way you want.

   ◆ To move text short distances in an outline or on a slide, drag the text to the new location. To copy text, press and hold the Ctrl key as you drag the text.

   ◆ To move or copy text between slides, click the Cut or Copy button on the Standard toolbar, click where you want to insert the text, and then click the Paste button.

Cut, Copy, and Paste buttons

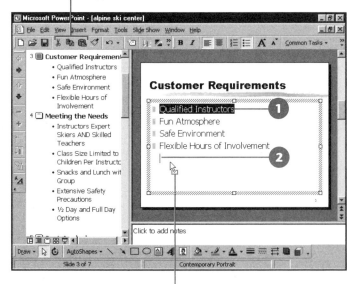

Mouse pointer to drag text

TIP

Use the Find command to search for text. *To find text in your presentation, click the Edit menu, click Find, type what you want to find, and then click Find Next.*

TIP

Delete text. *Select the text you want to delete, and then press Backspace or Delete.*

TIP

Use ScreenTips to help undo actions. *To find out what action PowerPoint will undo or redo, position the pointer over the Undo or Redo button. A ScreenTip appears, identifying the action.*

TIP

Redo one or more actions you just undid. *Click the Redo button on the Standard toolbar to redo one action. Click the Redo drop-down arrow on the Standard toolbar, and then click the actions you want to redo.*

SEE ALSO

See "Correcting Mistakes" on page 48 for more information on editing.

Find and Replace Text

1. Click the Edit menu, and then click Replace.

2. Type the text you want to locate.

3. Type the replacement text.

4. Click one of the following commands.

   - Click Find Next to find the next occurrence of the text.

   - Click Replace to find and replace this occurrence of the text.

   - Click Replace All to find and replace all occurrences of the text.

Click to replace only the instances of text that match the case of the entry you typed in the Find What box.

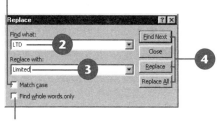

Click to replace only instances of text that are whole words.

Undo an Action

- To undo an action, click the Undo button on the Standard toolbar; click it repeatedly to undo previous actions.

- To undo multiple actions, click the Undo drop-down arrow on the Standard toolbar to view a list of the most recent changes, and then click the actions you want to undo.

List of actions to undo

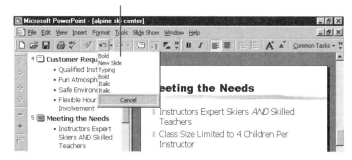

Developing an Outline

If you create your presentation using an AutoContent Wizard, PowerPoint generates an outline automatically. If you prefer to develop your own outline, you can create a blank presentation, and then type your outline in the outline pane of Normal view or in Outline view. As you develop an outline, you can add new slides and duplicate existing slides in your presentation. You can also insert an outline you created in another program, such as Microsoft Word. Make sure the document containing the outline is set up using outline heading styles. When you insert the outline in PowerPoint, it creates slide titles, subtitles, and bulleted lists based on those styles.

TIP

Outlining toolbar. *If the Outlining toolbar is not visible, right-click a visible toolbar, and then click Outlining.*

Enter Text in Outline View

1. In the outline pane of Normal view or in Outline view, click to place the insertion point where you want the text to appear.

2. Type the text you want to enter, pressing Enter after each line.

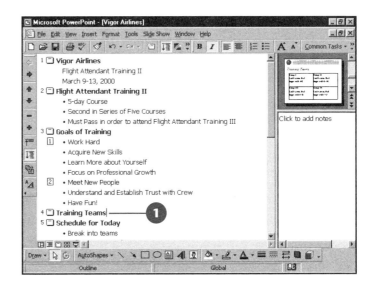

Add a Slide in Outline View

1. In the outline pane of Normal view or in Outline view, click at the end of the slide text where you want to insert a new slide.

2. Click the Insert New Slide button on the Standard toolbar, click a layout and click OK, or press Ctrl+Enter to insert a slide using the existing slide layout.

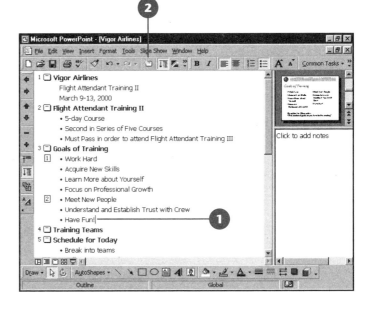

Show and hide formatting in Outline view. *Click the Show Formatting button on the Outlining toolbar to show or hide formatting.*

Different ways to delete a slide. *In Outline or Slide Sorter view, select the slide you want to delete, and then press Delete. In Slide view, select the slide you want to delete, click the Edit menu, and then click Delete Slide.*

Change the display view size. *Click the Zoom drop-down arrow on the Standard toolbar, and then select a view size.*

Open an outline from another program in PowerPoint. *Click the Open button on the Standard toolbar, click the Files Of Type drop-down arrow, click All Outlines, and then double-click the outline file you want to open.*

Duplicate a Slide

1. In the outline pane of Normal view or in Outline view, click the slide you want to duplicate.

2. Click the Edit menu, and then click Duplicate.

   The new slide appears directly after the slide duplicated.

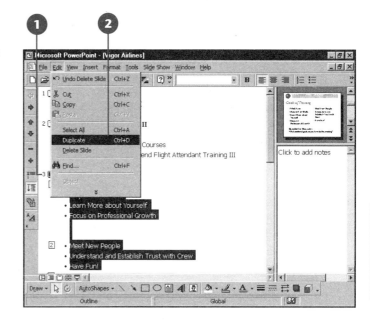

Insert an Outline from Another Program

1. In the outline pane of Normal view or in Outline view, click the slide after which you want to insert an outline.

2. Click the Insert menu, and then click Slides From Outline.

3. Locate and then select the file containing the outline you want to insert.

4. Click Insert.

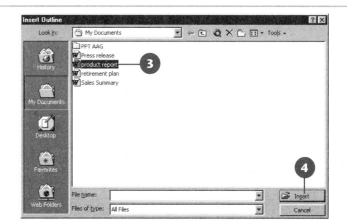

Indenting Text

Title text is usually the most prominent text object on a slide; next is subtitle text, and then body text, which you can indent or to which you can add bullets. You can indent paragraphs of body text up to five levels using the Promote and Demote buttons on the Formatting toolbar. In an outline, these tools let you demote text from a title, for example, to bulleted text. You can view and change the locations of the indent markers within a text object using the ruler.

Use the mouse to promote or demote text. *Move the mouse pointer over the bullet you want to promote or demote, and then when it changes to a four-headed arrow, drag the text to the left to promote it or to the right to demote it.*

Change the Indent Level

1. In Normal, Slide, or Outline view, click in the line of text you want to indent.

2. Click the Promote button on the Outlining toolbar to move the line up one level (to the left).

3. Click the Demote button on the Outlining toolbar to move the line down one level (to the right).

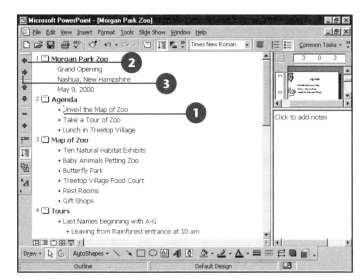

Display the Ruler

1. In Normal or Slide view, click the View menu, and then click Ruler.

   To hide the ruler, click the View menu, and then click Ruler again.

Vertical ruler   Horizontal ruler

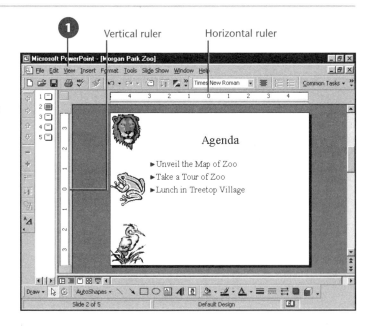

How does the ruler work?
When you select a text object and then view the ruler, the ruler runs the length of just that text object, and the origin (zero point) of the ruler is at the box borders, starting with the upper left. When you select an object other than text, the ruler runs the length of the entire slide, the origin is at the center, and measurements appear for the entire slide.

Assign indent levels using the keyboard. *Press Tab to indent text one level (demote it) or press Shift+Tab to move it back one level (promote it). If the insertion point is at the end of a line of title text, press Enter to insert a new slide. If the insertion point is at the end of a bulleted list item, press Enter to insert another bulleted list item or press Ctrl+Enter to create a new slide. Press Shift+Enter to start a new line of text in the same paragraph.*

Outlining toolbar. *If the Outlining toolbar is not visible, right-click a visible toolbar, and then click Outlining.*

Change the Indent

1. Display the ruler.

2. Select the text for which you want to change the indentation.

3. Change the indent level the way you want.

   - ◆ To change the indent for the first line of a paragraph, drag the first-line indent marker.

   - ◆ To change the indent for the rest of the paragraph, drag the left indent marker.

   - ◆ To change the distance between the indents and the left margin, but maintain the relative distance between the first-line and left indent markers, drag the rectangle below the left indent marker.

First-line indent marker   Left indent marker

Rectangle changes first-line indent and left indent simultaneously.

Setting Tabs

PowerPoint includes default tab stops at every inch; when you press the Tab key, the text moves to the next tab stop. You can control the location of the tab stops using the ruler. When you set a tab, tab markers appear on the ruler. Tabs apply to an entire paragraph, not a single line within that paragraph. You can also clear a tab by removing it from the ruler.

"How does a tab affect my text?"

SEE ALSO

See "Indenting Text" on page 36 for information on using the ruler and changing the indent level of text.

Set a Tab

1. Click the paragraph or select the paragraphs whose tabs you want to modify. You can also select a text object to change the tabs for all paragraphs in that object.

2. If necessary, click the View menu, and then click Ruler to display the ruler.

3. Click the Tab button until you see the type of tab you want.

4. Click the ruler where you want to set the tab.

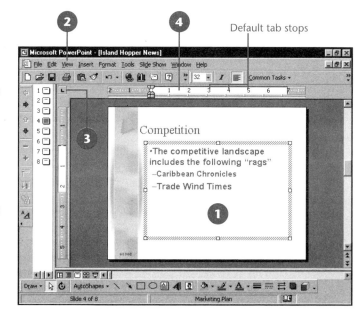

Default tab stops

TAB BUTTON ALIGNMENTS	
Tab button	**Aligns text with**
L	Left edge of text
⊥	Center of text
⌐	Right edge of text
⊥.	Decimal points in text

TIP

Use caution when you change a default tab. *When you drag a default tab marker to a new location, the spaces between all the tab markers change proportionally.*

SEE ALSO

See "Viewing Masters" on page 52 and "Controlling Slide Appearance with Masters" on page 54 for information on using masters to change tab settings for all slides in a presentation.

"I need to get rid of a tab."

Change the Distance Between Default Tab Stops

1 Select the text object in which you want to change the default tab stops.

2 If necessary, click the View menu, and then click Ruler to display the ruler.

3 Drag any default tab stop marker to a new position.

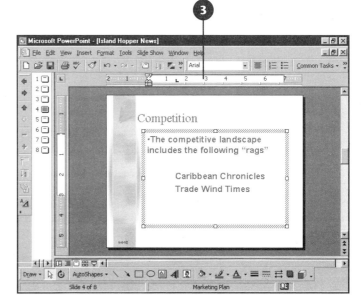

Clear a Tab

1 Drag the tab marker off the ruler.

The tab turns gray when you clear it.

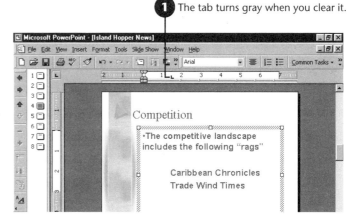

Rearranging Slides

You can instantly rearrange slides in an outline or in Slide Sorter view. You can use the drag-and-drop method or the Cut and Paste buttons to move slides to new locations. In the outline pane of Normal view or in Outline view, you can use the Move Up and Move Down buttons to move selected slides within the outline. You can also collapse the outline to its major points so you can more easily see its structure.

Rearrange Slides in Slide Sorter View

1. Click the Slide Sorter View button.

2. Click to select the slides you want to move.

3. Drag the selected slides to a new location. A vertical bar appears next to the slide where the slides will be moved when you release the mouse button.

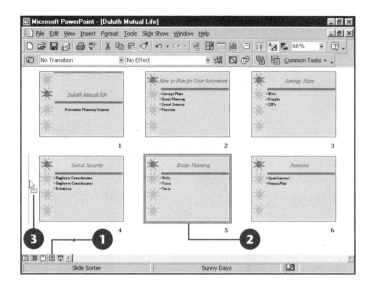

Rearrange Slides in an Outline

1. Click the Normal View or Outline View button.

2. If necessary, click the View menu, point to Toolbars, and then click Outlining to display the Outlining toolbar.

3. Click the slide icon of the slide you want to move.

4. Click the Move Up button to move the slide up, or click the Move Down button to move the slide down. Repeat until the slide is where you want it.

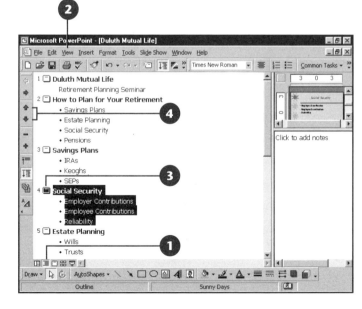

TIP

How can you tell when a slide is collapsed? *A horizontal line appears below a collapsed slide in Outline view.*

TIP

Expand or collapse the content on a slide. *In the outline pane of Normal view or in Outline view, double-click a collapsed slide to expand and show all bullets on that slide, or double-click an expanded slide to collapse the content to show only the title. This does not affect the content of the slide—just how you view it.*

SEE ALSO

See "Developing an Outline" on page 34 for more information on developing slide content.

TIP

Select one or more slides. *To select an entire slide, click the slide icon in Outline view or the slide miniature in Slide Sorter view. To select more than one slide, press and hold Shift while you click each slide.*

Collapse and Expand Slides in an Outline

1. In Outline or Normal view, select the slide, and then click the button you want.

   ◆ To collapse the selected slides, click the Collapse button.

   ◆ To expand the selected slides, click the Expand button.

   ◆ To collapse all slides, click the Collapse All button.

   ◆ To expand all slides, click the Expand All button.

Move a Slide with Cut and Paste

1. In Outline, Normal, or Slide Sorter view, select the slides you want to move.

2. Click the Cut button on the Standard toolbar.

3. Click the new location.

4. Click the Paste button on the Standard toolbar.

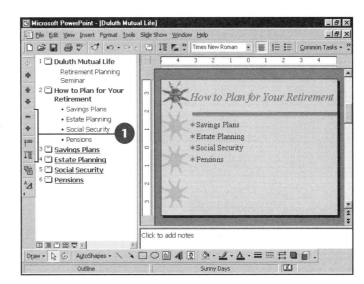

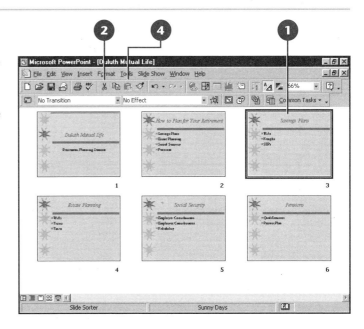

Formatting Text

Although PowerPoint's templates provide preformatted styles for text objects, you can change the formatting or add extra emphasis to a word or text object. The four most basic formats you can apply to text are bold, italic, underline, and shadow. Each has its own button on the Formatting toolbar. You can format a single letter, a word, a phrase, or all the text in a text object. You can also align text to make it stand out.

What's the difference between selecting text and selecting a text object? *When a selection box of slanted lines appears, your changes affect only the selected text. When a dotted selection box appears, changes apply to the entire text object.*

Format Text Using the Formatting Toolbar

① Select the text you want to format, or click the selection box of a text object to format all the text in the box.

② Click one or more of the format buttons on the Formatting toolbar: Bold, Italic, Underline, or Shadow.

If necessary, click the More Buttons drop-down arrow on the Formatting toolbar to display additional toolbar buttons.

Format the Text Font

① Select the text you want to format, or click the selection box of a text object to format all the text in the box.

② Click the Format menu, and then click Font.

③ Make any changes you want to the font: type, style, size, or effect.

④ Click OK.

Click to see more buttons on the Formatting toolbar.

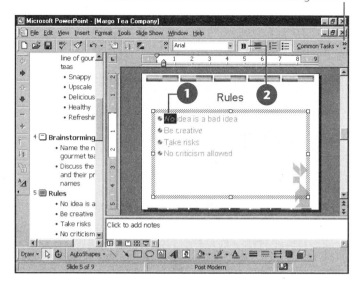

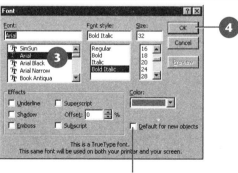

Click to set the current font format as the default for new text objects.

Show font names in their font. *Click the Tools menu, click Customize, click the Options tab, click to select the List Font Names In Their Font check box, and then click OK.*

Use the Font Size buttons to quickly increase or decrease font size. *Select a word, phrase, or text object, and click the Increase Font Size button or the Decrease Font Size button on the Formatting toolbar repeatedly until the font is the size you want.*

Pick up and apply a style using the Format Painter. *The Format Painter lets you "pick up" the style of one section of text and apply, or "paint," it to another. Select the word or text object whose format you want to pick up. Click the Format Painter button on the Standard toolbar, and then drag to select the text to which you want to apply the format.*

Change the Font Using the Formatting Toolbar

1. Select the text or text object whose font you want to change.

2. Click the Font drop-down arrow on the Formatting toolbar.

3. Click the font you want.

4. Click the Font Size drop-down arrow on the Formatting toolbar.

5. Click the font size you want.

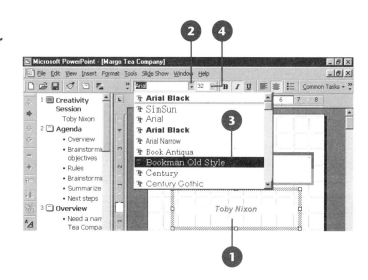

Align Text

1. Select the text or text object you want to align.

2. Click one of the alignment buttons on the Formatting toolbar—Align Left, Center, or Align Right—to align the text to the left margin, center, or right margin of the selection box border, respectively.

   If necessary, click the More Buttons drop-down arrow on the Formatting toolbar to display all the alignment buttons.

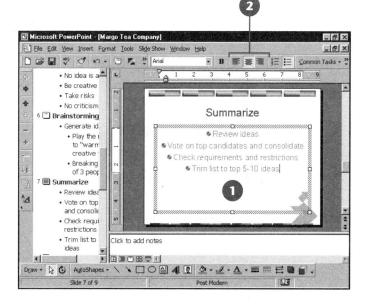

Modifying a Bulleted List

When you create a new slide, you can choose the Bulleted List AutoLayout to include a bulleted list placeholder. You can customize the appearance of your bulleted list in several ways. You have control over the appearance of your bullets, their size, and their color. You can change the bullets to numbers or import pictures to use as bullets. You can also adjust the distance between a bullet and its text using the PowerPoint ruler.

TIP

Create numbered bullets.
To change bullets to numbers, select the bulleted text, and then click the Numbering button on the Formatting toolbar.

SEE ALSO

See "Indenting Text" on page 36 for information on moving the indent markers on the ruler.

Add and Remove Bullets from Text

1. Click anywhere in the paragraph in which you want to add a bullet.

2. Click the Bullets button.on the Formatting toolbar.

3. Click anywhere in the paragraph from which you want to remove the bullet.

4. Click the Bullets button on the Formatting toolbar.

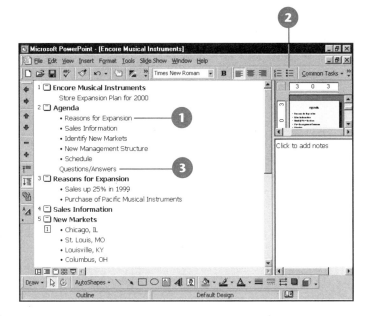

Change the Distance Between Bullets and Text

1. Select the text you want to indent.

2. If the ruler isn't visible, click the View menu, and then click Ruler.

3. Drag the indent markers on the ruler.

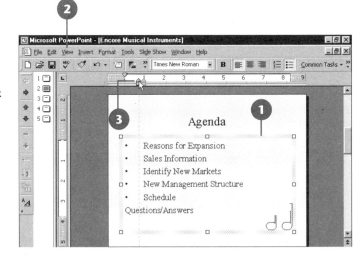

SEE ALSO

See "AutoFormatting Text and Numbered Lists" on page 50 for information on creating a numbered list from scratch.

"I want to use a check mark as my bullet character."

SEE ALSO

See "Entering Text" on page 30 for information on creating a bulleted list using a placeholder.

Change the Bullet or Number Character

1 Select the text or text object whose bullet character you want to change.

2 Click the Format menu, and then click Bullets And Numbering.

3 Click the Bulleted or Numbered tab.

4 Click one of the pre-defined styles or do one of the following.

- ◆ Click Character and click the character you want to use for your bullet character.

- ◆ Click Picture and click the picture you want to use for your bullet character.

5 To change the bullet's color, click the Color drop-down arrow, and then select the color you want.

6 To change the bullet's size, enter a percentage in the Size box.

7 Click OK.

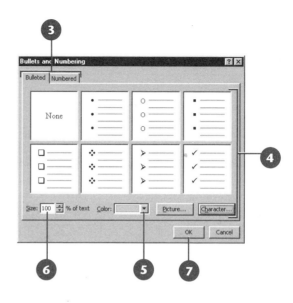

Click to select the numbering format you want to use.

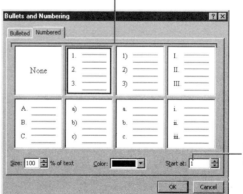

Enter the start number here.

Creating a Text Box

Usually you use the title, subtitle, and bulleted list placeholders to place text on a slide. However, when you want to add text outside one of the standard placeholders, such as for an annotation to a slide or chart, you can create a text box. Your text box doesn't have to be rectangular—you can also use one of PowerPoint's *AutoShapes*, a collection of shapes that range from rectangles and circles to arrows and stars. When you place text in an AutoShape, the text becomes part of the AutoShape. You can also orient text in text boxes, table cells, and AutoShapes vertically instead of horizontally. Use this feature when you are working with objects that are not typically shaped.

TIP

View text boxes. *Text boxes appear only in the slide pane of Normal view or in Slide view, but not in Outline view.*

Create a Text Box

1. In Normal or Slide view, click the View menu, point to Toolbars, and then click Drawing if necessary.

2. Click the Text Box button on the Drawing toolbar.

3. To add text that wraps, drag to create a box, and then start typing. To add text that doesn't wrap, click and then start typing.

4. Click outside the selection box to deselect the text box.

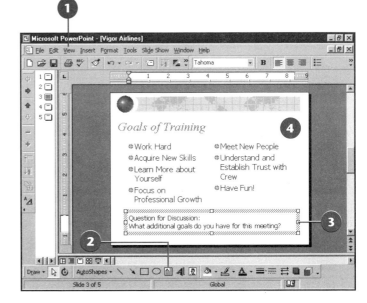

Format a Text Box

1. In Normal or Slide view, select the text box.

2. Click the Format menu, and then click Text Box.

3. Click the Text Box tab.

4. Select the format options you want.

5. Click OK.

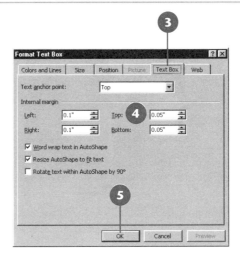

SEE ALSO

See "Drawing AutoShapes" on page 74 for more information on AutoShapes.

TIP

Edit a text box. *Click the text box, and then select the text you want to edit. Edit the text, and then click outside the text box to deselect it.*

TIP

Use sizing handles to adjust text boxes. *If you create a text box without word wrapping and then find that the text spills over the edge of your slide, use the sizing handles to resize the text box so it fits on your slide. The text then wraps to the size of the box.*

Add Text to an AutoShape

1. Click the AutoShapes button on the Drawing toolbar.

2. Point to the shape category you want to use.

3. Click the shape you want.

4. Drag to draw the shape on your slide.

5. Type your text.

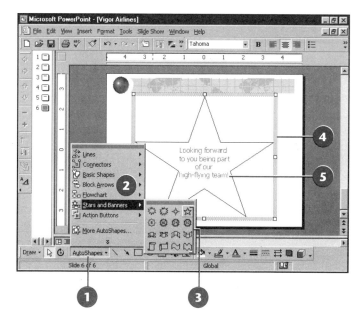

Change Text Orientation

1. In Normal or Slide view, select the text box, AutoShape, or table cell you want to change.

2. Click the Format menu, and then click Text Box, AutoShape, or Table.

3. Click the Text Box tab.

4. Click to select the Rotate Text Within AutoShape By 90° check box.

5. Click OK.

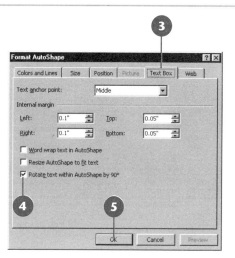

Correcting Mistakes

Misspellings and grammatical errors can distract your audience from your real message. PowerPoint provides several tools that help ensure accuracy. You can check a presentation's style for grammatical errors and control spelling errors. With AutoCorrect, you can replace common typing errors with the correct spelling as you type. For example, if you type *ahve*, AutoCorrect replaces it with *have*. You can check the spelling in an entire presentation after you've typed it using the Spelling command. You can enable the Spelling feature to alert you to a potentially misspelled word as you type, which you can correct on the spot. You can specify which style options you want the Presentation Assistant to check.

Add an Entry to AutoCorrect

1. Click the Tools menu, and then click AutoCorrect.

2. Click to select the check boxes of the AutoCorrect features you want to enable.

3. Type the abbreviation or misspelling you want to add to the list of AutoCorrect entries.

4. Type the replacement text for your AutoCorrect entry.

5. Click OK.

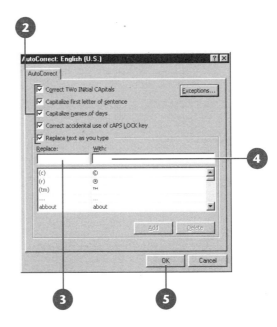

Check Spelling

1. Click the Spelling button on the Standard toolbar.

2. If the Spelling dialog box opens, click Ignore if the word is spelled correctly, or click the correct spelling, and then click Change.

3. Click OK when the spelling check is complete.

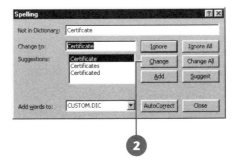

Correct Spelling as You Type

1. Click the Tools menu, and then click Options.

2. Click the Spelling And Style tab.

3. Click to select the Check Spelling As You Type check box.

4. Click OK.

5. If a red wavy line appears under a word as you type, right-click it and then click the correct spelling.

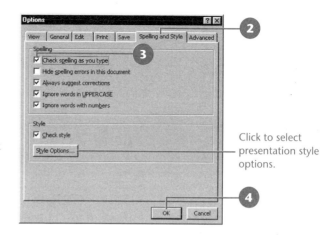

Click to select presentation style options.

Set Style Options for the Presentation Assistant

1. Click the Tools menu, and then click Options.

2. Click the Spelling And Style tab.

3. Click Style Options.

4. Click the appropriate tab, and then set the style options you want the Presentation Assistant to check.

5. Click OK.

6. Click OK.

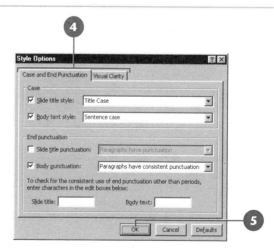

Auto-Formatting Text and Numbered Lists

PowerPoint recognizes ordinals, fractions, em-dashes and en-dashes, formatted AutoCorrect, entries and smart quotes followed by a number, and formats them as you type. For example, if you type *1/2*, PowerPoint replaces it with ½. You can also automatically number a list. PowerPoint recognizes your intent; when you enter a number followed by a period and a space, PowerPoint will format the entry and the subsequent entries as a numbered list. If you insert a new line in the middle of the numbered list, PowerPoint automatically adjusts the numbers.

SEE ALSO

See "Modifying a Bulleted List" on page 44 for information on numbered and bulleted lists.

AutoFormat Text as You Type

1. In Normal or Slide view, click to place the insertion point in the text where you want to type.

2. Type text you can AutoFormat, such as 1/2, and then press the Spacebar or Enter.

   PowerPoint recognizes this as a fraction and changes it to ½.

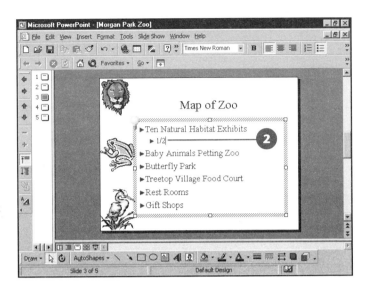

AutoNumber a List as You Type

1. In Normal or Slide view, click to place the insertion point in the text at the beginning of a blank line where you want to begin a numbered list.

2. Type 1., press the Spacebar, type text, and then press Enter.

   PowerPoint recognizes this as a numbered list and displays the next number in the list in gray.

3. Type text, and continue until you complete the list.

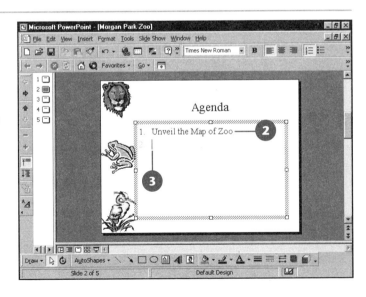

4

Designing a Look

The look you create for your presentation depends in part on your content and your audience. A goal-setting session for your company's sales group looks different from a presentation that recommends downsizing. Microsoft PowerPoint 2000 helps you design the look of your presentation in three ways: masters, color schemes, and templates.

Design Features

Masters, available for each part of your presentation—slides, handouts, and speaker's notes—contain the formatting information for your presentation.

A presentation's *color scheme* is a set of eight balanced colors that harmonizes your presentation's text, borders, fills, backgrounds, and so on.

PowerPoint features two kinds of templates. *Design templates* include professionally designed colors, graphics, and other visual elements you can apply to your presentation. *Content templates*, on the other hand, contain both designs and content. They are available through the AutoContent Wizard or on the Presentations tab of the New Presentation dialog box.

Viewing Masters

If you want to change the appearance of each instance of a slide element, such as all the title fonts or all the bullet characters, you don't have to change every slide individually. Instead, you change them all at once using a master. PowerPoint updates the existing slides, and applies your settings to any slides you add. Which master you open depends on what part of your presentation you want to change.

TIP

Use the scroll bar to switch between master views.
Click the vertical arrows to switch between the slide master and the title master.

TIP

View a master quickly. *Press and hold the Shift key, point to a view button to determine the master, and then click a view button to go to a master view.*

View the Slide Master

1 Click the View menu, point to Master, and then click Slide Master.

The slide master controls all slides that do not use the Title Slide AutoLayout.

The changes you make to the slide master do not affect the title slide.

2 Click the Close button on the Master toolbar.

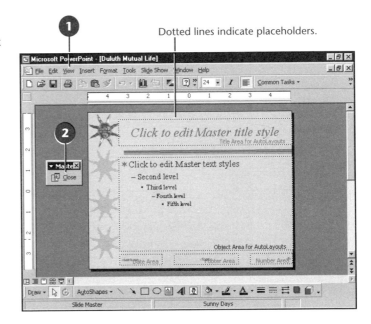

Dotted lines indicate placeholders.

View the Title Master

1 Click the View menu, point to Master, and then click Title Master.

The title master controls the look of your title slide.

The changes you make to the title master do not affect non-title slides.

2 Click the Close button on the Master toolbar.

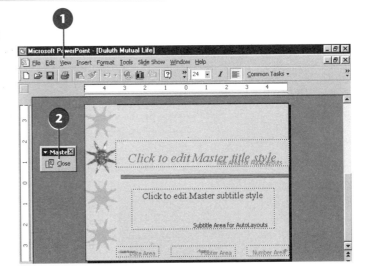

View the Notes Master

1 Click the View menu, point to Master, and then click Notes Master.

The notes master controls the look of your notes pages.

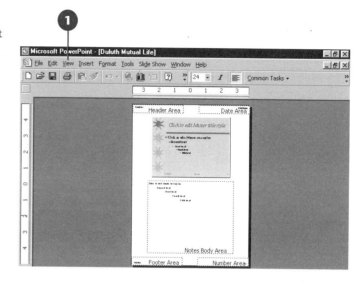

View the Handout Master

1 Click the View menu, point to Master, and then click Handout Master.

The handout master controls the look of your handouts.

2 Click the button on the Handout Master toolbar with the number of slides you want on your handout pages.

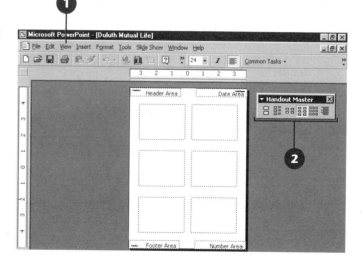

Controlling Slide Appearance with Masters

If you want an object, such as a company logo or clip art, to appear on every slide in your presentation (except the title slide), place it on the slide master. You can hide the object in any slide you want. You can also create unique slides that don't follow the format of the masters. If you change your mind, you can easily restore a master format to a slide you altered. As you view the master, you can view a sample miniature of the slide, complete with text and graphics, using the Slide Miniature window.

SEE ALSO

See "Working with Objects" on page 26 for more information on modifying the size and placement of an object.

Include an Object on Every Slide

1. Click the View menu, point to Master, and then click Slide Master.

2. Add the object you want and modify its size and placement.

3. Click the Close button on the Master toolbar.

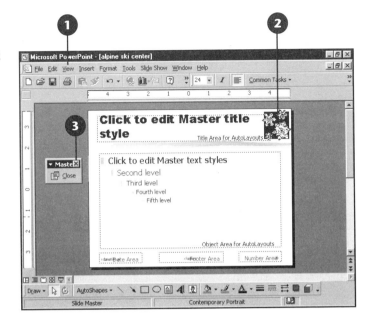

Hide Master Background Objects on a Slide

1. Display the slide whose background object you want to hide.

2. Click the Format menu, and then click Background.

3. Click to select the Omit Background Graphics From Master check box.

4. Click Apply.

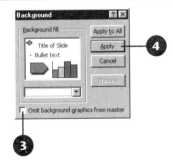

Make a slide format different from the master. *Display the slide you want to change, and then modify it. Your changes override master formatting, and even if you change the master, this slide retains the features you changed.*

Make changes to an individual slide. *If you change a slide and want the change to apply to all slides, click Apply To All instead of Apply.*

See "Indenting Text" on page 36 for information on changing the indent level between bullets and text for all slides in a presentation.

See "Setting Tabs" on page 38 for information on changing the distance between default tab stops for all slides in a presentation.

Reapply the Master to a Changed Slide

1. In Normal or Slide view, display the slide you want to reapply the master to.

2. Click the Format menu, and then click Slide Layout.

3. Click Reapply.

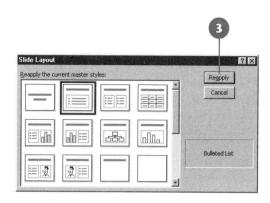

View a Slide Miniature in Slide Master or Notes Master View

1. Click the View menu, and then click Slide Miniature.

2. Click the Close button on the Slide Miniature window.

Slide miniature

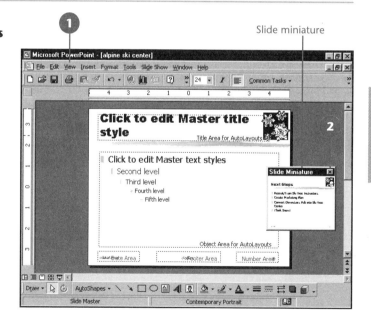

Inserting the Date, Time, and Slide Numbers

You can insert the date, the time, and slide numbers into the text of your presentation. For example, you might want today's date to appear in a stock market quote. Dates and times come in two formats: as a field or as text. If you insert the date as a field, PowerPoint inserts a code for the date and then every time you open the presentation, it automatically updates the date from your computer's clock. If you insert the date as text, the date remains the same until you change it. When you insert slide numbers, PowerPoint keeps track of your slide numbers for you. You can even start numbering with a number other than one. This is useful when your slides are a part of a larger presentation.

Insert the Date and Time

1. Click to place the insertion point in the text object where you want to insert the date or time.

2. Click the Insert menu, and then click Date And Time.

3. Click the date or time format you want.

4. Click OK.

Check if you want the date or time to be updated automatically whenever you open the presentation.

Insert Slide Numbering

1. Click to place the insertion point in the text object where you want to insert the current slide number.

2. Click the Insert menu, and then click Slide Number.

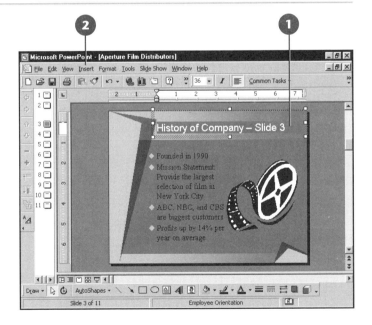

PowerPoint automatically updates slide numbering. *Slide numbering is updated automatically, regardless of whether you insert, delete, or reorder the slides in your presentation.*

Update the date and time automatically. *Click to select the Update Automatically check box in the Date And Time dialog box before you click OK.*

See "Adding a Header and Footer" on page 58 for information on adding the date, time, or slide number to every slide in your presentation.

Add slide numbers to the slide master. *View the slide master, and then click the View menu, click Header and Footer, click the Slide tab, click to select the Slide Number check box to add a slide number to every slide, and then click OK.*

Start Numbering with a Different Number

1. Insert the slide number if you need one on the slide or slide master.

2. Click the File menu, and then click Page Setup.

3. Click the Number Slides From up or down arrow to set the number you want.

4. Click OK.

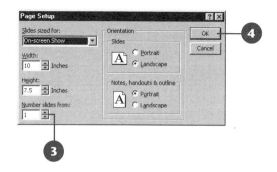

Adding a Header and Footer

A header and footer appear on every slide. You can choose to not have them appear on the title slide. They often include information such as the presentation title, slide number, date, and name of the presenter. Use the masters to place header and footer information on your slides, handouts, or notes pages. Make sure your header and footer don't make your presentation look cluttered. Their default font size is usually small enough to minimize distraction, but you can experiment by changing their font size and placement to make sure.

Add a Header and Footer

1. Click the View menu, and then click Header And Footer.

2. Click the Slide or Notes And Handouts tab.

3. Enter or select the information you want to include on your slide or your notes and handouts.

4. Click Apply to apply your selections to the current slide, or click Apply To All to apply the selections to all slides.

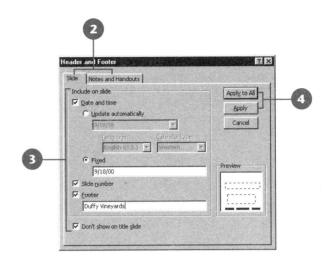

Change the Look of a Header or Footer

1. Click the View menu, and then point to Master.

2. Click the master you want to change.

3. Make the necessary changes to the header and footer. You can move or resize them or change their text attributes.

4. Click the Close button on the Master toolbar.

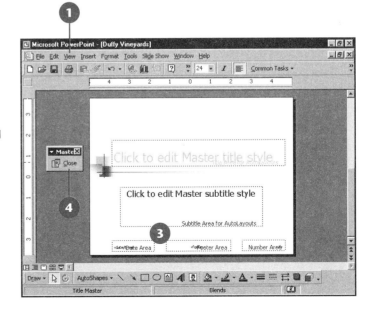

Understanding Color Schemes

If you've created a slide presentation with the AutoContent Wizard or with a presentation template, you've probably noticed that PowerPoint automatically assigns consistent colors to the objects you create.

These colors are chosen from the presentation's color scheme, the collection of eight well-matched colors that are the foundation of a presentation's look and feel.

Title Text
The color of the title text contrasts with the background color.

Accent And Followed Hyperlink
A color for objects and the color for a hyperlink you have already selected.

Accent And Hyperlink
A color for objects and the color for any hyperlinks you add to your presentation.

Accent
A color for objects, such as bars on a chart, or objects that make up the template design.

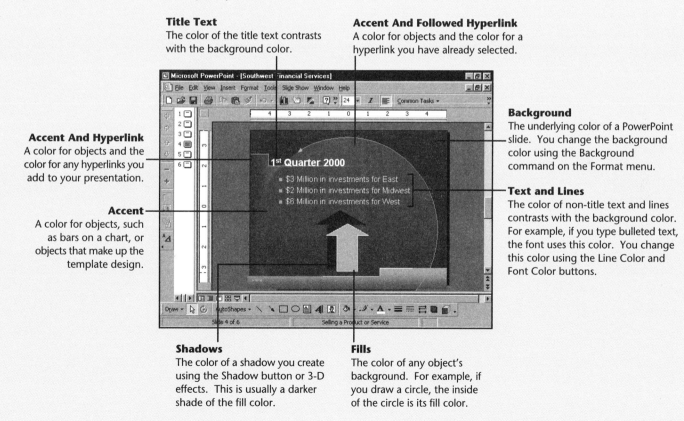

Background
The underlying color of a PowerPoint slide. You change the background color using the Background command on the Format menu.

Text and Lines
The color of non-title text and lines contrasts with the background color. For example, if you type bulleted text, the font uses this color. You change this color using the Line Color and Font Color buttons.

Shadows
The color of a shadow you create using the Shadow button or 3-D effects. This is usually a darker shade of the fill color.

Fills
The color of any object's background. For example, if you draw a circle, the inside of the circle is its fill color.

Working with Color Schemes

You can apply a color scheme to one slide or all slides in a presentation. You can choose from one or more standard color schemes in each template. You can also create your own color schemes and save them so you can apply them to other slides and even other presentations.

TIP

Which colors work better for on-screen presentations? *Use dark backgrounds for on-screen presentations and 35mm slides. Use a light background for overhead transparencies.*

TIP

Preview the color scheme. *Click the Preview button in the Color Scheme dialog box to preview the color scheme before you apply it.*

Choose a Color Scheme

1. Click the Format menu, and then click Slide Color Scheme.

2. Click the Standard tab to view the available color schemes.

3. Click the color scheme you want.

4. Click Apply to apply the color scheme to the slide you are viewing, or click Apply To All to apply the color scheme to the entire presentation.

Each box represents a different available color scheme.

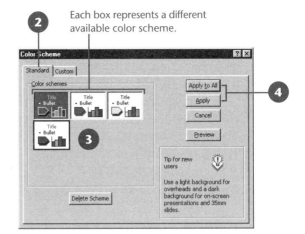

Delete a Color Scheme

1. Click the Format menu, and then click Slide Color Scheme.

2. Click the Standard tab to view the available color schemes.

3. Click the scheme you want to delete.

4. Click Delete Scheme.

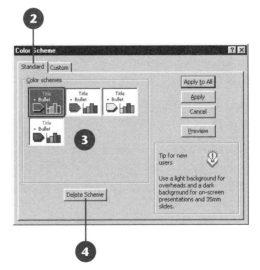

SEE ALSO

See "Changing the Color Scheme" on page 62 for information on changing a color in a color scheme and saving the result.

"I really like this color scheme—I'd like to apply it to a different slide."

SEE ALSO

See "Applying a Color to an Object" on page 64 for information on adding colors not in a color scheme to all menus with color options.

Apply the Color Scheme of One Slide to Another

1. Click the Slide Sorter View button.

2. Click the slide with the color scheme you want to apply.

3. Click the Format Painter button on the Formatting toolbar to apply the color scheme to one slide, or double-click the button to apply the color scheme to multiple slides.

4. Click the slides to which you want to apply the color scheme. The slides can be in the current presentation or in another open presentation.

5. If you are applying the scheme to more than one slide, press Esc to cancel Format Painter. If you are applying the scheme to only one slide, Format Painter is canceled automatically.

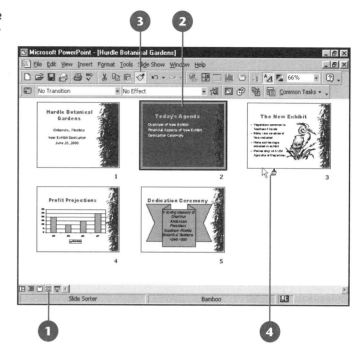

Changing the Color Scheme

You may like a certain color scheme except for one or two colors. You can change an existing color scheme and apply your changes to the entire presentation or to just a few slides. Once you change a color scheme, you can add it to your collection of color schemes so that you can make it available to any slide in the presentation.

"I need just the right color for this text."

Change a Color in a Standard Color Scheme

1. In Slide view, display the slide whose color scheme you want to change, click the Format menu, and then click Slide Color Scheme.

2. Click the Custom tab.

3. Click the element you want to change.

4. Click Change Color.

5. Click a color on the Standard tab.

6. Click OK.

7. Click Apply to apply the changed color scheme to the current slide, or click Apply To All to apply the changed scheme to all slides.

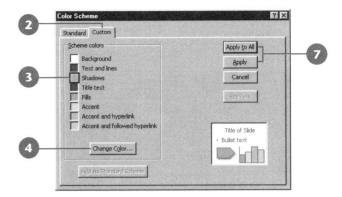

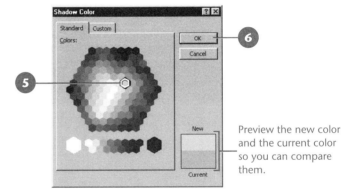

Preview the new color and the current color so you can compare them.

Choose a Custom Color

1. Click the Format menu, and then click Slide Color Scheme.

2. Click the Custom tab.

3. Click the element you want to customize in the Scheme Colors list.

4. Click Change Color.

THE PROPERTIES OF COLORS	
Characteristic	**Description**
Hue	The color itself; every color is identified by a number, determined by the number of colors available on your monitor.
Saturation	The intensity of the color. The higher the number, the more vivid the color.
Luminosity	The brightness of the color, or how close the color is to black or white. The larger the number, the lighter the color.

SEE ALSO

See "Working with Color Schemes" on page 60 for more information on color schemes.

TRY THIS

Prevent chart colors from being updated when you change a color scheme.
When you don't want the chart to take on the new colors of the color scheme, click the chart, click the Recolor Chart button on the Picture toolbar, and then click None.

"I'd like to be able to save this color scheme."

5 Click the Custom tab.

6 Drag across the palette until the pointer is over the color you want, or enter the Hue, Sat, Lum, Red, Green, and Blue values.

7 Click OK.

8 Click Apply to make the new color part of the color scheme for the current slide, or click Apply To All to make it part of the entire presentation.

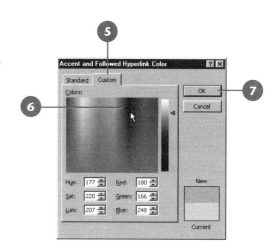

Save a Changed Color Scheme

1 Click the Format menu, and then click Slide Color Scheme.

2 Click the Custom tab.

3 Change the color scheme until all eight colors are as you want them.

4 Click Add As Standard Scheme. Your new scheme now appears on the Standard tab.

5 If you want to apply the scheme, click Apply or Apply To All, or click Cancel to close the dialog box.

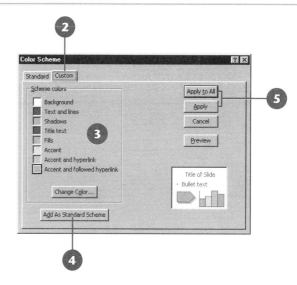

Applying a Color to an Object

When you want to change the color of only one element in your presentation on only one slide, you don't need to use the Color Scheme dialog box. Instead, you can select the object and open the Color dialog box for the color you want to change—the fill, border, line, text, and so on. The Color dialog box looks the same from one element to another. When you work with color, you should keep in mind whether you'll be printing handouts in black and white. PowerPoint makes it easy to preview color presentations in black and white. Note that different formatting effects appear differently in Black And White view.

Change an Object's Color

① Click the object whose color you want to change.

② Click the Fill Color, Line Color, or Text Color button on the Drawing toolbar to change an object's color.

③ Click a color from the color scheme, or click More Fill Colors, and then select a color.

To apply a fill effect to your object, click Fill Effects and select the effect you want.

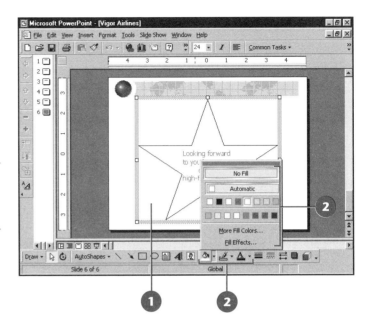

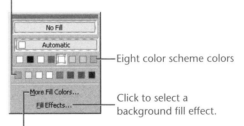

Additional colors not in color scheme

Eight color scheme colors

Click to select a background fill effect.

Click to select a non—color scheme color from the color palette.

SEE ALSO

See "Choosing Object Colors" on page 84 for more information about using fill effects.

TIP

Add colors to all color menus. *Any time you add a color, PowerPoint adds it to all the color menus—those that appear for text, shadows, bullets, background, and lines. PowerPoint "remembers" up to eight colors that you've added. If you add a ninth, it appears first on the palette, replacing the oldest.*

TRY THIS

Recolor a picture from the Clip Gallery. *Select the picture, and then click the Recolor Picture button on the Picture toolbar. You can click Colors to change any color in the picture or Fills to change only background or fill colors in the picture. To change the color or fill, click the appropriate drop-down arrow, select a color, and then click OK.*

Choose a Different Slide Background Color

1 Display the slide whose background you want to change.

2 Click the Format menu, and then click Background.

3 Click the Background Fill drop-down arrow.

4 Select the color you want.

5 Click Apply to apply the background color to only the current slide, or click Apply To All to apply the background color to the entire presentation.

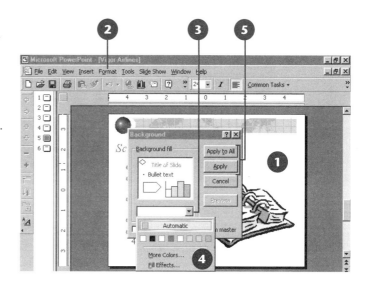

View a Presentation in Black and White

1 Click the Grayscale Preview button on the Standard toolbar.

2 Click the Grayscale Preview button on the Standard toolbar again to view your presentation in color.

4

Choosing a Fill Effect

The *fill* is the inside pattern or color of an object or background. For example, if you have drawn a square, the fill is the color inside the border. A *fill effect* is the look you give to the fill of an object or the background of your slides, such as a pattern or texture. Fill effects are often based on a color or collection of colors that fill the area with a pattern. PowerPoint fill effects include gradients, textures, patterns, and pictures. When you apply the fill effect you want, it fills the selected area, such as an arrow or the entire slide background.

SEE ALSO

See "Choosing Object Colors" on page 84 for information on changing colors, lines, and arrow options.

Select a Background Fill Effect

1. Click the Format menu, and then click Background.

2. Click the Background Fill drop-down arrow, and then click Fill Effects.

3. Click the Gradient, Texture, Pattern, or Picture tab to display the available fill effects.

4. Click the fill effect you want.

5. Click OK.

6. Click Apply to apply the fill effect to the current slide, or click Apply To All to apply the fill effect to all slides.

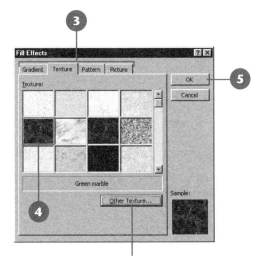

Click to get other textures.

Apply a Picture Fill

1. Select the object you want to fill, click the Fill Color drop-down arrow on the Drawing toolbar, and then click Fill Effects.

2. Click the Picture tab.

3. Click Select Picture.

4. Locate the picture you want, and then double-click it.

5. Click OK.

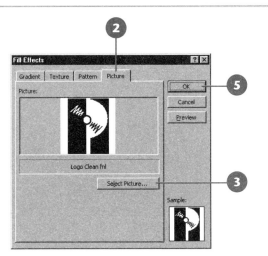

Apply fill effects to other objects. *You can also apply fill effects to objects such as lines and WordArt.*

"I'd like to use a pattern as my fill."

Apply a Gradient Fill

1 Select the object you want to fill, click the Fill Color drop-down arrow on the Drawing toolbar, and then click Fill Effects.

2 Click the Gradient tab.

3 Click the color or color combination you want.

4 Click the shading style option you want.

5 Click the variant you want.

6 Click OK.

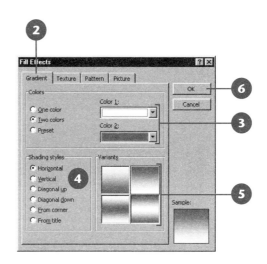

Apply a Pattern Fill

1 Select the object you want to fill, click the Fill Color drop-down arrow on the Drawing toolbar, and then click Fill Effects.

2 Click the Pattern tab.

3 Click the Foreground drop-down arrow to select the color you want in the foreground.

4 Click the Background drop-down arrow to select the color you want in the background.

5 Click the pattern you want.

6 Click OK.

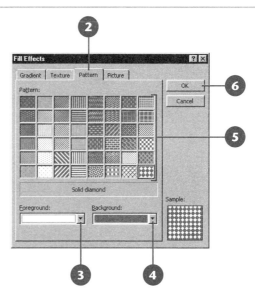

Saving a Template

You can save any presentation as a template. When you create a new presentation from that template, its content and design can form the basis of your next presentation. Although you can store your template anywhere you want, you may find it handy to store it in the Templates folder that PowerPoint uses to store its templates. If you store your design templates in the Presentation Designs folder and your AutoContent templates in the Presentations folder, those templates appear as options when you choose the New command on the File menu. You can also change existing templates. For example, you can change the Blank Presentation template so that it includes your company's colors or logo.

Create a Template

1. Open any presentation—a blank one, one created with an existing design template, or an existing presentation.

2. Click the Format menu, click Slide Color Scheme, select or create a color scheme, and then click Apply To All.

3. Format the placeholders on the slide and title masters.

4. Place objects or insert pictures on the slide and title masters.

5. Add the footer and header information you want to include.

6. Click the File menu, click Save As, and then enter a name for your template.

7. Click the Save As Type drop-down arrow, and then click Design Template.

   The template will appear on the General tab of the New Presentation dialog box.

8. Click Save.

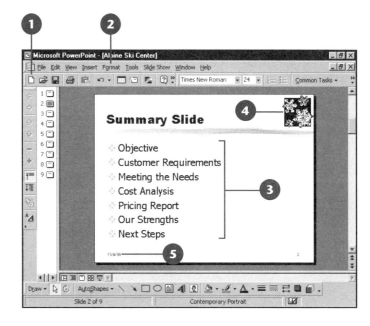

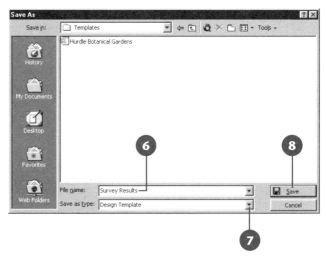

Change an Existing Design Template

1. Click the File menu, and then click Open.

2. Click the Files Of Type drop-down arrow, and then click Design Templates.

3. If necessary, click the Look In drop-down arrow, and select the folder containing the template you want to open.

4. Double-click the template you want to change.

5. Make your changes to the template.

6. Click the File menu, and then click Save As.

7. Click the Save As Type drop-down arrow, and then click Design Template.

8. Click Save.

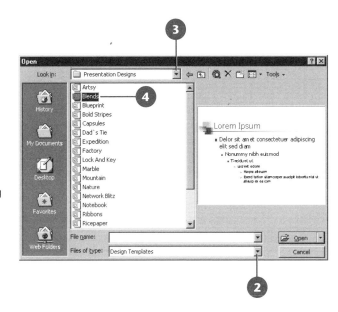

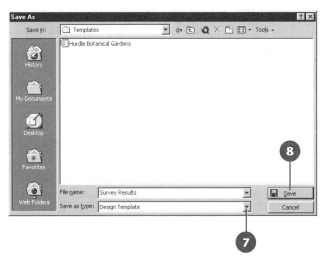

Applying a Design Template

PowerPoint design templates feature customized color schemes, slide and title masters, and fonts that come together to create a particular impression. You can apply a design template to a presentation at any time—even if you created the presentation with a different template. When you apply a design template to a presentation, the masters and color scheme of the new template replace the original ones.

SEE ALSO

See "Saving a Template" on page 68 for information on creating a template.

TIP

Use a toolbar button to apply a design template. *Click the Common Tasks button on the Formatting toolbar, click Apply Design Template, select the template you want, and then click Apply.*

Apply a New Template

1. Click the Format menu, and then click Apply Design Template.

2. Locate and select the design template you want to apply.

3. Click Apply.

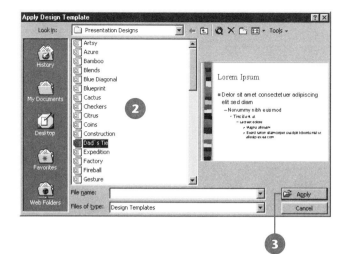

Apply a Design from an Existing Presentation

1. Click the Format menu, and then click Apply Design Template.

2. Click the Files Of Type drop-down arrow, and then click Presentations And Shows.

3. Locate and select the presentation whose design you want to apply.

4. Click Apply.

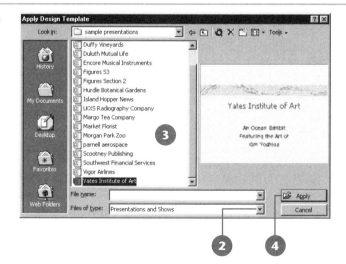

5

Drawing and Modifying Objects

W hen you want to add pictures to your presentations, you can use Microsoft PowerPoint 2000 as a drawing package. You can choose from a set of predesigned shapes, or you can use tools to draw and edit your own shapes and forms.

Drawing Objects

You can add three types of drawing objects to your presentations: lines, AutoShapes, and freeforms. *Lines* are simply the straight or curved lines (arcs) that connect two points. *AutoShapes* are preset shapes, such as stars, circles, or ovals. A *freeform* is an irregular curve or polygon that you can create as a freehand drawing.

Once you create a drawing object, you can manipulate it by rotating it, coloring it, or changing its style, for example. PowerPoint also provides special effects, including drop shadows and 3-D. When you add shadows to an image, you can control the shadow's color, location, or angle. You can also transform your two-dimensional shapes into three-dimensional surfaces. You can rotate, tilt, and revolve the object in three-dimensions, control the object's perspective, and specify the surface texture.

Drawing Lines and Arrows

The most basic drawing objects you create on your slides are lines and arrows. Use the Line tool to create line segments. The Drawing toolbar's Line Style and Dash Style tools let you determine the type of line you draw—solid, dashed, or a combination. You can add arrowheads to any lines on your slide. Use the Arrow tool to create arrows that emphasize key features of your presentation. You can edit the style of the arrow using the Arrow style tool.

TRY THIS

Use keyboard controls as you draw your lines. *Press and hold the Shift key as you drag the pointer to constrain the angle of the line to 15-degree increments. Press and hold Ctrl as you drag the pointer to draw the line from the center out, rather than from one endpoint to another.*

Draw a Straight Line

1 Click the Line button on the Drawing toolbar.

2 Drag the pointer to draw a line. The endpoints of the line are where you start and finish dragging.

3 Release the mouse button when the line is the correct length. Sizing handles appear at both ends of the line. Use these handles to resize your line or move an endpoint.

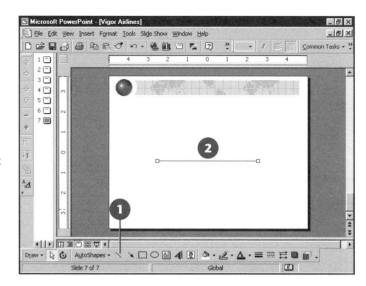

Edit a Line

1 Click the line you want to edit.

2 Click the Line Style button on the Drawing toolbar to select a line thickness.

3 Click the Dash Style button on the Drawing toolbar to select a style.

4 Click the Line Color drop-down arrow on the Drawing toolbar to select a color.

5 Drag a sizing handle to change the size or angle of the line.

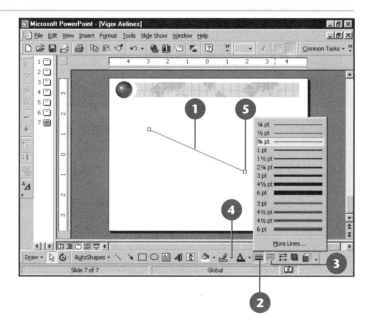

SEE ALSO

See "Drawing AutoShapes" on page 74 for information on creating block arrows using the AutoShape drawing tools.

TIP

Increase the size of an arrow. *Because of its size, you may not see the arrowhead when you draw a default arrow. To increase the size of the arrowhead, click the Arrow Style button, click More Arrows, and then increase the Weight setting or End Size setting.*

TIP

Change the default size of an arrow. *Click an arrow object, click the Arrow Style button, click More Arrows, and change the line and arrow settings to the default format you want, click to select the Default For New Objects check box, and then click OK.*

Draw an Arrow

1. Click the Arrow button on the Drawing toolbar.

2. Drag the pointer from the base of the arrow to the arrow's point.

3. Release the mouse button when the arrow is correct length and angle.

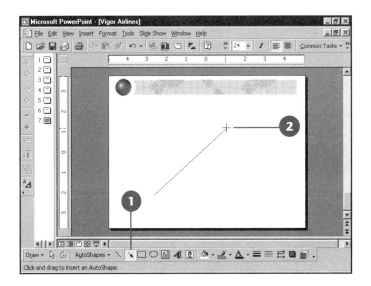

Edit an Arrow

1. Click the arrow you want to edit.

2. Click the Arrow Style button on the Drawing toolbar.

3. Click the arrow type you want to use, or click More Arrows.

4. If you clicked More Arrows, modify the arrow type in the Format AutoShape dialog box as necessary, and then click OK.

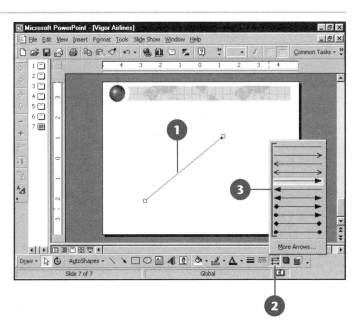

5

Drawing AutoShapes

PowerPoint supplies 155 different AutoShapes, ranging from hearts to lightening bolts to stars. The two most common AutoShapes, the oval and the rectangle, are available directly on the Drawing toolbar. The rest of the AutoShapes are organized into categories you can select from the AutoShapes menu on the Drawing toolbar. Once you have placed an AutoShape on a slide, you can resize it using the sizing handles. Many AutoShapes have an *adjustment handle*, a small yellow diamond located near a resize handle that you can drag to alter the shape of the AutoShape. In addition to drawing AutoShapes, you can insert AutoShapes, such as computers and furniture, from the Clip Gallery.

Draw an Oval or Rectangle

1. Click the Oval or Rectangle button on the Drawing toolbar.

2. Drag the pointer on the slide where you want to place the oval or rectangle. The shape you draw uses the line and fill color defined by the presentation's color scheme.

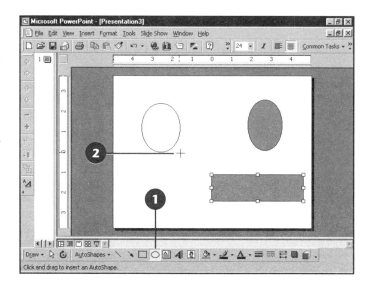

Draw an AutoShape

1. Click the AutoShapes button on the Drawing toolbar, and then point to the AutoShape category you want to use.

2. Click the symbol you want.

3. Drag the pointer on the slide until the drawing object is the shape and size that you want.

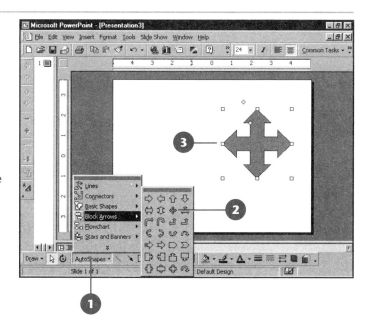

SEE ALSO

See "Moving and Resizing a Drawing Object" on page 80 for information on resizing an AutoShape.

TIP

Draw a circle or square. *To draw a perfect circle or square, click the Oval or Rectangle button on the Drawing toolbar, and then press and hold Shift as you drag.*

TIP

Replace an AutoShape. *You can replace one AutoShape with another, while retaining the size, color, and orientation of the AutoShape. Click the AutoShape you want to replace, click the Draw button on the Drawing toolbar, point to Change AutoShape, and then click the new AutoShape you want.*

TIP

View the full More AutoShapes dialog box. *Click the Change To Full Window button on the toolbar.*

Adjust an AutoShape

1. Click the AutoShape you want to adjust.

2. Click one of the adjustment handles (small yellow diamonds), and then drag the handle to alter the form of the AutoShape.

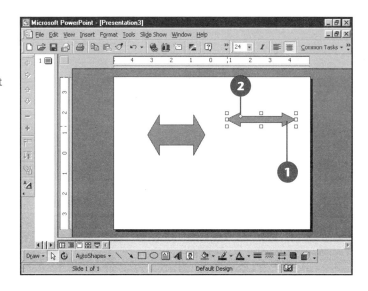

Insert an AutoShape from the Clip Gallery

1. Click the AutoShapes button on the Drawing toolbar, and then click More AutoShapes.

2. Click a category with the type of AutoShape you want to insert.

3. Click the AutoShape you want, and then click Insert Clip.

4. When you're finished, click the Close button.

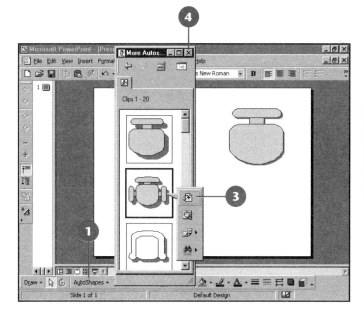

Creating Freeforms

When you need to create a customized shape, use the PowerPoint freeform tools. Choose a freeform tool from the Lines category in the list of AutoShapes. Freeforms are like the drawings you make with a pen and paper, except that you use a mouse for your pen and a slide for your paper. A freeform shape can either be an open curve or a closed curve.

Freeform button

Draw a Freeform Polygon

1 Click the AutoShapes button on the Drawing toolbar, and then point to Lines.

2 Click the Freeform button.

3 Click the slide where you want to place the first vertex of the polygon.

4 Move the pointer to the second point of your polygon, and then click. A line joins the two points.

5 Continue moving the mouse pointer and clicking to create additional sides of your polygon.

6 Finish the polygon. For a closed polygon, click near the starting point. For an open polygon, double-click the last point in the polygon.

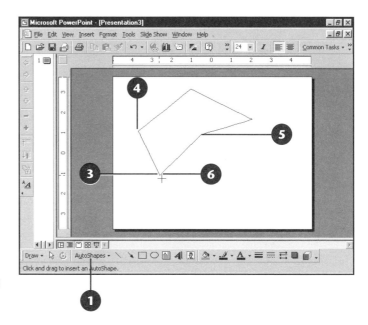

Switch between a closed curve and an open curve. *Right-click the freeform drawing. To switch from an open curve to a closed curve, click Close Curve, or to switch from a closed curve to an open curve, click Open Curve.*

Curve button

Format freeforms and curves. *You can enhance freeforms and curves just as you can AutoShapes. For example, you can add color or a pattern, change the line style, flip or rotate them, and add shadow or 3-D effects.*

Scribble button

What is a vertex? *A vertex is a corner in an irregular polygon or a bend in a curve.*

Draw a Curve

1 Click the AutoShapes button on the Drawing toolbar, and then point to Lines.

2 Click the Curve button.

3 Click the slide where you want to place the curve's starting point.

4 Click where you want your curve to bend. Repeat this step as often as you need to create bends.

5 Finish the curve. For a closed curve, click near the starting point. For an open curve, double-click the last point in the curve.

Scribble

1 Click the AutoShapes button on the Drawing toolbar, and then point to Lines.

2 Click the Scribble button.

3 Drag the pointer across the screen to draw freehand.

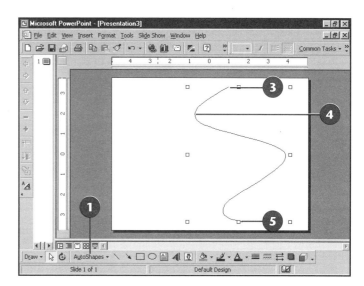

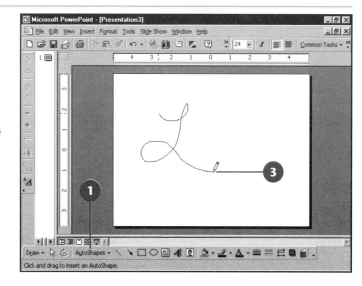

5

Editing Freeforms

You can edit a freeform by using the Edit Points command to alter the vertices that create the shape. Each *vertex* (a corner in an irregular polygon and a bend in a curve) has two attributes: its position and the angle at which the curve enters and leaves it. You can move the position of each vertex and control the corner or bend angles. You can also add or delete vertices as you like. When you delete a vertex, PowerPoint recalculates the freeform and smooths it among the remaining points. Similarly, if you add a new vertex, PowerPoint adds a corner or bend in your freeform.

TIP

Access the Edit Points command from a shortcut menu. *Right-click a freeform, and then click Edit Points.*

Move a Vertex in a Freeform

1. Click the freeform object you want to edit.

2. Click the Draw button on the Drawing toolbar, and then click Edit Points.

3. Drag one of the freeform vertices to a new location.

4. Click outside the freeform when you are finished.

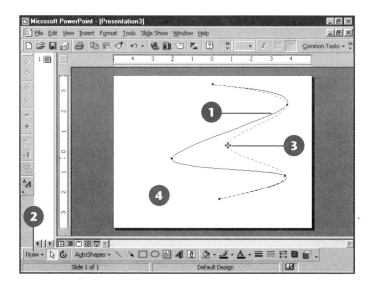

Insert a Freeform Vertex

1. Click the freeform object in which you want to insert a vertex.

2. Click the Draw button on the Drawing toolbar, and then click Edit Points.

3. Position the pointer on the curve or polygon border (not on a vertex), and then drag in the direction you want the new vertex.

4. Click outside the freeform to set the new shape.

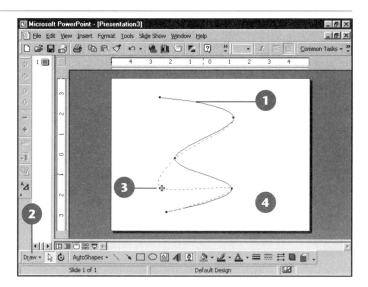

Gain control over your freeform. *After you click Edit Points, right-click a vertex. PowerPoint displays a shortcut menu with options for other types of vertices you can use to refine the shape of the freeform. These commands let you specify, for example, a smooth point, a straight point, or a corner point.*

"How do I change the angle of one of my freeforms?"

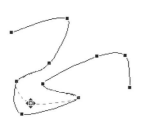

Delete a Freeform Vertex

1 Click the freeform object you want to edit.

2 Click the Draw button on the Drawing toolbar, and then click Edit Points.

3 Press and hold the Ctrl key while clicking the point you want to delete.

4 Click outside the freeform to set the shape of the freeform.

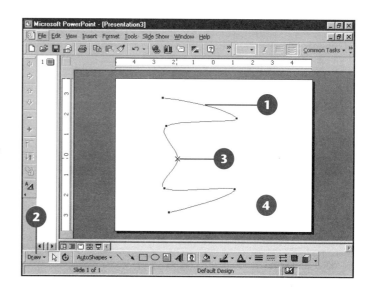

Modify a Vertex Angle

1 Click the freeform object.

2 Click the Draw button on the Drawing toolbar, and then click Edit Points.

3 Right-click a vertex and click Smooth Point, Straight Point, or Corner Point. Angle handles appear.

4 Drag one or both of the angle handles to modify the shape of the line segments going into and out of the vertex.

5 Click outside the freeform to set its shape.

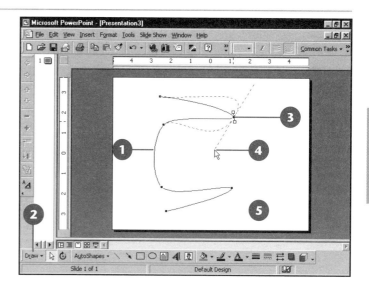

Moving and Resizing a Drawing Object

After you create a drawing object, you can resize or move it. You can quickly move and resize objects using the mouse. If you want precise control over the object's size and position, use PowerPoint's Format command to specify the location and size of the drawing object. You can also use the Nudge command to move drawing objects in tiny increments up, down, left, or right.

Move a Drawing Object

1. Drag the object to a new location on the slide.

   Make sure you aren't dragging a sizing handle or adjustment handle. If you are working with a freeform and you are in Edit Points mode, drag the interior of the object, not the border, or you will end up resizing or reshaping the object, not moving it.

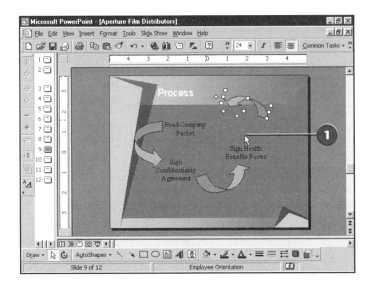

Nudge a Drawing Object

1. Click the object you want to nudge.

2. Click the Draw button on the Drawing toolbar.

3. Point to Nudge and then click Up, Down, Left, or Right.

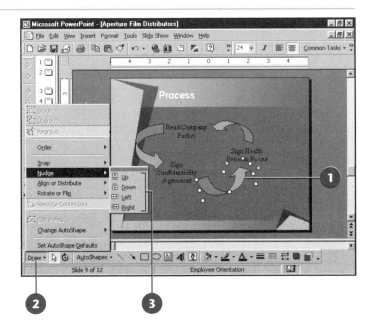

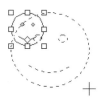

Resize a Drawing Object with the Mouse

(1) Click the object you want to resize.

(2) Drag one of the sizing handles.

◆ To resize the object in the vertical or horizontal direction, drag a sizing handle on the side of the selection box.

◆ To resize the object in both the vertical and horizontal directions, drag a sizing handle on the corner of the selection box.

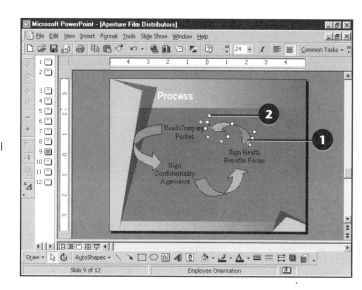

TRY THIS

Set your mouse to the slowest tracking speed. *You have more control when you draw slowly. Click the Start button on the taskbar, point to Settings, click Control Panel, double-click the mouse icon, click the Motion tab, and then move the Pointer Speed slider all the way to the left.*

TIP

Double-click the object to display the Format AutoShape dialog box. *This allows you to set the fill and line colors, the size and position of the object, and any Web text you want to associate with the object.*

Move or Resize an Object with Precision

(1) Click the Format menu, and then click AutoShape.

(2) Click the Position tab to move the object and change settings as necessary.

(3) Click the Size tab to resize the object and change settings as necessary.

(4) Click OK.

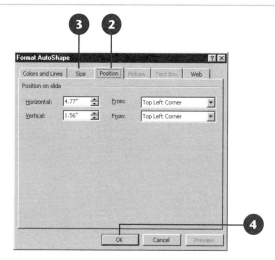

Rotating and Flipping a Drawing Object

If you need to change the orientation of a drawing object, you can rotate or flip it. For example, if you want to create a mirror image of your object, you can flip it, or if you want to turn an object on its side, you can rotate it 90 degrees. Rotating and flipping tools work with drawing and text objects. Some pictures, graphs, and organization charts that you import can't be rotated or flipped because they weren't created in PowerPoint.

TIP

Different ways to rotate objects. *Click the Draw button on the Drawing toolbar, and then point to Rotate. To rotate the object 90 degrees to the left, click Rotate Left. To rotate the object 90 degrees to the right, click Rotate Right. To flip the object horizontally, click Flip Horizontal. To flip the object vertically, click Flip Vertical.*

Rotate an Object to any Angle

1. Click the object you want to rotate.

2. Click the Free Rotate button on the Drawing toolbar.

3. Drag a rotation handle to rotate the object.

4. Click outside the object to set the rotation.

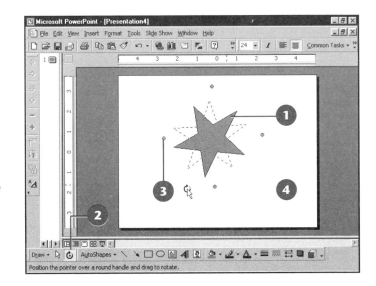

Rotate or Flip a Drawing Using Preset Increments

1. Click the object you want to rotate.

2. Click the Draw button on the Drawing toolbar.

3. Point to Rotate Or Flip, and then click the option you want.

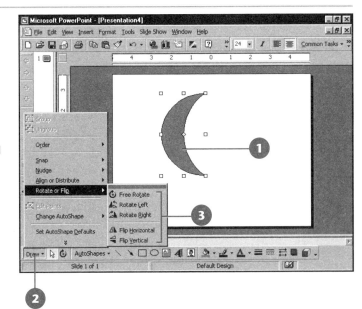

"I want to rotate this arrow by 70 degrees."

Rotate a Drawing Object Around a Fixed Point

1. Click the object you want to rotate.

2. Click the Free Rotate button on the Drawing toolbar.

3. Click the rotate handle opposite the point you want to rotate, and then press and hold the Ctrl key as you rotate the object.

4. Click outside the object to set the rotation.

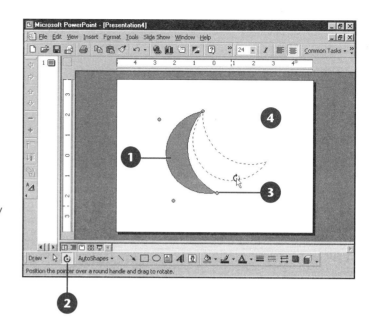

Rotate a Drawing Precisely

1. Right-click the object you want to rotate, and then click Format AutoShape.

2. Click the Size tab.

3. Enter the angle of rotation, or click the up arrow or down arrow.

4. Click OK.

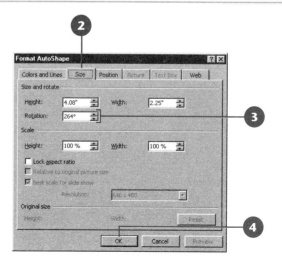

5

Choosing Object Colors

When you create a closed drawing object such as a square, it uses two colors from the color scheme: the Fill color and the Line color. When you create a line drawing object, it uses the color scheme Line color. You can change the Fill and Line color settings for drawing objects using the same color tools for changing a slide's background or text color. You can use fill effects as well, including gradients, patterns, and even clip art pictures.

TIP

Apply the current fill color.
An easy way to apply the current fill color to an object is to select the object and then click the Fill Color button.

Change a Drawing Object's Fill Color

1 Click the drawing object whose fill color you want to change.

2 Click the Fill Color drop-down arrow on the Drawing toolbar.

3 Select the fill color you want.

4 Click Fill Effects if you want to change the fill effect too.

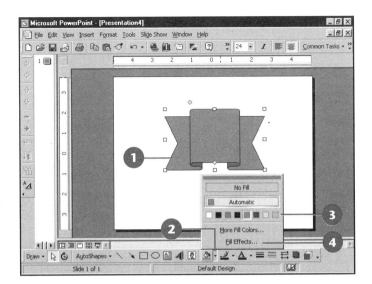

Remove a Fill

1 Click the drawing object whose fill you want to change.

2 Click the Fill Color drop-down arrow on the Drawing toolbar.

3 Click No Fill.

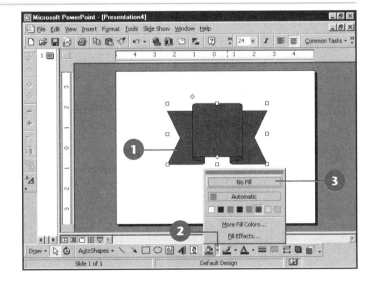

SEE ALSO

See "Choosing a Fill Effect" on page 66 for information on using fill effects and patterns.

TIP

Change the fill to match the background. *Select the object, click the Format menu, click Colors And Lines, click the Fill Color drop-down arrow, and then click Background.*

SEE ALSO

See "Applying a Color to an Object" on page 64 for information on selecting and creating customized colors.

TIP

Set the color and line style for an object as the default. *Right-click the object, and then click Set AutoShape Defaults. Any new objects you create will use the same styles.*

Create a Fill Pattern

1. Click the drawing object whose fill you want to change.

2. Click the Fill Color drop-down arrow, and then click Fill Effects.

   ◆ Click the Gradient tab and select the gradient color and shading style.

   ◆ Click the Texture tab and select a texture.

   ◆ Click the Pattern tab and select a pattern and foreground and background color.

   ◆ Click the Picture tab to select a picture.

3. Click OK.

Click a tab to select a fill effect style

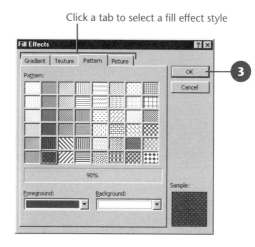

Change Colors and Lines in the Format Dialog Box

1. Click the drawing object you want to modify.

2. Click the Format menu, and then click AutoShape.

3. Click the Colors And Lines tab.

4. Set color, line, and arrow options.

5. Click OK.

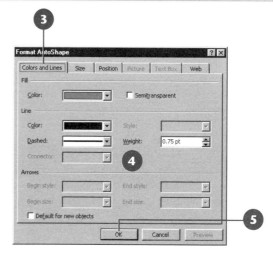

Creating Shadows

You can give objects on your slides the illusion of depth by adding shadows. PowerPoint provides several preset shadowing options, or you can create your own by specifying the location and color of the shadow. If the shadow is falling on another object in your slide, you can create a semitransparent shadow that blends the color of the shadow with the color of the object underneath it.

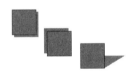

TIP

Remove a shadow. *Click the drawing object with the shadow, click the Shadow button on the Drawing toolbar, and then click No Shadow.*

Use a Preset Shadow

1. Click the drawing object to which you want to add a preset shadow.

2. Click the Shadow button on the Drawing toolbar.

3. Click a shadow style.

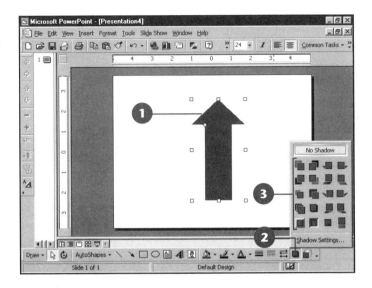

Change the Location of a Shadow

1. Click the drawing object with the shadow.

2. Click the Shadow button on the Drawing toolbar, and then click Shadow Settings.

3. Click the tool that creates the effect you want. The Nudge buttons move the shadow location slightly up, down, right, or left.

4. Click the Close button on the Shadow Settings toolbar.

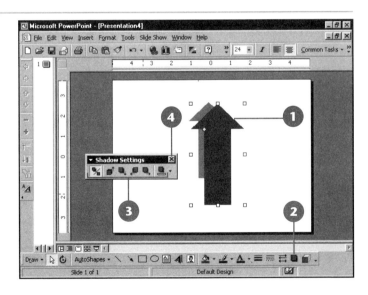

SEE ALSO

See "Choosing Object Colors" on page 84 for information on selecting colors.

TRY THIS

Add an embossed or engraved effect to an object. *Select the object, and then click the Shadow button on the Drawing toolbar. To add an embossed effect, click Shadow Style 17. To add an engraved effect, click Shadow Style 18. Adding one of these effects to your company name or logo gives it a polished look.*

A B C

SEE ALSO

See "Creating a 3-D Object" on page 88 for information on adding a 3-D style to an object.

Change the Color of a Shadow

1. Click the drawing object with the shadow.

2. Click the Shadow button on the Drawing toolbar, and then click Shadow Settings.

3. Click the Shadow Color drop-down arrow on the Shadow Settings toolbar, and then select a new color.

4. Click the Close button on the Shadow Settings toolbar.

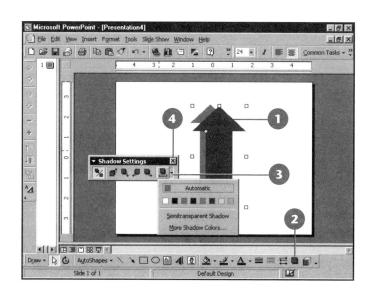

Add a Shadow to Text

1. Click the text object to which you want to add a shadow.

2. Click the Shadow button on the Drawing toolbar.

3. Click a shadow style.

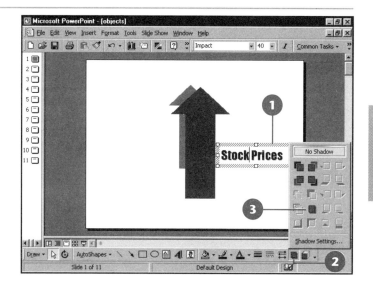

Creating a 3-D Object

You can add the illusion of depth to your slides by using the 3-D tool. Although not all objects can be turned into 3-D objects, most of the AutoShapes can. You can create a 3-D effect using one of the 20 preset 3-D styles supported by PowerPoint, or you can use the 3-D tools to customize your own 3-D style. The settings you can control with the customization tools include the spin of the object, or the angle at which the 3-D object is tilted and rotated, the depth of the object, and the direction of light falling upon the object.

Apply a Preset 3-D Style

1. Click the drawing object you want to change.

2. Click the 3-D button on the Drawing toolbar.

3. Click a 3-D style.

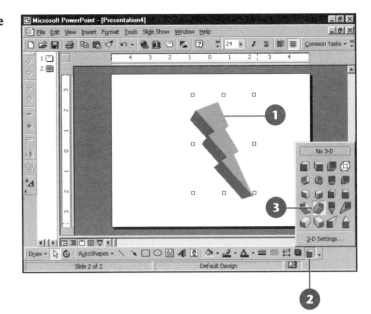

Spinning a 3-D Object

1. Click the 3-D object you want to change.

2. Click the 3-D button on the Drawing toolbar, and then click 3-D Settings.

3. Click the spin setting you want.

4. Click the Close button on the 3-D Settings toolbar.

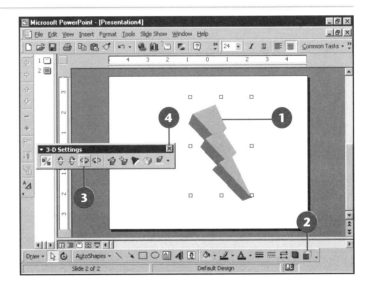

Troubleshooting 3-D objects. *You cannot use both drop shadows and 3-D effects on the same object.*

Add a different surface to your 3-D object. *You can apply interesting surfaces, such as wire frame, matte, plastic, or metal, to your 3-D object by clicking the Surface button on the 3-D Settings toolbar.*

Change the direction of a 3-D object. *Click the Direction button on the 3-D Settings toolbar. You can also use this button to add perspective to your objects or align them along a parallel.*

Set Lighting

1. Click the 3-D object, click the 3-D button on the Drawing toolbar, and then click 3-D Settings.

2. Click the Lighting button.

3. Click the spotlight that creates the effect you want.

4. Click the Close button on the 3-D Settings toolbar.

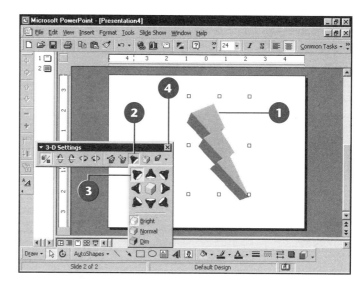

Set 3-D Depth

1. Click the 3-D object, click the 3-D button on the Drawing toolbar, and then click 3-D Settings.

2. Click the Depth button.

3. Click the size of the depth in points, or enter the exact number of points you want in the Custom box.

4. Click the Close button on the 3-D Settings toolbar.

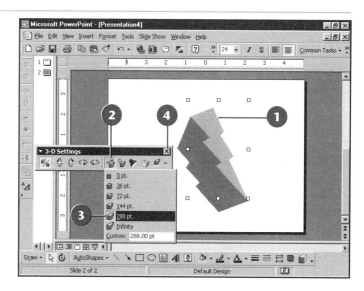

5

Controlling Object Placement

PowerPoint offers several tools for controlling where you place objects on the slide. One tool is the *grid*, an invisible matrix of lines. When the grid is on, an object *snaps* or aligns to the nearest point on the grid. PowerPoint also can snap objects to other shapes so that as you place new objects on the slide they align themselves with preexisting shapes. Another way of controlling placement is with *alignment guides*, horizontal and vertical lines superimposed on the slide to help manually align objects. When an object is close to a guide, its corner or center, whichever is closer, snaps to the guide.

> **TIP**
>
> **Select multiple objects.**
> *Press and hold the Shift key and then click each object you want selected.*

Set Objects to Snap into Place

1. Click the Draw button on the Drawing toolbar, and then point to Snap.

2. Click To Grid or To Shape.

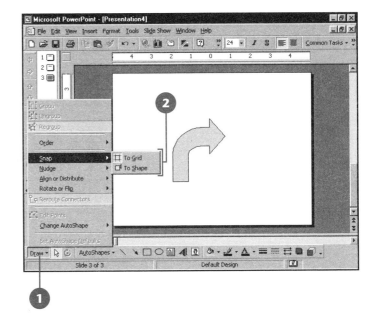

Align an Object to a Guide

1. Click the View menu, and then click Guides to display a horizontal and vertical guide.

2. Drag the object's center or edge near the guide. PowerPoint aligns the center or edge to the guide.

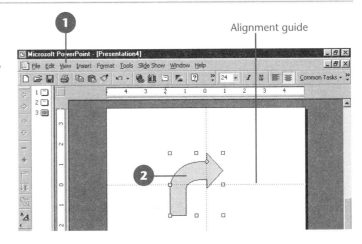

Alignment guide

Use the keyboard to override grid settings. *To temporarily override settings for the grids and guides, press and hold the Alt key as you drag an object.*

See "Indenting Text" on page 36 for information on viewing the ruler when you want to set guides.

See "Working with Objects" on page 26 for information on selecting, resizing, and moving objects.

Add, Move, or Remove a Guide

◆ To move a guide, drag it.

◆ To add a new guide, press and hold the Ctrl key, and then drag the line to the new location. You can place a guide anywhere on the slide.

◆ To remove a guide, drag the guide off the slide.

As you drag, a number appears that indicates the guide's position relative to the ruler.

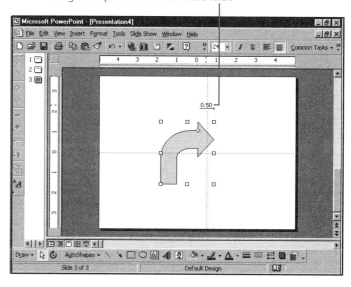

Aligning and Distributing Objects

Often when you work with three similar or identical objects, they look best when aligned with each other. For example, you can align three objects with the leftmost object in the selection so that the tops of all three objects match along an invisible line. PowerPoint also lets you distribute your items horizontally and vertically. You can specify whether the distribution should occur for only the space currently occupied by the objects or across the entire slide.

SEE ALSO

See "Controlling Object Placement" on page 90 for information on aligning objects to a grid, shape, or guide.

Align Objects with Other Objects

1. Select the objects you want to align.

2. Click the Draw button on the Drawing toolbar, and then point to Align Or Distribute.

3. Select Relative To Slide if you want the objects to align relative to the slide, or deselect Relative To Slide if you want the objects to align relative to each other.

4. Click the alignment command you want.

   ◆ Click Align Left to line up the objects with the left edge of the selection or slide.

   ◆ Click Align Center to line up the objects with the center of the selection or slide.

   ◆ Click Align Right to line up the objects with the right edge of the selection or slide.

   ◆ Click Align Top to line up the objects with the top edge of the selection or slide.

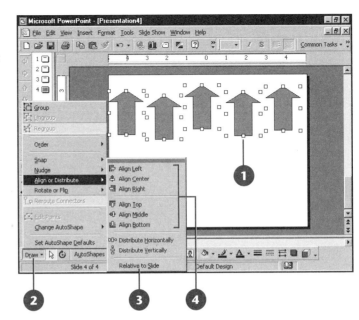

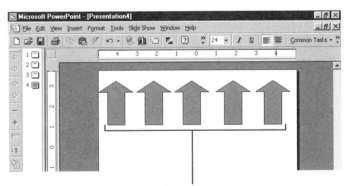

Objects aligned to their tops

Objects don't move where I want them. *Make sure Relative To Slide on the Align Or Distribute submenu isn't selected. When this command is selected, objects will move in relation to the slide as well as to other objects.*

"How can I make sure these three objects are the same distance apart?"

◆ Click Align Middle to line up the objects vertically with the middle of the selection or slide.

◆ Click Align Bottom to line up the objects with the bottom of the selection or slide.

Distribute Objects

1. Select the objects you want to distribute.

2. Click the Draw button on the Drawing toolbar, and then point to Align Or Distribute.

3. Click the distribution option you want.

◆ Click Distribute Horizontally to evenly distribute the objects horizontally.

◆ Click Distribute Vertically to evenly distribute the objects vertically.

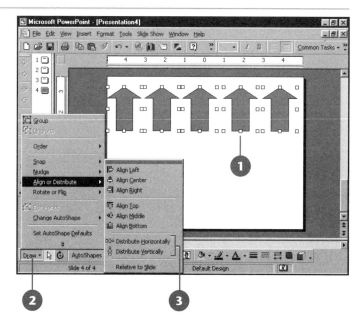

Arranging and Grouping Objects

When a slide contains multiple objects, consider how they interact with each other. If the objects overlap, the most recently created drawing is placed on top of older drawings. You can change the order of this stack of objects. If you create a collection of objects that work together, you can group them to create a new drawing object that you can move, resize, or copy as a single unit.

TIP

Use the Tab key to select objects in order. *You can move between the drawing objects on your slide (even those hidden behind other objects) by pressing the Tab key.*

Arrange a Stack of Objects

1 Select the objects you want to arrange.

2 Click the Draw button on the Drawing toolbar, point to Order, and then click the option you want.

◆ Click Bring To Front or Bring Forward to move a drawing to the top of the stack or up one location in the stack.

◆ Click Send To Back or Send Backward to move a drawing to the bottom of the stack or back one location in the stack.

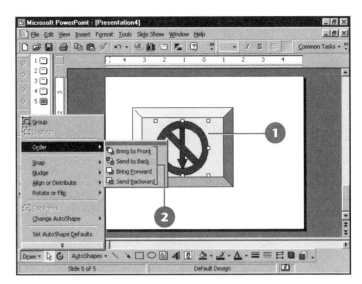

Group Objects Together

1 Select the objects you want to group together.

2 Click the Draw button on the Drawing toolbar, and then click Group.

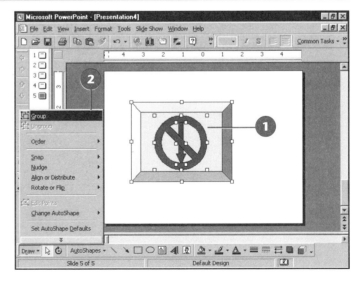

Use the shortcut menu to select the Order and Grouping commands. *Right-click the objects you want to group or reorder, and then point to Grouping or Order and make your selections.*

Troubleshoot arranging objects. *If you have trouble selecting an object because another object is in the way, try moving the first object out of the way temporarily.*

Add effects to a group of objects. *Select the group to which you want to add special effects. Then click the 3-D, Shadow, or Free Rotate button on the Drawing toolbar.*

Ungroup a Drawing

1. Select the grouped object you want to ungroup.

2. Click the Draw button on the Drawing toolbar, and then click Ungroup.

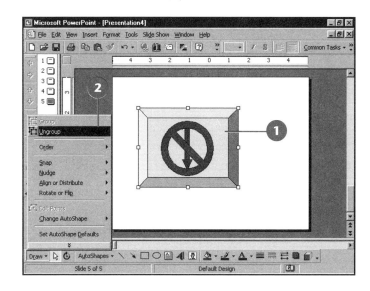

Regroup a Drawing

1. Select one of the objects in the group of objects you want to regroup.

2. Click the Draw button on the Drawing toolbar, and then click Regroup.

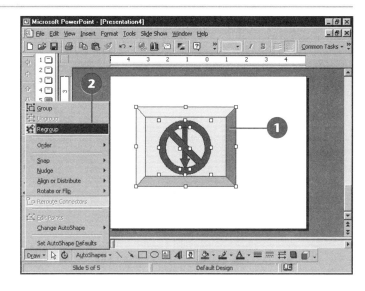

Adding a Drawing Object to the Clip Gallery

After spending time creating an object, you might want to save it for use in future presentations. You can add any object you create to the Microsoft Clip Gallery, an organized collection of clip art, pictures, videos, and sounds that come with PowerPoint. You can also find a picture in the Clip Gallery and use it as the basis for the logo for your home business. For example, you could use the basket of bread image for a home bakery.

SEE ALSO

See "Locating Clips" on page 99 and "Inserting Clips" on page 100 for more information on using the Microsoft Clip Gallery.

Add Your Own Drawing Object to the Clip Gallery

① Select the drawing object you created.

② Click the Copy button on the Standard toolbar.

③ Click the Insert Clip Art button on the Drawing toolbar.

④ Click the category in the Clip Gallery to which you want to add the drawing object.

⑤ Click the Paste button on the Insert ClipArt toolbar.

⑥ Enter a description for the object.

⑦ Click OK.

⑧ Click the Close button.

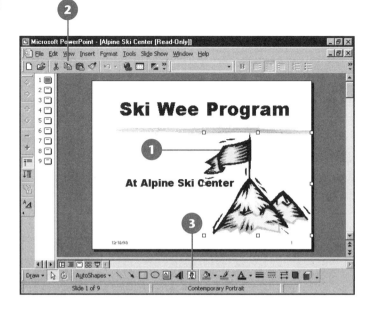

Category name

6

Adding Multimedia Clips

Although well-illustrated slides can't make up for a lack of content, you can capture your audience's attention if your slides are vibrant and visually interesting. You can easily enhance a slide by adding a picture—one of your own or one of the hundreds that come with Microsoft PowerPoint 2000. If you have the appropriate hardware, such as a sound card and speakers, you can also include sound files and video clips in your presentation.

You can also insert other multimedia objects into your presentation, such as clip art and videos. If you have used other Microsoft Office 2000 products, you are probably already familiar with the tools you use to insert these types of objects. Make sure you have the necessary accessories installed before you perform all the tasks in this section. For example, you need the PowerPoint 2000 or Office 2000 CD, a sound card, speakers, a microphone, and access to the Internet.

Inserting Multimedia Clips

A vast collection of multimedia clips come with PowerPoint. These clips include clip art, pictures, photographs, sounds, and videos. All Office 2000 programs provide a feature called the *Microsoft Clip Gallery,* which organizes these objects into categories and gives you tools to help locate the clips you need quickly. You can extend the usefulness of the Clip Gallery by importing your own objects.

Clip Art

Clip art objects (pictures and animated pictures) are images made up of geometric shapes, such as lines, curves, circles, squares, and so on. These images, known as *vector images*, are mathematically defined, which make them easy to resize and manipulate. A picture in the Microsoft Windows Metafile (.WMF) file format is an example of a vector image.

Pictures

Pictures, on the other hand, are not mathematically defined. They are *bitmaps*, images that are made up of dots. Bitmaps do not lend themselves as easily to resizing because the dots can't expand and contract when you enlarge or shrink your picture. You can create a picture using a bitmap graphics program such as Windows *Paint, Microsoft PhotoDraw 2000,* or *Microsoft Photo Editor,* by drawing or scanning an image or by taking a digital photograph.

Sounds

A *sound* is a file that makes a sound. Some sounds play on your computer's internal speakers (such as the beep you hear when your operating system alerts you to an error), but others require a sound card and speakers. You can use the Windows accessory called *Windows Media Player* to listen to sound clips.

Videos

A *video* can be animated pictures, such as cartoons, or it can be digital video prepared with digitized video equipment. Although you can play a video clip on most monitors, if it has sound, you need a sound card and speakers to hear the clip.

Locating Clips

You can use the Clip Gallery's Search feature to locate a particular clip. You search for clips using one or more keywords. A *keyword* describes the clip and can be part of the clip's filename. Imagine, for example, that you need a piece of clip art to show how a recent bull market affected your company's returns. If you enter the keyword *bull*, the Clip Gallery displays all images associated with bulls—from the animal to a bulldozer. You can also locate clips based on other clips. For example, you might want all of the clips in the presentation to represent a certain theme or artistic style.

TIP

Display all the categories in Clip Gallery. *Click the All Categories button on the Insert ClipArt toolbar.*

Locate a Clip by Keyword

1. Click the Insert menu, point to Picture, and then click Clip Art.

2. Click the tab representing the type of clip you are looking for (Pictures, Sounds, or Motion Clips).

3. Click the Search For Clips box, and then type the keyword(s) associated with the clip you are looking for.

4. Press Enter.

   Matching clips appear.

5. Click the Close button.

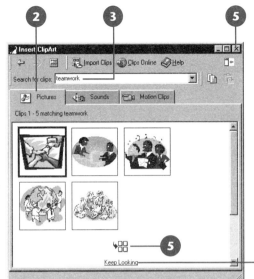

Click to see more matching clips.

Find Similar Clips

1. Click the Insert menu, point to Picture, and then click Clip Art.

2. Click a clip similar to the ones you want to find.

3. Click the Find Similar Clips button on the shortcut menu.

4. Click Artistic Style, Color & Shape, or one of the keywords to narrow your search.

5. Click the Close button.

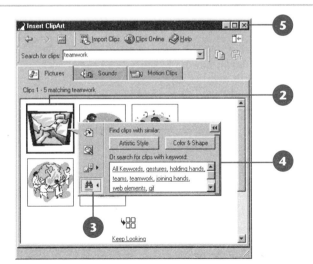

6

Inserting Clips

PowerPoint offers several easy methods for inserting clips. If you're including a clip on a new slide, you can choose an AutoLayout that includes a placeholder for a clip. To insert a clip on an existing slide, use the Insert menu. The Insert menu contains commands for inserting pictures (from the Clip Gallery, a file, or a scanner or digital camera) and for inserting movies and sounds. You can insert clips from Microsoft's Clip Gallery or from your own files. You can also add your own clips to the Clip Gallery.

Insert Clip Art button

> **TIP**
>
> **Drag a picture.** *You can also drag a picture from the Clip Gallery to your slide.*

Insert a Clip on a New Slide

1. Click the New Slide button on the Standard toolbar.

2. Click the AutoLayout that includes the clip type you want to insert, such as Clip Art, and then click OK.

3. Double-click the place-holder for the object type you want to insert.

4. Click the tab for the type of clip you want, and then click a category you want.

5. Click the clip you want, and then click the Insert Clip button.

6. Click the Close button.

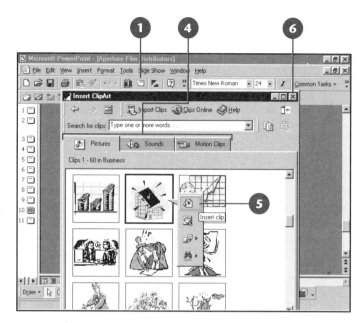

Insert a Clip on an Existing Slide

1. Click the Insert Clip Art button on the Drawing toolbar.

2. Click the tab for the type of clip you want, and then click a category you want.

3. Click the clip you want, and then click the Insert Clip button.

4. Click the Close button.

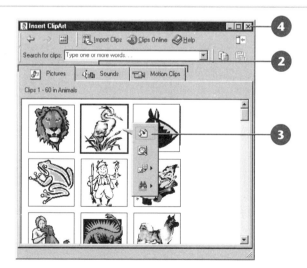

TIP

Use the Picture toolbar to insert a picture. *To insert an picture from a file, click Insert Picture From File on the Picture toolbar.*

SEE ALSO

See "Inserting and Playing Videos and Sounds" on page 112 for information on importing those types of clips.

TIP

Move back or forward in the Clip Gallery. *To go back to a previous screen or forward to one you've already visited, click the Back or Forward button on the Insert ClipArt toolbar.*

TIP

Get Clip Gallery Help. *To get more information about the Clip Gallery, click the Help button on the Insert ClipArt toolbar.*

Insert a Picture from a File

1. Click the Insert menu, point to Picture, and then click From File.

2. Click the Look In drop-down arrow, and then select the drive and folder that contain the file you want to insert.

3. Click the file you want to insert.

4. Click Insert.

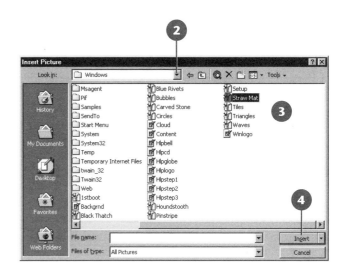

Insert a Picture from a Scanner or Camera

1. Click the Insert menu, point to Picture, and then click From Scanner Or Camera.

2. Click the Device drop-down arrow, and then select the device connected to your computer.

3. Select the resolution (the visual quality of the image).

4. Click Insert or Custom Insert.

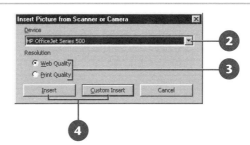

6

Adding and Removing Clips

You can import your own clips (pictures, photo-graphics, sounds, and videos) into the Clip Gallery. For example, if you have a company logo that you plan to include in more than one presentation, add it to the Clip Gallery. You can also add groups of clips to the Clip Gallery or remove individual ones.

SEE ALSO

See "Accessing the Clip Gallery Live on the Web" on page 104 for information on downloading clip art you can add to the Clip Gallery.

SEE ALSO

See "Adding a Drawing Object to the Clip Gallery" on page 96 for more information on adding PowerPoint objects to the Clip Gallery.

Add a Clip

1 Click the Insert Clip Art button on the Drawing toolbar, and then click the Import Clips button.

2 Click the Look In drop-down arrow, and then select the drive and folder that contain the clip you want to import.

3 Click the Files Of Type drop-down arrow, and then select the file type.

4 Click the clip you want to import.

5 Click a Clip Import option.

6 Click Import.

7 Set the clip properties, and then click OK.

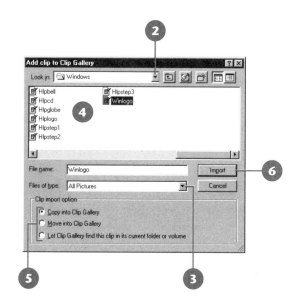

Remove a Clip

1 Click the Insert Clip Art button on the Drawing toolbar, and then click the clip you want to remove.

2 Press Delete.

3 To delete the clip from all Clip Gallery categories, click OK.

To remove the clip from just one category, click Cancel and use the Clip Properties dialog box.

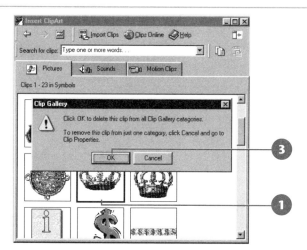

Organizing Clips into Categories

The clips that come with PowerPoint 2000 are already organized, but if you've added clips without organizing them, it's probably hard to find what you need in a hurry. To help you locate a clip quickly, you can place it in one or more categories. You can also assign one or more keywords to a clip and modify the description of a clip.

TIP

Create a new category. *In the Clip Gallery, click the All Categories button to display all the categories, click New Category, type a new category name, and then click OK.*

New Category

Categorize a Clip

1. Click the Insert Clip Art button on the Drawing toolbar, and then click the clip you want to categorize.

2. Click the Add Clip To Favorites Or Other Category button on the shortcut menu.

3. Click the drop-down arrow, and select the category to which you want to add the clip.

4. Click Add.

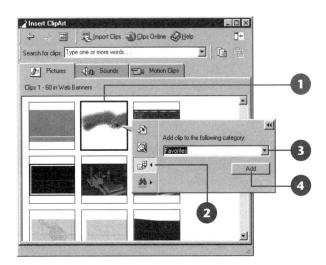

Change Clip Properties

1. Click the Insert Clip Art button on the Drawing toolbar.

2. Right-click the clip you want to categorize, and then click Clip Properties.

3. Click the Description tab to enter a description for the clip.

4. Click the Categories tab to select one or more categories where you want the clip to appear.

5. Click the Keywords tab to add or remove keywords for the clip.

6. Click OK.

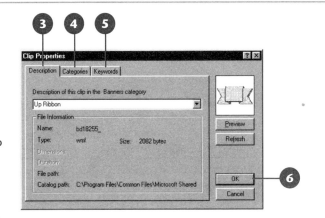

6

Accessing Clip Gallery Live on the Web

If you have an Internet connection, you can go to a Web page from the Clip Gallery to browse through additional clips. You can then download those clips to your hard disk. Any clips you select are added to the Clip Gallery.

SEE ALSO

See "Adding and Removing Clips" on page 102 to import your own clips into the Clip Gallery.

Open Clip Gallery Live

1. Click the Insert Clip Art button on the Drawing toolbar, and then click the Clips Online button.

2. If a message appears telling you about the Web feature, click OK. Windows initiates your computer's Internet connection.

3. Connect to the Web using the dialog box that appears.

   Your Web browser displays the Microsoft Clip Gallery Live Web page.

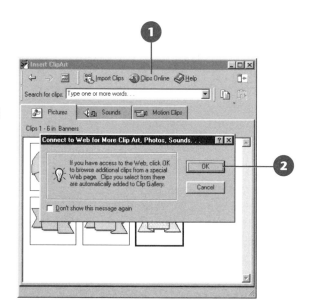

View Clips in a Category

1. If necessary, click the Accept button on the Clip Gallery Live Web page.

2. Click the tab for the media type you want: Clip Art, Pictures, Sounds, or Motion.

3. Click the Browse Clips By Category drop-down arrow, and then click the category you want.

4. Click More to see more clips in the category.

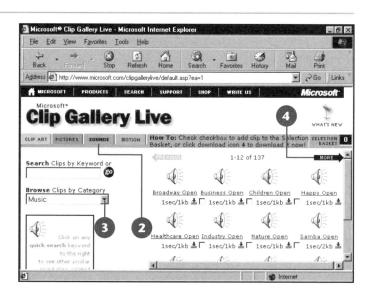

TIP

Use the Selection Basket.
You can add clips to the Selection Basket by clicking the check box below the clip. That way, you can mark the clips but not download them until you are ready to "check out."

TRY THIS

Download the contents of the Selection Basket. *Once you have finished searching for clips, you can download the contents of the Selection Basket rather than downloading the clips one at a time. Click the Selection Basket, click Download, and then click Download Now!*

SEE ALSO

See "Organizing Clips into Categories" on page 103 for more information on how to change a clip's properties.

Search for a Clip

1. Click the tab for the media type you want: Clip Art, Pictures, Sounds, or Motion.

2. Click the Search Clips By Keyword box.

3. Type a keyword.

4. Click Go.

5. Click Yes if you are asked if you want to continue.

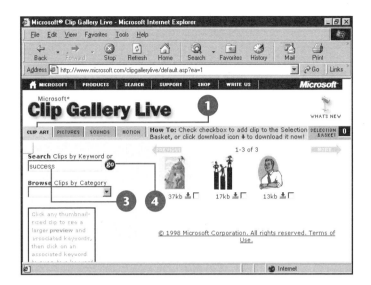

Download a Clip

1. Once you have displayed a list of clips on the Clip Gallery Live Web page, click the Download Clip icon below the clip you want.

2. If a virus warning dialog box appears, click the Save It To Disk option button, and then click OK to add the clip to the Clip Gallery.

3. Click one of the tabs to change the properties of the clip.

4. Click OK. The clip is stored on your hard disk and added to the Clip Gallery.

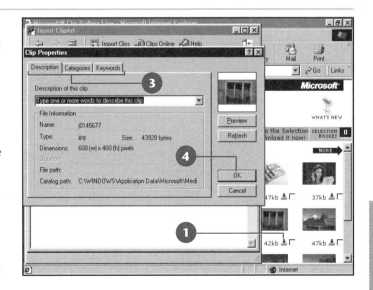

Modifying a Picture

Once you have inserted clip art and other objects into your presentation, you can adapt them to meet your needs. Perhaps the clip is too small to be effective, or you don't quite like the colors it uses. Like any object, you can resize or move the clip art. You can also control the image's colors, brightness, and contrast using the Picture toolbar. You can use these same methods with bitmapped pictures.

TIP

Show the Picture toolbar.
If the Picture Toolbar didn't appear when you selected an image, right-click any toolbar, and then click Picture.

TIP

Add a border to a picture.
Select the picture, click the Line Style button on the Picture toolbar, and then click the line style you want.

Resize an Object

1. Click the object you want to resize.

2. Drag one of the sizing handles to increase or decrease the object's size.

   ◆ Drag a middle handle to resize the object up, down, left, or right.

   ◆ Drag a corner handle to resize the object proportionally.

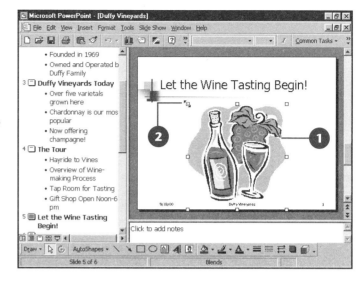

Change Contrast

1. Click the picture whose contrast you want to increase or decrease.

2. Choose the contrast you want.

   ◆ Click the More Contrast button on the Picture toolbar to increase color intensity, resulting in less gray.

   ◆ Click the Less Contrast button on the Picture toolbar to decrease color intensity, resulting in more gray.

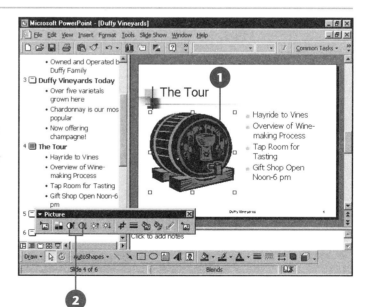

TIP

Ungroup and modify clip art. When you insert a picture from the Clip Gallery, you can convert it into separate PowerPoint objects. Then you can use the drawing tools to edit the objects. Double-click the Clip Gallery picture you want to modify, and then click Yes to ungroup the picture.

TIP

What happens when you reset a picture? Resetting a picture restores its previous size and its original contrast and brightness.

"I made changes to my clip, but I'd like to restore its original settings."

Change Brightness

1 Click the picture whose brightness you want to increase or decrease.

2 Choose the image brightness you want.

◆ Click the More Brightness button on the Picture toolbar to lighten the object colors by adding more white.

◆ Click the Less Brightness button on the Picture toolbar to darken the object colors by adding more black.

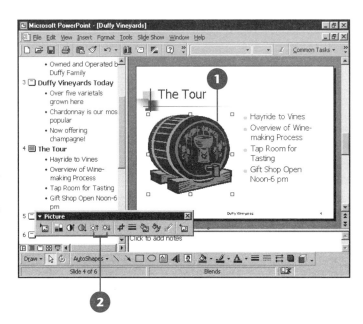

Restore Original Settings

1 Click the picture whose settings you want to restore.

2 Click the Reset Picture button on the Picture toolbar.

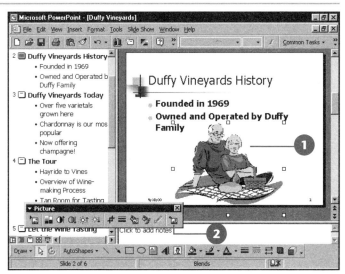

6

Recoloring a Picture

You can recolor clip art and other objects to match the color scheme of your presentation. For example, if you use a flower clip art as your business logo, you can change shades of pink in the spring to shades of orange in the autumn. You can also use a transparent background in your clip art to avoid conflict between its background color and your slide's background. With a transparent background, the clip art takes on the same background as your slide presentation.

TIP

Can't modify some pictures in PowerPoint.
If the picture is a bitmap (.BMP, .JPG, .GIF, or .PNG), you need to edit its colors in an image editing program, such as Microsoft Photo Editor or Microsoft PhotoDraw 2000.

Choose a Color Type

1. Click the picture whose color you want to change.

2. Click the Image Control button on the Picture toolbar.

3. Click one of the Image Control options.

    ◆ Automatic gives the image the default coloring.

    ◆ Grayscale converts the default coloring into whites, blacks, and grays scaled between white and black.

    ◆ Black & White converts the default coloring into only white and black. You may lose detail in your object when you choose this option.

    ◆ Watermark converts the default coloring into whites and very light colors. This option makes a nice slide background.

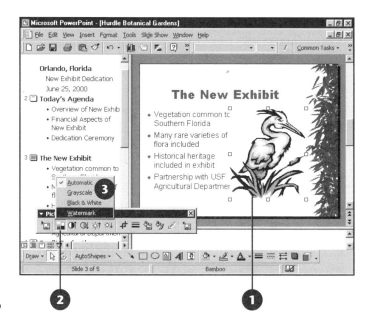

Recolor Picture button

Recolor a Picture

1. Click the picture you want to recolor.

2. Click the Recolor Picture button on the Picture toolbar.

3. Click the check box next to the original color you want to change.

4. Click the corresponding New drop-down arrow, and then select a new color.

5. Repeat steps 3 and 4 for as many colors as you want.

6. Click OK.

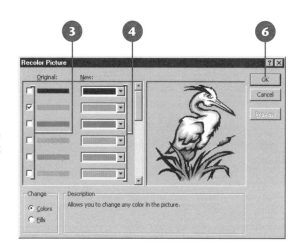

Set a Transparent Background

1. Click the picture you want to change.

2. Click the Set Transparent Color button on the Picture toolbar.

3. Move the pointer over the object until the pointer changes shape.

4. Click the color you want to set as transparent.

5. Click outside the image when you are finished.

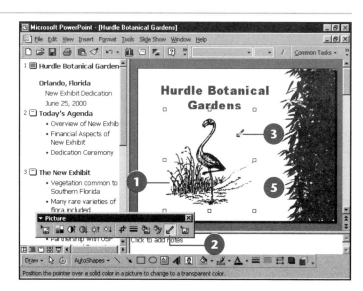

Cropping a Picture

You can crop clip art to isolate just one portion of the picture. Because clip art uses vector image technology, you can *crop*, or cut out, even the smallest part of it and then enlarge it, and the clip art will still be recognizable. You can also crop bitmapped pictures, but if you enlarge the area you cropped, you lose picture detail. You can crop an image by hand using the Crop button on the Picture toolbar. You can also crop using the Format Picture dialog box, which gives you precise control over the dimensions of the area you want to crop.

SEE ALSO

See "Inserting Multimedia Clips" on page 98 for more information on vector image technology.

Crop a Picture Quickly

1. Click the picture you want to crop.

2. Click the Crop button on the Picture toolbar.

3. Drag the sizing handles until the borders surround the area you want to crop.

4. Click outside the image when you are finished.

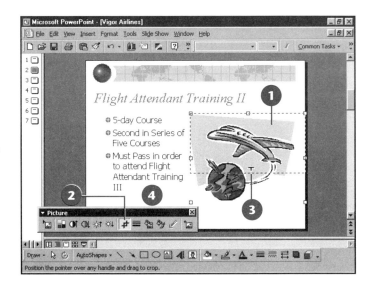

Redisplay a Cropped Picture

1. Click the picture you want to restore.

2. Click the Crop button on the Picture toolbar.

3. Drag the sizing handles to reveal the areas that were originally cropped.

4. Click outside the image when you are finished.

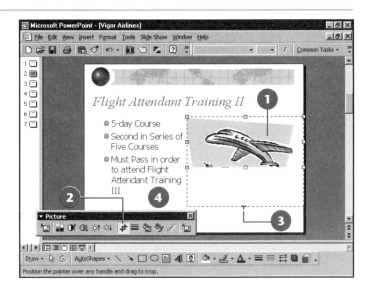

TIP

Adjust cropping from values. *Values represent distance from the border of the image. When you first insert an image, the values are all 0. If you enter, for example, a value of 2" in the Left box, the leftmost two inches of the image will be cropped off.*

TIP

Can't make some changes to an animated GIF. *You cannot crop, group, or change the fill, border, shadow, or transparency of an animated GIF. Make these changes in an animated GIF editing program, and then insert the file on the slide again.*

Crop a Picture Precisely

1. Right-click the picture you want to format, and then click Format Picture.

2. Click the Picture tab.

3. Adjust the values in the Left, Right, Top, and Bottom boxes to crop the image to the exact dimensions you want.

4. Click OK.

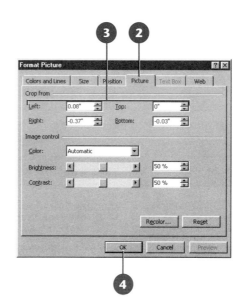

Inserting and Playing Videos and Sounds

You can insert videos or sounds into a presentation by inserting them from the Clip Gallery or a file. Videos can be either *animated pictures,* also known as animated GIFs, such as cartoons, or they can be digital videos prepared with digitized video equipment. Videos and sounds are inserted as PowerPoint objects. When you insert a sound, a small icon appears representing the sound file. You can modify videos and sounds so they play continuously or just one time. To play individual sounds, or sounds from video, you need a sound card and speakers.

SEE ALSO

See "Embedding and Linking an Object" on page 122 for information on inserting an emdedded object, such as Media Player, if PowerPoint doesn't support a particular media type.

Insert a Clip Gallery Movie or Sound

1. Click the Insert menu, and then point to Movies And Sounds.

2. Click Sound From Gallery or Movie From Gallery.

3. Click the media clip you want to insert, and then click the Insert Clip button.

4. Click the Close button.

5. Click Yes or No to play the media clip in slide show.

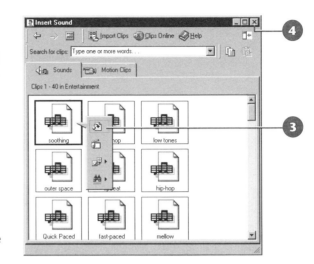

Insert a Movie or Sound on a New Slide

1. Click the Insert New Slide button on the Standard toolbar.

2. Click the Media Clip & Text or Text & Media Clip AutoLayout, and then click OK.

3. Double-click the Media Clip placeholder.

4. Click the media clip you want to insert, and then click the Insert Clip button.

5. Click the Close button.

6. Click Yes or No to play the media clip in slide show.

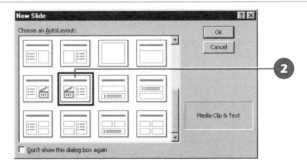

Set slide show multimedia options for a video or sound. *For example, you can have the video object fly in from the left and then begin playing in an animation sequence. Select the video object or sound icon for which you want to set play options. Click the Slide Show menu, click Custom Animation, and then click the Multimedia Settings tab. Select the options you want or click More Options. You can't set play options for animated pictures.*

Play a Movie or Sound

◆ To play a movie or sound in Normal or Slide view, double-click the movie object or sound icon.

◆ To play a movie, sound, or animated picture in Slide Show view, click the Slide Show button, and then display the slide with the media you want to play.

Depending on your slide show multimedia options, you may need to click the movie object or sound icon to play it.

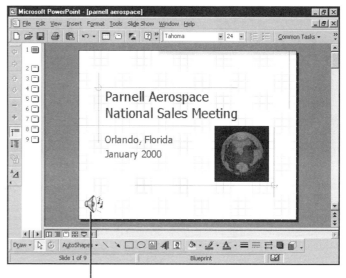

This icon appears when you insert a sound.

Insert a CD audio track on a slide. *Display the slide to which you want to add a CD audio track. (You do not need the CD in the drive to set this up.) Click the Insert menu, point to Movies And Sounds, and then click Play CD Audio Track. Select the track and timing options you want, and then click OK. A CD icon appears on the slide. Click Yes or No to automatically play the CD sound in slide show. You can preview the music in Normal view by double-clicking the CD icon.*

Edit a Movie or Sound

1 Right-click the sound icon or movie object, and then click Edit Sound Object or Edit Movie Object.

2 Change the sound or movie settings.

◆ Click the Loop Until Stopped check box to play the sound or movie continuously.

◆ Click the Rewind Movie When Done Playing check box if you are inserting a movie.

3 Click OK.

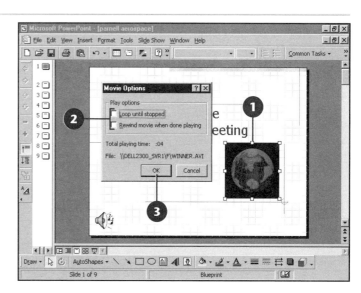

6

Recording Sounds

You can record your own sounds and include them in your PowerPoint presentations. You might want to include a message from the company president in your presentation or maybe the voice of someone who can't attend the presentation. To record sounds, you need a microphone and Windows Sound Recorder.

TIP

Use Sound Recorder to edit a sound. *If you want to cut a part from your recording, click the Edit menu, and then click Delete Before Current Position or Delete After Current Position.*

TIP

Use Sound Recorder to add special sound effects. *You can add special effects to a sound object such as Reverse or Echo options available on the Effects menu.*

Record a Sound

1. Click the Insert menu, point to Movies And Sounds, and then click Record Sound.

2. Type a name for the sound.

3. Click the Record button.

4. Click the Stop button when you are finished.

5. Click OK.

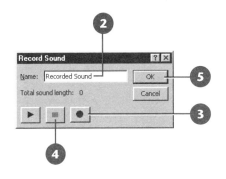

Record a Sound File Using Sound Recorder

1. Click the Start button on the taskbar, point to Programs, point to Accessories, point to Entertainment, and then click Sound Recorder.

2. Click the Record button.

3. Click the Stop button when you are finished.

4. Click the File menu, and then click Save As.

5. Click the Save In drop-down arrow, and then select a location to store the sound file.

6. Enter a filename.

7. Click Save.

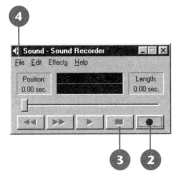

7

Inserting Linked and Embedded Objects

An effective presentation draws on information from many sources. Microsoft PowerPoint 2000 helps you seamlessly integrate information such as tables like those in Microsoft Word, Microsoft Excel worksheet and charts, Microsoft WordArt styled text, and Microsoft Organization Chart charts into your presentations. *Microsoft WordArt* lets you create interesting textual effects. *Microsoft Organization Chart* allows you to create an organization chart, usually to display the personnel or reporting structure within an organization.

Object Linking and Embedding

In PowerPoint, you can insert an object created in another program into a presentation using technology known as *object linking and embedding* (OLE). OLE is a critical feature for many PowerPoint users because it lets you share objects among compatible programs when you create presentations. When you share an object using OLE, the menus and toolbars from the program that created the object are available to you from within your PowerPoint presentation. You can edit inserted information without having to leave PowerPoint.

Sharing Information Among Documents

Object linking and embedding is one of the great recent innovations in personal computing. OLE lets you insert an object created in one program into a document created in another program. Terms that you'll find useful in understanding how you can share objects among documents include:

TERM	DEFINITION
source program	The program that created the original object
source file	The file that contains the original object
destination program	The program that created the document into which you are inserting the object
destination file	The file into which you are inserting the object

For example, if you place an Excel chart in your Power-Point presentation, Excel is the source program and PowerPoint is the destination program. The chart is the source file; the presentation is the destination file.

There are three ways to share information in Windows programs: pasting, embedding, and linking.

Pasting

You can cut or copy an object from one document and then paste it into another using the Cut, Copy, and Paste buttons on the source and destination program toolbars.

Embedding

When you *embed* an object, you place a copy of the object in the destination file, and when you activate the object, the tools from the source program become available in your presentation. For example, if you insert and then click an Excel chart in your PowerPoint presentation, the Excel menus and toolbars replace the PowerPoint menus and toolbars, so you can edit the chart if necessary. With embedding, any changes you make to the chart in the presentation do not affect the original file.

Linking

When you *link* an object, you insert a representation of the object itself into the destination file. The tools of the source program are available, and when you use them to edit the object you've inserted, you are actually editing the source file. Moreover, any changes you make to the source file are reflected in the destination file.

Copying and Pasting Objects

You can copy or cut an object on a slide and paste it to another location in your presentation or a different destination file. When you copy or cut an object, Windows temporarily stores the object on the *Windows Clipboard* (a temporary area in memory). You can paste the object on a slide or into the destination file using the Paste button or the Paste Special command, which gives you more control over how the object appears in the destination file.

TIP

Be careful of file size when pasting objects. *When you click Paste, you are sometimes actually embedding. Because embedding can greatly increase file size, use Paste Special if disk space is at a premium. With Paste Special you can paste the object as a simple picture or text instead of as an embedded object.*

Paste an Object into a Presentation

1. Select the object in the source program.

2. Click the Copy button on the source program's toolbar.

3. Switch to PowerPoint and display the slide on which you want to paste the object.

4. Click the Paste button on the PowerPoint Standard toolbar.

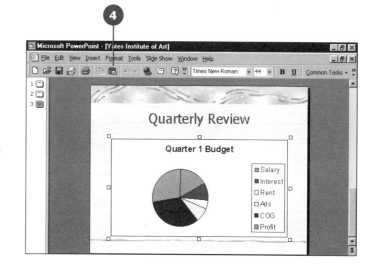

Paste Information in a Specified Format

1. Select the object in the source program.

2. Click the Copy button on the source program's toolbar.

3. Switch to PowerPoint and display the slide on which you want to paste the object.

4. Click the Edit menu, and then click Paste Special.

5. Click the object type you want.

6. Click OK.

The objects that appear depend on what object is on the Clipboard.

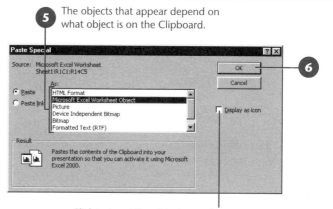

Click to insert the object as an icon.

Storing Multiple Objects

With PowerPoint 2000, you can use the *Microsoft Office Clipboard* to store multiple pieces of information from several different sources in one storage area shared by all Office programs. Unlike the Windows Clipboard, which stores only a single piece of information at a time, the Office Clipboard allows you to copy up to twelve pieces of text or pictures from one or more documents. When you copy multiple items in an Office program, you see the Office Clipboard, showing all the items you stored there. You can paste these pieces of information into any Office program, either individually or all at once.

Copy Data to the Office Clipboard

1. Click the View menu, point to Toolbars, and then click Clipboard.

2. Select the object you want to copy.

3. Click the Copy button on the Office Clipboard or Standard toolbar.

   The object is copied into the first empty position on the Office Clipboard toolbar.

4. Click the Close button.

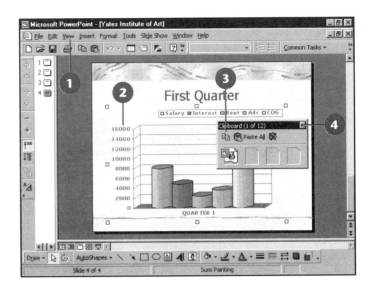

Paste Data from the Office Clipboard

1. Click the View menu, point to Toolbars, and then click Clipboard.

2. In Normal or Slide view, display the slide in which you want to paste the object.

3. Click the Office Clipboard toolbar item you want to paste.

4. Click the Close button.

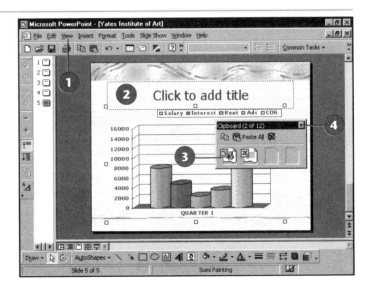

Inserting a Table

A *table* organizes information neatly into rows and columns. The intersection of a column and row is called a *cell*. You enter text into cells just as you would anywhere else in PowerPoint, except that pressing the Tab key moves you from one cell to the next. PowerPoint tables behave much like tables in Word. You don't need to have Microsoft Word installed on your computer to create tables in your presentations.

TIP

Create a new slide with a table. *Click the New Slide button, click the Table AutoLayout, and then click OK. Double-click the table placeholder on the new slide to enter the table information.*

TIP

Insert a tab in a table cell. *Position the insertion point where you want to insert a tab, and then press Ctrl+Tab.*

Insert a Table Quickly

1. In Normal or Slide view, display the slide to which you want to add a table.

2. Click the Insert Table button on the Standard toolbar.

3. Drag to select the number of rows and columns you want.

4. Release the mouse button to insert a blank grid in the document. Press Esc to cancel the selection.

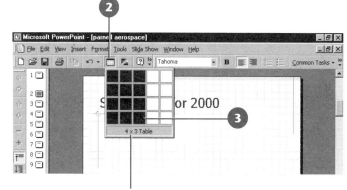

The first number indicates the number of rows. The second number indicates the number of columns.

Enter Text and Move Around a Table

The insertion point shows where text you type will appear in a table. Choose one of the following after you type text in a cell.

◆ Press Return to start a new paragraph within that cell.

◆ Press Tab to move the insertion point to the next cell to the right (or to the first cell in the next row).

◆ Use the arrow keys or click anywhere in the table to move the insertion point to a new location.

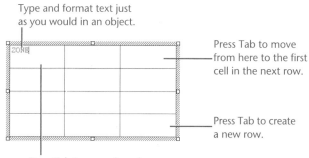

Type and format text just as you would in an object.

Press Tab to move from here to the first cell in the next row.

Press Tab to create a new row.

Press Tab to move from here to the next cell to the right.

Modifying a Table

After you create a table or begin to enter text in one, you might want to add more rows or columns to accomodate the text you are entering in the table. PowerPoint makes it easy for you to format your table. You can change the alignment of the text in the cells (by default, text is aligned on the left of a cell).

TIP

Open the Tables And Borders toolbar. *Click the View menu, point to Toolbars, and then click Tables And Borders.*

TIP

Use the pencil and eraser to add and remove cells. *Click the Pencil button on the Tables And Borders toolbar, and then drag the pencil pointer from one boundary to another to add cells. Click the Eraser button, and then drag over a border to erase a cell.*

Insert and Delete Columns and Rows

1. Click in a table cell next to where you want the new column or row to appear.

2. Click the Table drop-down arrow on the Tables And Borders toolbar.

3. To insert columns and rows, click one of the insert column or insert row commands.

4. To delete columns and rows, click Delete Columns or Delete Rows.

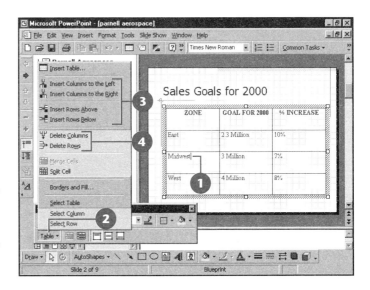

Align Text Within Cells

1. Select the text you want to align in the cells, rows, or columns.

2. Click one of the alignment buttons on the Formatting or Tables And Borders toolbar.

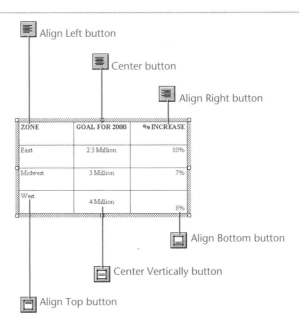

Align Left button

Center button

Align Right button

Align Bottom button

Center Vertically button

Align Top button

TIP

Select a row, column, or table. *Click in a cell in the row, column, or table you want to select, click the Table drop-down arrow on the Tables And Borders toolbar, and then click the appropriate Select command.*

TIP

Merge or split cells. *Select the cells you want to merge or the cell you want to split, and then click the Merge or Split button on the Tables And Borders toolbar.*

TIP

Add shading to a table cell. *Select the cell you want to shade, click the Shading Color drop-down arrow on the Tables And Borders toolbar, and then select the background shading you want inside the cell.*

SEE ALSO

See "Creating a Text Box" on page 46 for information on changing table text orientation.

Modify Cell Borders

1. Select the cells or text whose border(s) you want to modify.

2. Click the Border Style drop-down arrow, and then select a border line style.

3. Click the Border Width drop-down arrow, and then select a line thickness.

4. Click the Border Color drop-down arrow, and then select a border color.

5. Click the Outside Borders drop-down arrow, and then select a border style. The current border styles appear selected.

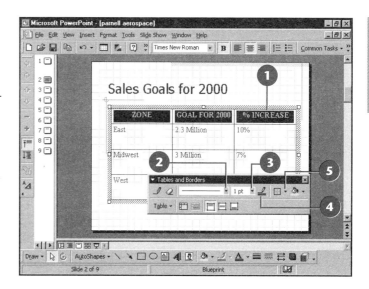

Adjust Row Height and Column Width

1. Move the pointer over the boundary of the row or column you want to adjust until the pointer changes into a resizing pointer.

2. Drag the boundary to adjust the row or column to the size you want.

Embedding and Linking an Object

You can embed or link objects in several ways. If you are creating a new object you want to embed or link, use the Insert Object command. If you want to embed an existing file, you can also use Insert Object and specify whether you want to also link the object. If your object is already open in its source program, you can copy the object, and in some cases, paste it onto a slide, automatically embedding it. Finally, you can use the Paste Special command to *paste link* a copied object—pasting and linking it at the same time.

Insert a New Object

1 Click the Insert menu, and then click Object.

2 Click the Create New option button.

3 Click the type of object you want to insert.

4 Click OK.

5 Use the source program tools to edit the object.

6 Click outside the object when you are finished.

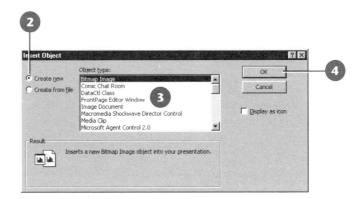

Insert a File

1 Click the Insert menu, and then click Object.

2 Click the Create From File option button.

3 Click Browse.

4 Click the Look In drop-down arrow, and then select the file you want to insert. Click OK.

5 To embed the object, click to deselect the Link check box. To link it, click to select the Link check box.

6 Click OK.

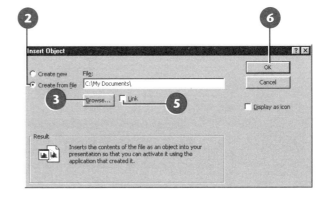

Paste Link an Object

1. In the source program, select the object you want to paste link.

2. Click the Cut or Copy button on the Standard toolbar in the source program.

3. Switch to your presentation.

4. Click the Edit menu, and then click Paste Special.

5. Click the Paste Link option button.

6. Click the object type you want.

7. Click OK.

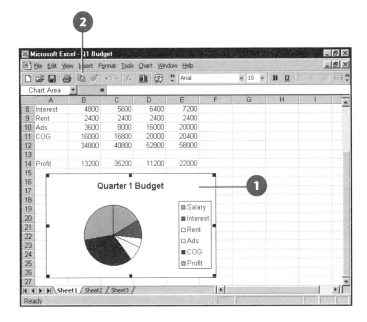

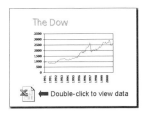

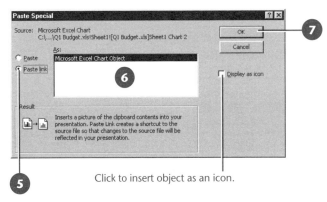

Click to insert object as an icon.

Modifying Links

When you modify a linked object, it is usually updated in the destination document. However, you can choose to update the link manually. All Office 2000 programs give you control over the links you have established. You can change the source file and you can break a link at any time. You can also convert a linked object to another object type.

Edit an embedded object in the source program.
Double-click the embedded object to open it. Make the changes you want to the object. If you edit the object in the open program, click anywhere outside the object to return to the destination file. If you edit the object in the source program, click the File menu, and then click Exit to return to the destination file.

Update Links

1. Open the presentation that contains the links you want to update.

2. Click the Edit menu, and then click Links.

3. Click the link you want to update.

4. Click Update Now.

5. Click Close.

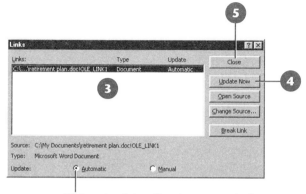

Click so that links will update automatically whenever the document is reopened.

Change the Source of a Linked Object

1. Click the Edit menu, and then click Links.

2. Click the link whose source you want to change.

3. Click Change Source.

4. Locate and double-click the new source file.

5. Click Close.

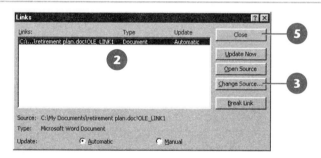

Breaking a link. *After you break the connection to a linked object, you must reinsert the object into your presentation to reconnect.*

"How can I ensure that changes I make to the source file won't affect the object in my presentation?"

Set up an OLE object to open during a presentation. *Select the object you want to open, click the Slide Show menu, and then click Action Settings. To open the OLE object by clicking it during a slide show, click the Mouse Click tab. To open the OLE object by moving the mouse pointer over it, click the Mouse Over tab. Click Object Action and then click Open.*

Break a Link

1. Click the Edit menu, and then click Links.

2. Click the link you want to break.

3. Click Break Link.

   The link no longer appears in the Links dialog box.

4. Click Close.

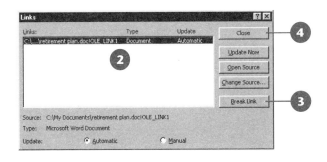

Convert a Linked Object

1. Click the linked object whose file type you want to convert.

2. Click the Edit menu, and then point to Linked Object. This command might appear as Linked Chart Object, or some other file type, depending on the object type.

3. Click Convert.

4. Click the new object type you want.

5. Click OK.

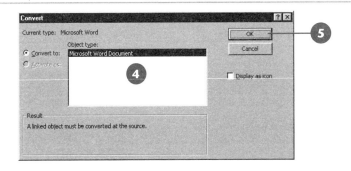

Inserting an Excel Object

You can insert several types of Excel objects into your presentation. Two of the most common are worksheets and charts. You can insert a new Excel worksheet and then add data to it, or you can insert an existing Excel worksheet. You can also insert a chart from an Excel workbook.

TIP

Display only a certain portion of a worksheet.
Double-click the embedded Excel object, and then drag the sizing handles until only the rows and columns you want are displayed. You can also use the Crop button on the Picture toolbar to crop unwanted portions.

SEE ALSO

See "Embedding and Linking an Object" on page 122 for more information on inserting objects.

Insert a New Excel Chart or Worksheet

1. Click the Insert menu, and then click Object.

2. Click the Create New option button.

3. Click Microsoft Excel Chart or Microsoft Excel Worksheet, depending on which object you want to insert.

4. Click OK.

5. Use the source program tools to edit the object.

6. Click outside the object when you are finished.

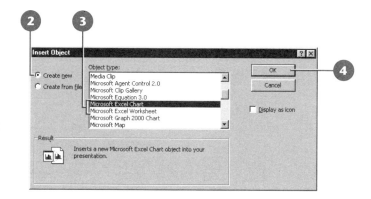

Import a Microsoft Excel Worksheet or Chart

1. Display the slide on which you want to insert the Excel worksheet.

2. Click the Insert menu, and then click Object.

3. Click the Create From File option button, click the Browse button, locate and select the worksheet you want, and then click OK.

4. To link the worksheet, click the Link check box.

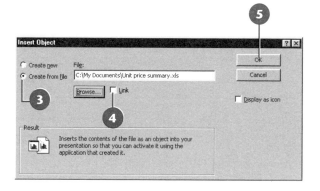

SEE ALSO

See "Inserting a Graph Chart" on page 140 for information on inserting a chart using Microsoft Graph—an alternative if you need a chart in your presentation but don't have a program like Excel.

5 Click OK.

6 If necessary, edit the worksheet using the Excel tools.

7 Click outside the worksheet when you are finished.

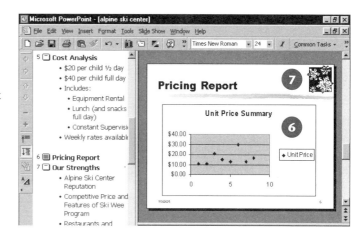

TIP

Drag a chart from Excel to PowerPoint. *Open both Excel and PowerPoint, select the chart in Excel, and then drag it into PowerPoint. If the PowerPoint presentation is not visible, drag the chart to the presentation button on the taskbar to display PowerPoint.*

Insert an Existing Excel Chart

1 Open the worksheet containing the chart in Excel.

2 Click the chart, and then click the Copy button on Excel's Standard toolbar.

3 Switch to PowerPoint and open the slide on which you want to add the chart.

4 Click the Paste button on the Standard toolbar.

5 Click outside the chart to deselect it.

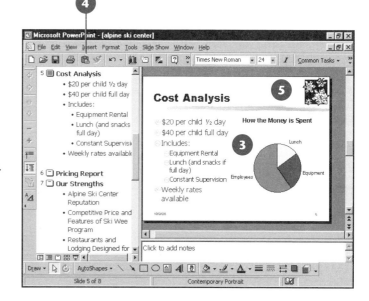

Creating WordArt Text

The WordArt feature lets you create stylized text to draw attention to your most important words. Most users apply WordArt to short phrases or even just a word, such as *Our Customers Come First* or *Welcome*. You should apply WordArt to a slide sparingly. Its visual appeal and unique look require uncluttered space. When you use WordArt, you can choose from a variety of text styles that come with the WordArt feature, or you can create your own using tools on the WordArt toolbar.

Insert WordArt button

SEE ALSO

See "Modifying WordArt Text" on page 130 for information on changing the shape, color, and alignment of the WordArt text.

Insert WordArt

1. Click the Insert WordArt button on the Drawing toolbar.

2. Click one of the WordArt styles. If you want to create your own WordArt, click OK without selecting a WordArt style.

3. Click OK.

4. Type the text you want WordArt to use.

5. If applicable, use the Font, Size, Bold, and Italic options to modify the text you entered.

6. Click OK.

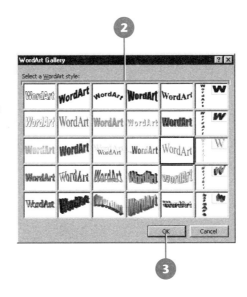

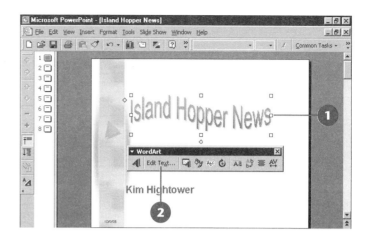

TIP

Edit WordArt text quickly.
Double-click the WordArt object to open the Edit WordArt Text dialog box.

TIP

Display the WordArt toolbar. *Right-click any toolbar, and then click WordArt.*

TRY THIS

Change a WordArt style.
You can vary a WordArt style by experimenting with different fonts. Apply a WordArt style, click the Edit Text button on the WordArt toolbar, change the font, font size, and format attributes, and then click OK.

SEE ALSO

See "Applying WordArt Text Effects" on page 132 for information on changing the letter height, justification, and spacing of the WordArt text.

Edit WordArt Text

1. Click the WordArt object you want to edit.

2. Click the Edit Text button on the WordArt toolbar.

3. Edit the text.

4. Click OK.

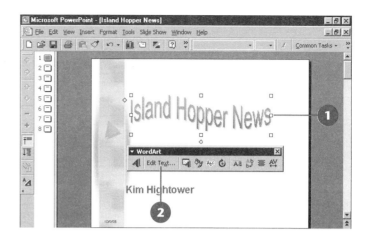

Apply a Different WordArt Style to Existing WordArt

1. Click the WordArt object whose style you want to change.

2. Click the WordArt Gallery button on the WordArt toolbar.

3. Click the WordArt Gallery style you want to apply.

4. Click OK.

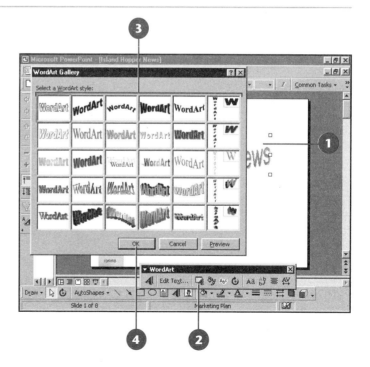

Modifying WordArt Text

With WordArt, in addition to applying one of the preformatted styles, you can also create your own style by shaping your text into a variety of shapes, curves, styles, and color patterns. The WordArt toolbar gives you tools for coloring, rotating, and shaping your text. You can also format your WordArt using tools on the Drawing toolbar. The Drawing toolbar makes it easy to see your format changes.

TIP

Format the WordArt text.
Click the Edit Text button on the WordArt toolbar, edit the WordArt text, or click the Bold or Italic button, and then click OK.

Change the Shape of WordArt

1. Click the WordArt object.

2. Click the WordArt Shape button on the WordArt toolbar.

3. Click the shape you want to apply to the text.

4. Click outside the object to deselect it.

Rotate WordArt

1. Click the WordArt object.

2. Click the Free Rotate button on the WordArt toolbar.

3. Drag one of the green rotate handles to rotate the object in any direction you want.

4. When you are finished, click the Free Rotate button.

5. Click outside the object to deselect it.

Color WordArt

1. Click the WordArt object.

2. Click the Fill Color drop-down arrow on the Drawing toolbar, and then click the fill color you want.

3. Click the Line Color drop-down arrow on the Drawing toolbar, and then click the line color you want.

4. Click outside the object to deselect it.

Align WordArt

1. Click the WordArt object.

2. Click the WordArt Alignment button on the WordArt toolbar.

3. Click the alignment you want.

4. Click outside the object to deselect it.

Applying WordArt Text Effects

You can apply a number of text effects to your WordArt objects that determine letter heights, justification, and spacing. The effects of some of the adjustments you make are more pronounced for certain WordArt styles than others. Some of these effects make the text unreadable for certain styles, so apply these effects carefully.

SEE ALSO

See "Creating WordArt Text" on page 128 and "Modifying WordArt Text" on page 130 for more information on working with WordArt text.

Make Letters the Same Height

1 Click the WordArt object.

2 Click the WordArt Same Letter Heights button on the WordArt toolbar.

3 Click outside the object to deselect it.

Format Text Vertically

1 Click the WordArt object.

2 Click the WordArt Vertical Text button on the WordArt toolbar.

3 Click outside the object to deselect it.

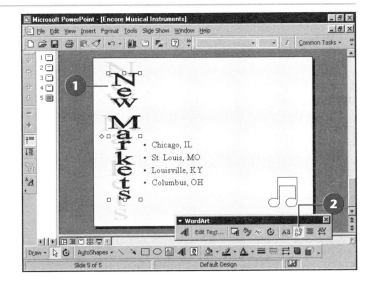

Change WordArt character spacing. *Although the default spacing for the WordArt Gallery objects is usually optimal, if you change the font you might want to experiment with character spacing.*

Change WordArt text to semitransparent. *Click the WordArt object, click the Format WordArt button on the WordArt toolbar, click the Colors And Lines tab, click to select the Semitransparent check box, and then click OK.*

Change the WordArt size or position. *Click the WordArt object, click the Format WordArt button on the WordArt toolbar, click the Size or Position tab, change the size or positioning settings, and then click OK.*

Adjust Character Spacing

1. Click the WordArt object.

2. Click the WordArt Character Spacing button on the WordArt toolbar.

3. Click a spacing setting— Very Tight, Tight, Normal, Loose, or Very Loose— to determine the amount of space between characters.

4. If you want, select or clear the Kern Character Pairs option to adjust the space between characters.

5. Click outside the object to deselect it.

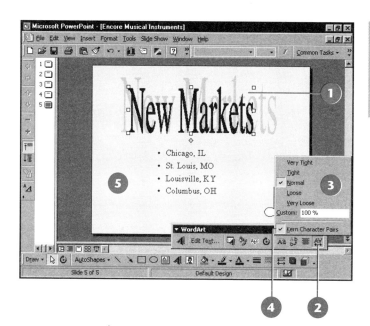

Creating an Organization Chart

An *organization chart*, also known as an *org chart*, shows the personnel structure in an organization. You can include an organization chart in a PowerPoint presentation using Microsoft Organization Chart, a program that comes with the Office 2000 suite. When you start Organization Chart, chart boxes appear into which you enter company personnel. Each chart box is identified by its position in the chart. Managers, for example, are at the top, while Subordinates are below, Co-Workers to the sides, and so on.

SEE ALSO

See "Structuring an Organization Chart" on page 136 for information on reorganizing your organization chart.

Create an Organization Chart

1. Start Microsoft Organization Chart in one of the following ways.

   ◆ On an existing slide, click the Insert menu, point to Picture, click Organization Chart, and then click OK.

   ◆ On a new slide, click the Insert New Slide button on the Standard toolbar, click the Organization Chart AutoLayout icon, click OK, and then double-click the org chart placeholder to add an org chart.

2. Use the Organization Chart tools and menus to design your organization chart.

3. Click the File menu, and then click Exit And Return To [File Name] to return to your presentation.

4. Click Yes to update the presentation.

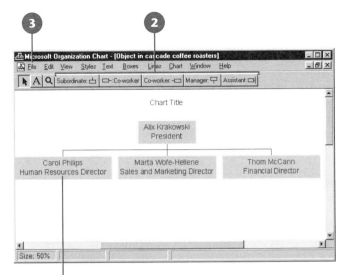

Each chart box represents one person or group in your company's structure. You can enter up to four lines of information in each box.

SELECT AND DESELECT CHART BOXES

To	Do this
Select a single chart box	Click a chart box using the arrow pointer
Select a set of chart boxes or chart objects	Click the Edit menu, point to Select, and then click the set you want
Select one or more levels of chart boxes	Click the Edit menu, click Select Levels, enter the levels you want, and then click OK
Deselect a chart box	Click outside the chart box

Use the Enter key to scroll through a chart box.
Within a chart box, you can continue to press Enter to scroll through the lines and edit them, if necessary.

See "Formatting an Organization Chart" on page 138 for information on enhancing the elements of an org chart.

"How can I add a title to my organization chart?"

Enter Text into a Chart Box

1 If necessary, double-click a chart box in which you want to enter text.

2 Type a person's name, and then press Enter.

3 Type a person's title, and then press Enter.

4 Type up to two lines of comments. If you don't want to include comments, leave the comment line placeholders blank.

5 When you are finished, click outside the chart box.

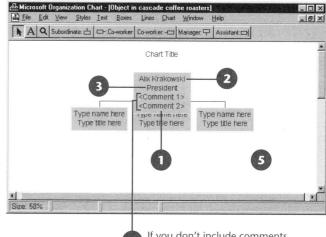

4 If you don't include comments, PowerPoint automatically removes the comment line placeholders from the chart box after you click outside it.

Add a Title

1 Highlight the sample title text *Chart Title* at the top of the organization chart.

2 Type a title you want for your org chart.

3 When you are finished, click outside the title area.

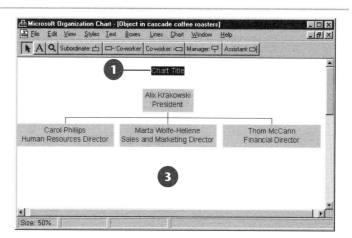

Structuring an Organization Chart

Chart boxes are related to each other. For example, if you want to add a Subordinate chart box, first select the chart box to which you want to attach it. The buttons on the toolbar show the relationship between the different chart boxes you can add. When you add a Subordinate, it is automatically placed below the selected chart box. You can, however, display the chart box levels in a different structure, and you can customize the organization chart's appearance using the formatting options.

Add a Chart Box

1. If necessary, double-click the org chart you want to modify.

2. Click a chart box button on the Organizational Chart toolbar, such as Subordinate or Co-Worker.

3. Click the existing chart box to which you want to attach the new chart box.

4. Enter the information in the box you just added.

5. Click outside the box.

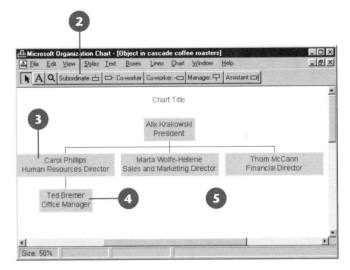

Change the Structure Style

1. Double-click the org chart you want to change, if necessary.

2. Select one or more chart boxes whose style you want to change. (Press and hold Shift to select more than one box.)

3. Click the Styles menu.

4. Click the button that provides the structure you want to use.

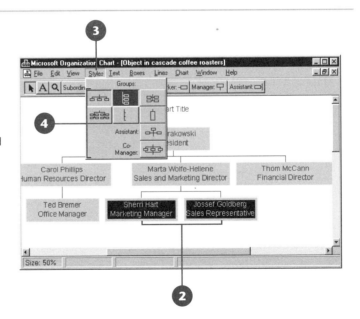

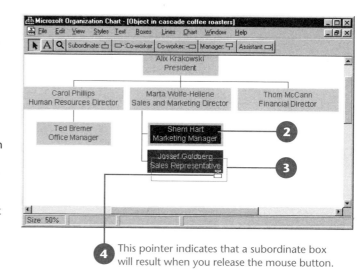

TIP

Open an existing organization chart. *Double-click the Organization Chart object.*

TIP

Work with Microsoft Organization Chart. *If you receive an error message saying the program can't start, your computer may not have enough memory to run Microsoft Organization Chart. Try shutting down all programs except PowerPoint and closing all PowerPoint files except the one with which you are working.*

Reporting Structure

Rearrange a Chart Box

1 Double-click the org chart you want to change, if necessary.

2 Make sure the chart box you want to move is not selected.

3 Drag the chart box over an existing chart box. The pointer changes to a four-headed arrow.

4 Continue to drag the chart box in the direction you want, and notice that the pointer changes.

◆ A left arrow appears when you drag over the left side of a box.

◆ A right arrow appears when you drag over the right side of a box.

◆ A double-headed arrow and a small chart box appear when you drag over the bottom of a box.

◆ A subordinate shape appears when you drag over a manager box.

5 Release the mouse button when the chart box is in the correct position.

4 This pointer indicates that a subordinate box will result when you release the mouse button.

Formatting an Organization Chart

You can format the text and appearance of an organization chart with the same tools you use for other PowerPoint objects. You can modify text, colors, and lines. Remember to use formatting wisely and keep in mind the overall design of your presentation.

TIP

Align text in a chart box.
You can align the text in a chart box by selecting text in the chart box, clicking the Text menu, and then clicking Left, Center, or Right.

SEE ALSO

See "Creating an Organization Chart" on page 134 for information on different ways to select chart objects.

Format an Organization Chart

1. Double-click the org chart you want to format.

2. Click the Edit menu, point to Select, and then click the chart object or objects you want to format.

3. Click the format menu you want to use.

   ◆ Use the Text menu to format the text in a chart box by choosing a new font and font size, color, and alignment.

   ◆ Use the Boxes menu to change the color, shadow effect, border style, border color, and border line style of a selected chart box.

   ◆ Use the Lines menu to format the lines that connect the chart boxes, including their thickness, style, and color.

   ◆ Use the Chart menu to change the background of the entire chart.

4. Make the formatting changes you want.

5. Click OK.

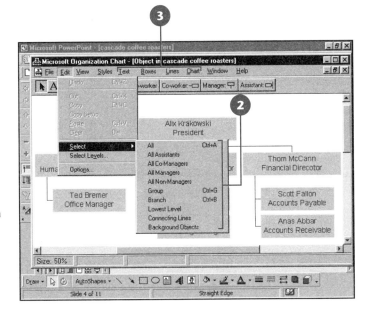

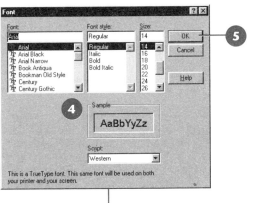

Use this dialog box to format an organization chart's text.

Inserting Charts with Microsoft Graph

8

When you create a presentation with numeric information, such as statistics and comparisons, you may want to present this information in a visual format. The best way to do this is to insert a graph into your presentation. If you don't have separate graphing software, you can include a graph in a Microsoft PowerPoint 2000 presentation using an add-in accessory that comes with all the Office 2000 programs: *Microsoft Graph*. With Graph, you can insert the data that make up the graph and then generate the graph automatically.

Microsoft Graph Features

Microsoft Graph is a very versatile accessory. With it, you can enter new data and import or paste existing data from almost any source. Graph offers a variety of spreadsheet tools that make it easy to move, format, and manipulate the data that forms the basis of your chart.

You can also apply a variety of looks to your chart using predesigned chart types or by creating your own. Finally, Graph offers advanced graphing techniques that help your chart provide statistical information to your audience.

Inserting a Graph Chart

Instead of adding a table of dry numbers, insert a Microsoft Graph chart. Charts add visual interest and useful information represented by lines, bars, pie slices, or other markers. Graph uses two views to display the information in a graph: the *datasheet*, a spreadsheet-like grid of rows and columns that contains your data, and the *chart*, the graphical representation of the data.

A datasheet contains cells to hold your data. A *cell* is the intersection of a row and column. A group of data values from a row or column of data makes up a *data series*. Each data series has a unique color or pattern on the chart.

SEE ALSO

See "Selecting a Chart Type" on page 150 for information on selecting a different chart type.

Create a Graph Chart

1. Start Microsoft Graph in one of the following ways.

   ◆ To create a graph on an existing slide, display the slide on which you want the graph to appear, and then click the Insert Chart button on the Standard toolbar.

   ◆ To create a graph on a new slide, click the Insert New Slide button on the Standard toolbar, click a Chart AutoLayout icon, click OK, and then double-click the chart place-holder to add the chart and datasheet.

2. Replace the sample data in the datasheet with your own data.

3. Edit and format the data in the datasheet as appropriate.

4. Click the Close button on the datasheet to close it and view the chart.

5. If necessary, change the chart type, and format the chart.

6. Click outside the chart to quit Microsoft Graph.

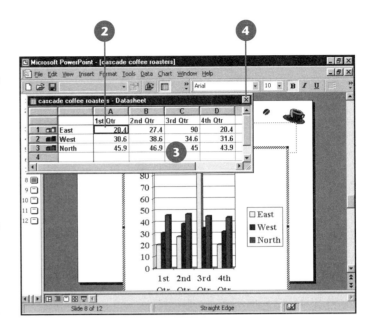

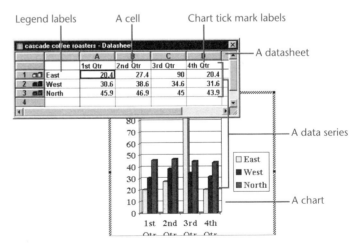

Legend labels   A cell   Chart tick mark labels — A datasheet — A data series — A chart

Opening an Existing Chart

Like any inserted object, you can open an existing chart in PowerPoint by double-clicking it. Then you can make any changes you want using the Graph commands and toolbars. Close the datasheet to view the chart.

SEE ALSO

See "Selecting a Chart Type" on page 150 for information on selecting a different chart type, and see "Formatting Chart Objects" on page 152 for information on formatting a chart.

Open and View a Chart in Microsoft Graph

1. In PowerPoint, display the slide that contains the chart you want to open.

2. Double-click the chart to start Microsoft Graph. The Datasheet and Graph toolbars and menus appear.

3. Click the View Datasheet button on the Standard toolbar to close the datasheet.

A chart consists of the following elements.

- ◆ Data markers: A graphical representation of a data point in a single cell in the datasheet. Typical data markers include bars, dots, or pie slices. Related data markers constitute a data series.

- ◆ Legend: A pattern or color that identifies each data series.

- ◆ X-axis: A reference line for the horizontal data values.

- ◆ Y-axis: A reference line for the vertical data values.

- ◆ Tick marks: Marks that identify data increments.

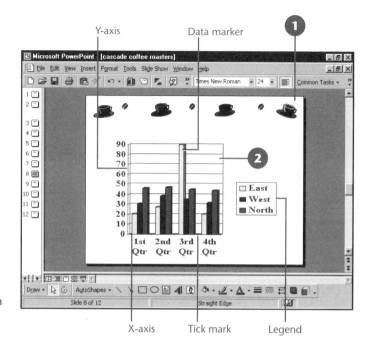

Selecting Graph Data

Use the datasheet to edit your data. Select the data first in the datasheet. If you click a cell to select it, anything you type replaces the contents of the cell. If you double-click the cell, however, anything you type is inserted at the location of the cursor.

TIP

Help with Microsoft Graph. *You can get help specific to Microsoft Graph by clicking the Help button on the Graph Standard toolbar or by pressing F1 when you are in Graph.*

SEE ALSO

See "Formatting Graph Data" on page 148 for information on changing the appearance of selected cells.

Select Data in the Datasheet

1. In Microsoft Graph, click the View Datasheet button on the Standard toolbar.

2. Use one of the following to select a cell, row, column, or datasheet.

   ◆ To select a cell, click it.

   ◆ To select an entire row or column, click the row heading or column heading button.

   ◆ To select a range of cells, drag the pointer over the cells you want to select, or click the upper-left cell of the range, press and hold Shift, and then click the lower-right cell. When you select a range of cells, the active cell has a thick border, and all other selected cells are highlighted in black.

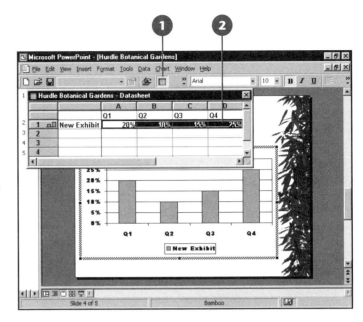

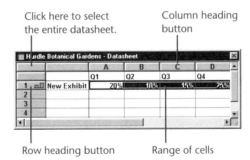

Click here to select the entire datasheet.

Column heading button

Row heading button

Range of cells

Entering Graph Data

You enter graph data in the datasheet either by typing it or by inserting it from a different source. The datasheet is designed to make data entry easy, so direct typing is best when you're entering brief, simple data. For more complex or longer data, and when you're concerned about accuracy, insert and link your data to the graph object.

When you first insert a graph, the datasheet contains sample labels and numbers. If you're entering data by typing, click a cell to make it the *active cell*, and then select the sample information and replace it with your own.

SEE ALSO

See "Importing Data" on page 144 for information on importing data from other sources into your datasheet.

Enter Data in the Datasheet

1. In Microsoft Graph, click the View Datasheet button on the Standard toolbar.

2. To delete the sample data, click the upper-left heading button to select all the cells, and then press Delete.

3. Click a cell to make it active.

4. Type the data you want to enter in the cell.

5. Press Enter to move the insertion point down one row to the next cell, or press Tab to move the insertion point right to the next cell.

6. Click outside the graph to return to PowerPoint.

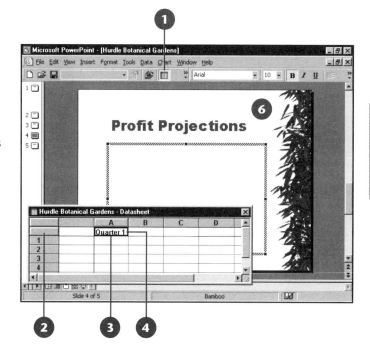

Importing Data

Microsoft Graph makes it easy to insert data from other sources, such as a plain text file or a Microsoft Excel worksheet. You have control over how much of the data in a file you want to insert, and, in the case of an imported text file, you can indicate how Graph should arrange your data once it is imported.

TIP

How much data can a datasheet accept? *Microsoft Graph can accept 4,000 rows and 4,000 columns of data and can display up to 255 data series.*

SEE ALSO

See "Selecting Graph Data" on page 142 for information on selecting data in a datasheet.

Import Data into the Datasheet

1 In Microsoft Graph, click the View Datasheet button on the Standard toolbar.

2 Click the cell where you want the data to begin.

3 Click the Edit menu, and then click Import File.

4 Double-click the file that contains the data you want to import.

5 If you are importing a text file, follow the Text Import Wizard steps. If you are importing Excel worksheet data, select the sheet that contains the data you want to import in the Import Data Options dialog box.

◆ To import all the sheet data, click the Entire Sheet option button.

◆ To import only a range, click the Range option button, and type the range of data. For example, to import cells A1 through C10, type A1:C10.

◆ If you selected a cell in step 2, click to clear the Overwrite Existing Cells check box.

6 Click OK.

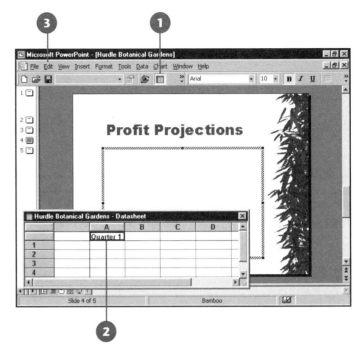

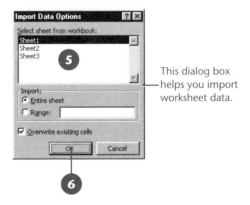

This dialog box helps you import worksheet data.

TIP

Use the first column and row to enter labels. *Enter row labels in the first column and column labels in the first row so that Microsoft Graph uses those values to label the X- and Y-axes.*

TIP

Turn on the Selection After Enter option. *With this option turned on, the active cell changes after you press Enter. Click the Tools menu, click Options, click Datasheet Options, click to select the Move Selection After Enter check box, and then click OK.*

TIP

Turn on the Cell Drag And Drop option. *With this option turned on, you can drag data from one cell to another. Click the Tools menu, click Options, click Datasheet Options, click to select the Cell Drag And Drop check box, and then click OK.*

Paste Data into the Datasheet

1. In the source program, open the file that contains the data you want to paste.

2. Select the data you want to paste.

3. Click the Edit menu, and then click Copy.

4. Switch to PowerPoint, display the slide that contains the Microsoft Graph object, and then double-click the graph object.

5. If necessary, switch to the datasheet and clear its contents.

6. Paste the data into the datasheet using one of the following methods.

   ◆ To paste the data without linking it, click the Edit menu, and then click Paste.

   ◆ To link the data, click the Edit menu, click Paste Special, click the Paste Link option button, and then click OK.

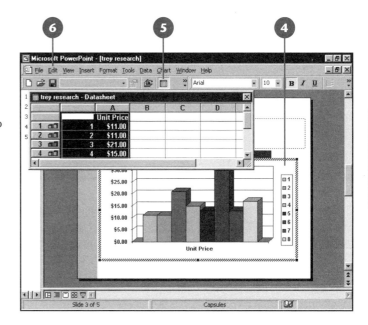

Editing Graph Data

Although most of the time you edit Microsoft Graph data in the datasheet, you can also change data in the chart by dragging a data marker. You can edit data one cell at a time, or you can manipulate blocks of adjacent data called *ranges*. If you are familiar with worksheets, such as Microsoft Excel, you will find that Microsoft Graph uses many of the same data editing techniques.

TIP

Switch the data series around. *You can change the data series to display by row or column. Click the Data menu, and then click Series In Row or Series In Column.*

Edit Cell Contents

1. In the datasheet, click the cell you want to edit.

   ◆ To replace the cell contents, type the new data into the cell. It replaces the previous entry.

   ◆ To edit the cell contents, double-click the selected cell where you want to edit.

   ◆ Press Delete or Backspace to delete one character at a time, and then type the new data.

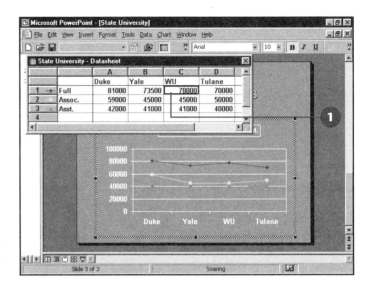

Edit Data by Dragging Data Markers

1. In the chart, click the data series that contains the data marker you want to change.

2. Click the data marker. When you select a data marker, a box appears that identifies the series and the value.

3. Drag the data marker for line or scatterplots, the top-center selection handle for bar or column charts, and the largest selection handle on the edge of a pie chart.

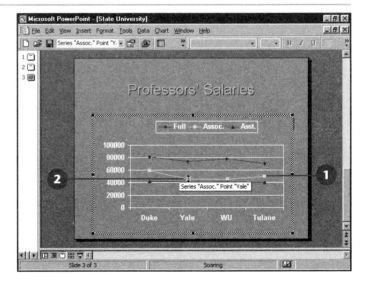

How does Graph create a legend? *Microsoft Graph derives the legend and data labels from the first row and column in the datasheet, so if you type new ones, the datasheet values are no longer used.*

Exclude or include row or column data. *Instead of deleting data, you can exclude row or column data from a graph and then include it later. Select the row or column you want, click the Data menu, and then click Exclude Row/Col or Include Row/Col.*

Clear data from a datasheet. *You can clear the contents, format, or both of a cell or range. When you clear both, it is the same as deleting the data. To clear data, click the Edit menu, point to Clear, and then click Contents, Formats, or All.*

Insert Cells

1 In the datasheet, click where you want to insert cells.

◆ To insert a column, click the column heading to the right of where you want the new column.

◆ To insert a row, click the row heading below where you want the new row.

◆ To insert a single cell, click an adjacent cell.

2 Click the Insert menu, and then click Cells.

3 Select how you want to insert the cells.

4 Click OK.

Delete Data from a Datasheet or a Graph

◆ Select the cell or range in the datasheet that contains the data you want to delete, and then press Delete.

◆ Click the data series in the graph, and then press Delete.

Click the column heading button to select an entire column.

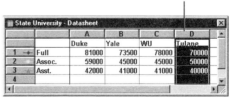

8

Formatting Graph Data

You may need to reformat the datasheet itself—its size and how it displays the data—to make it easier to read. For example, you can format numbers in currency, accounting, percentage, and scientific formats. You can also change the fonts used in the graph and change the column widths.

"I want to format my numbers with percentages."

TIP

AutoCorrect Microsoft Graph text. *AutoCorrect works the same in Microsoft Graph as it does in PowerPoint. To change AutoCorrect options, click the Format menu, click AutoCorrect, change the options you want, and then click OK.*

Change the Datasheet Font

1. In the datasheet, click any cell.

2. Click the Format menu, and then click Font.

3. Make any changes to the font settings.
   - ◆ Font, style, and size
   - ◆ Underline and color
   - ◆ Strikethrough, super-script, and subscript

4. Click OK.

   Changes you make to the font affect all the data in the datasheet.

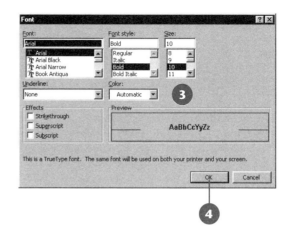

Format Datasheet Numbers

1. In the datasheet, select the data you want to format.

2. Click the Format menu, and then click Number.

3. Click the style you want to apply.

4. Select the options you want.

5. Click OK.

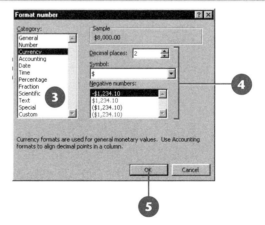

The column width is too narrow. *If a series of number signs (#) appears in the datasheet cell, it means that the cell is not wide enough to display the entire contents of the cell. Widen the column to view the data in that cell.*

Change the Width of a Column

◆ To increase or decrease the width of a column, position the pointer on the vertical line to the right of the column heading, and then drag the pointer until the column is the correct width.

◆ To adjust a datasheet column to display the widest data entered (also known as Best Fit), position the pointer on the line to the right of the column heading, and then double-click to adjust the column width.

Double-click the column heading to resize the column to the widest entry.

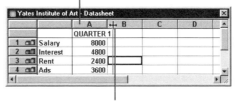

Drag to resize a column.

Reset the column width. *If you want to reset the column width to its default size, click the cell in the column you want to format, click the Format menu, click Column Width, and then click to select the Use Standard Width check box.*

Enter a Precise Column Width

1 Click a cell in the column you want to format.

2 Click the Format menu, and then click Column Width.

3 Enter a new column width.

4 Click OK.

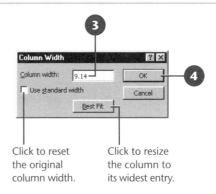

Click to reset the original column width.

Click to resize the column to its widest entry.

Selecting a Chart Type

Your chart is what your audience sees, so make sure to take advantage of PowerPoint's chart formatting options to make the chart appealing and visually informative. You start by choosing the chart type that is suited for presenting your data. There are 18 chart types, available in 2-D and 3-D formats, and for each chart type you can choose from a variety of formats. If you want to format your chart beyond the provided formats, you can customize a chart. Save your customized settings so that you can apply that chart formatting to any chart you create.

TIP

My Chart Type button looks different. *The image on the Chart Type button changes depending on which chart type is selected.*

Select a Chart Type

1. In Microsoft Graph, close the datasheet to view the chart, if necessary.

2. Click the Chart Type drop-down arrow on the Standard toolbar.

3. Click the button corresponding to the chart type you want.

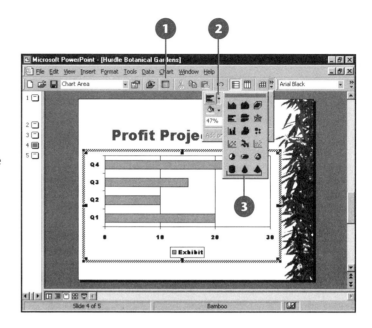

Apply a Standard Chart Type

1. Click the Chart menu, and then click Chart Type.

2. Click the Standard Types tab.

3. Click the chart type you want.

4. Click the chart sub-type you want. *Sub-types* are variations of the chart type.

5. Click OK.

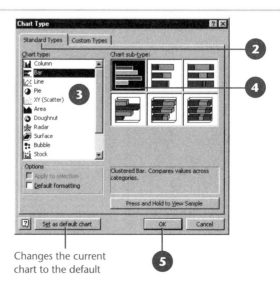

Changes the current chart to the default

TIP

Use chart options to add a title to your chart. *To add a title to your chart, click the Chart menu, click Chart Options, click the Titles tab, and then enter a title.*

SEE ALSO

See "Formatting Chart Objects" on page 152 for more information on customizing chart elements.

Apply a Custom Chart Type

1. Click the Chart menu, and then click Chart Type.

2. Click the Custom Types tab.

3. Click the Built-In option button.

4. Click the chart type you want.

5. Click OK.

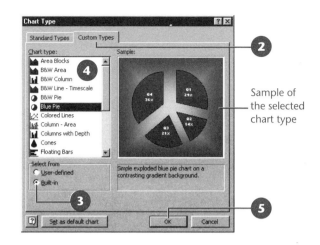

Sample of the selected chart type

TIP

Show chart tips. *When you point to a chart name or value, a chart tip appears with the information. Click the Tools menu, click Options, click the Chart tab, click to select the Show Names Or Show Values check box, and then click OK.*

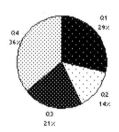

Create a Custom Chart Type

1. Select the chart you want to use to make a custom chart type.

2. Click the Chart menu, and then click Chart Type.

3. Click the Custom Types tab.

4. Click the User-Defined option button.

5. Click Add.

6. Type a name and description for the chart.

7. Click OK.

8. Click OK.

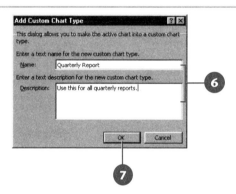

Formatting Chart Objects

Chart objects are the individual elements that make up a chart, such as an axis, the legend, or a data series. The *plot area* is the bordered area where the data are plotted. The *chart area* is the area between the plot area and the Microsoft Graph object selection box. As with any Microsoft add-in accessory, Graph treats all these elements as objects, so you can format and modify them individually.

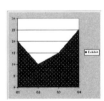

TIP

Use the Selected command on the Format menu to format a selected object. *For an axis, for example, the command is Selected Axis.*

Select a Chart Object

1. Click the Chart Objects drop-down arrow on the Standard toolbar.

2. Click the chart object you want to select.

   When a chart object is selected, selection handles appear.

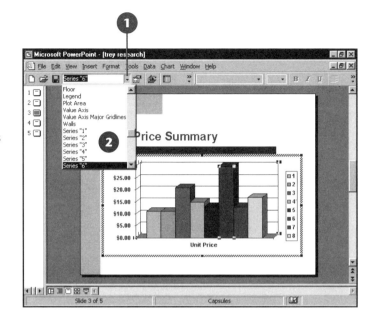

Format a Chart Object

1. Right-click the chart object you want to format, such as an axis, legend, or data series.

2. Click the appropriate Format command. For an axis, for example, the command is Format Axis.

3. Click the appropriate tab(s), and select the options you want to apply.

4. Click OK.

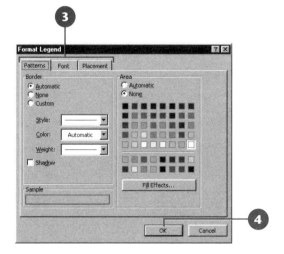

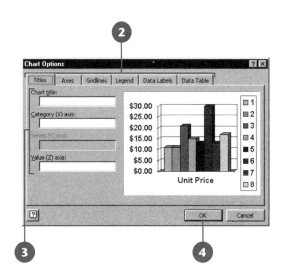

TIP

Zoom before you select a chart. *You can click a chart object to select it, but this can be tricky because the chart objects are often quite small. Increase the zoom percentage to enlarge your view before using the mouse pointer to select chart objects.*

SEE ALSO

See "Selecting a Chart Type" on page 150 for information on applying a different chart type.

TIP

Rotate the chart axis labels. *To change the angle of an axis label, right-click the axis, click Format Axis, click the Alignment tab, and then select a rotation.*

TIP

Change the placement of objects on a chart. *Select the chart objects whose placement you want to change, click the Format menu, point to Placement, and then click Bring To Front, Send To Back, or Group.*

Customize a Chart

1. Click the Chart menu, and then click Chart Options.

2. Click the tab corresponding to the chart object you want to customize.

   Each tab will display options that are specific to the chart object you want to customize.

3. Make the necessary changes.

4. Click OK.

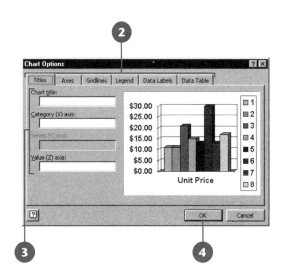

Change the View of a 3-D Chart

1. Select the 3-D chart you want to change.

2. Click the Chart menu, and then click 3-D View.

3. Click the left or right rotation button.

4. Click the up or down elevation button.

5. Click OK.

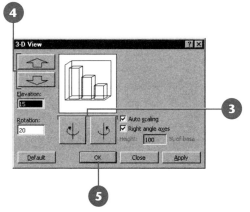

Choosing Advanced Features

Microsoft Graph offers a number of advanced graphing techniques that you can explore using the abundant information in online Help for Microsoft Graph. You can:

◆ Add *trendlines* derived from regression analysis to show a trend in existing data and make predictions.

◆ Create a *moving average*, a sequence of averages from grouped data points, that smooths the fluctuations in data so you can more easily identify trends.

◆ Add *error bars* that express the degree of uncertainty attached to a given data series.

◆ Add drawing objects, including arrows, text boxes, and pictures, to your charts.

◆ Fill chart elements such as bars, areas, and surfaces with textures, imported pictures, or gradient fills.

◆ Animate bars, data points, or other chart data for added multimedia impact.

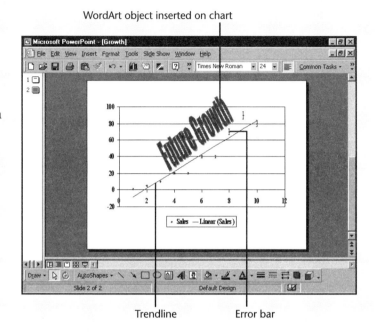

WordArt object inserted on chart

Trendline   Error bar

9

9

Finalizing a Presentation and Its Supplements

As you finish developing your presentation, you can add some last-minute enhancements by creating a summary slide or presentation supplements, or by including speaker notes and handouts, for example. When your presentation is complete, you can send it to others in your company, convert it to 35mm slides, or save it in different formats.

Creating Supplements

Handouts are printed materials that you supply to your audience. Typically handouts include an outline for the audience to follow as you speak, a copy of the slides in your presentation (printed one or more slides to a page), or a set of pages with blank lines next to reduced images of the slides for note taking. PowerPoint gives you many options for printing handouts, including editing and formatting them in Microsoft Word. Most speakers feel more comfortable giving a presentation with a script in front of them, and you can easily create one in Notes Page view. You can also work with your notes in Word.

Finalizing a Presentation in Slide Sorter View

Slide Sorter view helps you assess the final order of your slides because you can see them all at once. Slide Sorter view allows you to display the slides with or without color and formatting so that you can identify individual slides more easily. Slide Sorter view is also the easiest place to copy and paste slides between presentations. At the end of the presentation, you can create a *summary slide* that compiles the titles of selected slides into one slide. It is an easy way to create a presentation agenda.

TIP

Switch to Slide view quickly from Slide Sorter view. *If you are in Slide Sorter view and you want to open a slide in Slide view, double-click the slide.*

View Slides in Slide Sorter View

◆ To view only a slide's title in Slide Sorter view, press and hold Alt and click a slide.

◆ To view slides in black and white, click the View menu, and then click Black And White.

The selected slide appears with a thick black border.

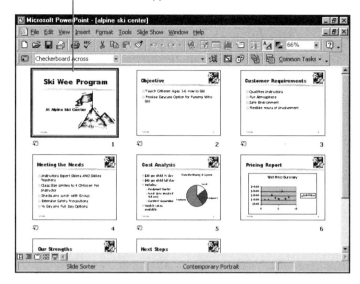

Create a Summary Slide

① In Slide Sorter, Normal, or Outline view, select the slides you want to include on your summary slide.

② Click the Summary Slide button on the Slide Sorter or Outlining toolbar.

A new slide appears with the title *Summary Slide* and a bulleted list of the select slide titles.

Summary slide

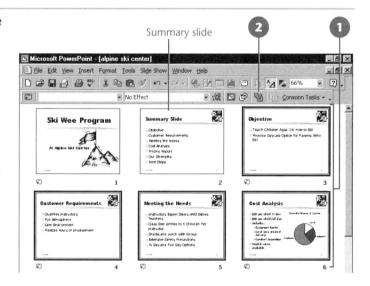

TIP

Use the mouse to copy slides from one present-ation to another. *You can drag slides from one presentation to another. Open both presentations in Slide Sorter view, click the Window menu, click Arrange All, and then drag the slides from one presentation into the other.*

"How can I insert slides from a different presentation?"

SEE ALSO

See "Rearranging Slides" on page 40 for information on rearranging slides in Slide Sorter view.

Copy Slides from Other Presentations

1. Open the presentation that contains the slides you want to use.

2. In Slide Sorter view, select one or more slides you want to copy.

3. Click the Copy button on the Standard toolbar.

4. Switch to the presentation you are working on.

5. In Slide Sorter view, click before or after the slide to place the insertion point.

6. Click the Paste button on the Standard toolbar.

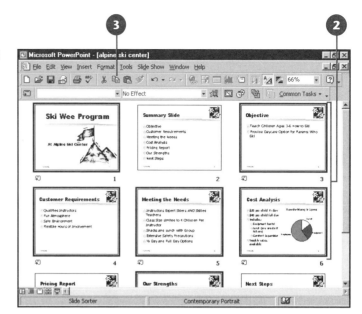

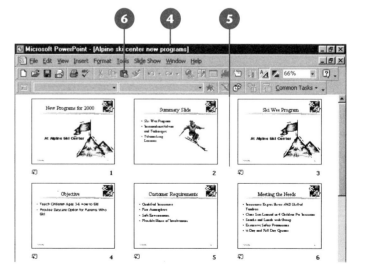

Inserting Slides from Other Presentations

To insert slides from other presentations in a slide show, you can open the presentation and copy and paste the slides you want, or you can use the *Slide Finder* feature. With Slide Finder, you don't have to open the presentation first; instead, you view a *miniature* of each slide in a presentation and then insert only the ones you select. With Slide Finder, you can also create a list of favorite presentations you can use as source material for future slide shows.

> **TIP**
>
> **Look up reference material.** *Select the word or phrase you want to look up, click the Tools menu, click Look Up Reference, click Microsoft Bookshelf Basics, click OK, view the information that appears, click a topic, and then click the Close button when you're done.*

Insert Slides from Slide Finder

1. Click the Insert menu, and then click Slides From Files.

2. Click the Find Presentation tab.

3. Click Browse, locate and select the file you want, and then click Open.

4. Click Display to display a miniature of each slide.

5. Select the slides you want to insert.

   ◆ To insert just one slide, click the slide and then click Insert.

   ◆ To insert multiple slides, click each slide you want to insert, and then click Insert.

   ◆ To insert all the slides in the presentation, click Insert All.

6. Click Close.

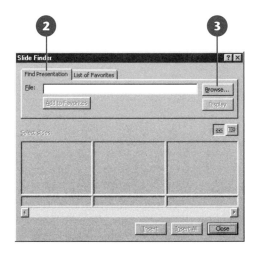

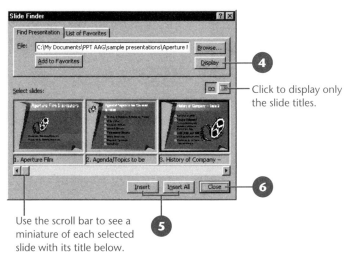

Click to display only the slide titles.

Use the scroll bar to see a miniature of each selected slide with its title below.

Use the keyboard to select more than one slide. *To select a group of adjacent slides, click the first slide, press and hold Shift, and then click the last slide. To select a group of nonadjacent slides, press and hold Ctrl and click each slide you want to select.*

Remove a presentation from your list of favorites. *Click the presentation on the List Of Favorites tab in Slide Finder, and then click Remove.*

Insert slides over a network. *To insert slides from presentations stored on other computers in your company's network, click the Insert menu, click Slides From File, click the Browse button, click the Look In drop-down arrow, and then click the network drive that contains the presentation you want to use. Slide Finder gives you the same access to those slides as it would to slides on your local hard disk drive.*

Display Slide Titles in Slide Finder

1 In Slide Finder, click the Titles button.

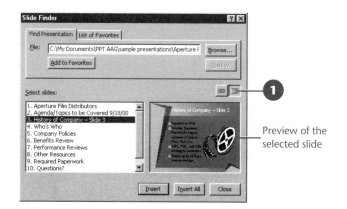

Preview of the selected slide

Add a Presentation to List of Favorites

1 In Slide Finder, locate the file you want to add to the list of favorites.

2 Click the Add To Favorites button on the Find Presentation tab.

3 Click the List Of Favorites tab.

4 Click the presentation file to display the slides.

5 If necessary, click Display.

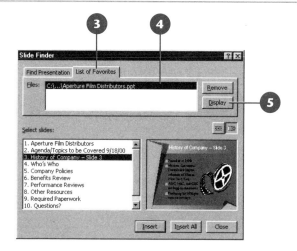

9

Inserting Comments

If a colleague asks you to review a presentation, you can enter your comments right into the presentation file. When you return the presentation to your colleague, he or she can view the comments to consider your remarks, deleting each comment as it is considered. Note that you can review these comments only in Normal, Slide, and Outline views.

Display the Reviewing toolbar to access comment commands.
Reviewers might find it handy to display the Reviewing toolbar, which provides buttons for adding, viewing, deleting, and e-mailing comments. Click the View menu, point to Toolbars, and then click Reviewing to display the Reviewing toolbar.

Insert a Comment

1. Select the slide to which you want to add a comment.

2. Click the Insert menu, and then click Comment.

3. Type your comment.

   PowerPoint automatically inserts the name of the evaluator so the presentation developer knows who inserted the comment.

4. Click outside the comment selection box when you are finished.

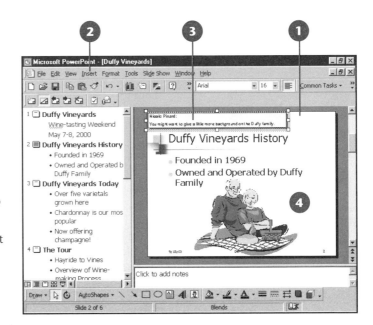

View or Hide Comments

1. Click the Show/Hide Comments button on the Reviewing toolbar.

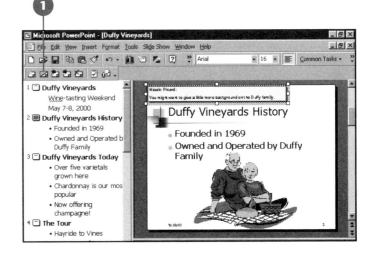

Insert a comment quickly.
*Click the Insert Comment
button on the Reviewing toolbar
to quickly add a comment.*

*"I've read a
comment and
now I want to
delete it."*

**Review all the comments
in a presentation.** *Click the
Previous Comment and Next
Comment buttons on the
Reviewing toolbar to read all of
the comments in a presentation.*

*See "Creating Shadows" on
page 86 and "Creating a 3-D
Object" on page 88 for
information on formatting other
objects in a presentation.*

Delete a Comment

1. Click the comment box
   you want to delete.

2. Click the Delete Comment
   button on the Reviewing
   toolbar.

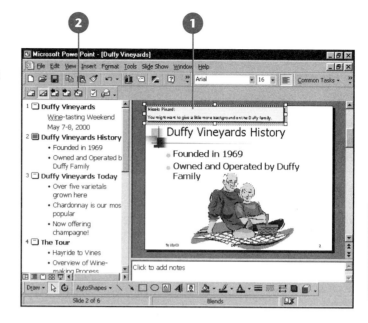

Format a Comment

1. Click the comment box
   you want to format.

2. Click the Format menu,
   and then Comment.

3. Make the formatting
   changes you want.

4. Click OK.

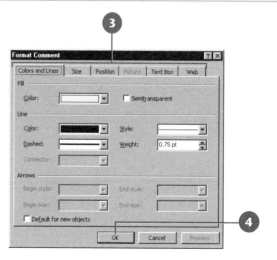

9

Working with Fonts

PowerPoint offers an assortment of tools for working with the fonts in your presentation. If you are using nonstandard fonts, you can embed the fonts you use so they "travel" with your presentation. If you decide to replace one font with another, you can easily do so with a single command.

Embed TrueType Fonts in a Presentation

1. Click the File menu, and then click Save As.

2. Click the Tools button, and then click Embed TrueType Fonts.

3. If necessary, enter a filename and select a location for your presentation.

4. Click Save.

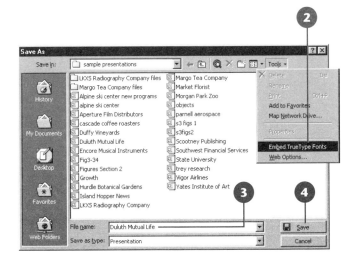

Replace Fonts

1. Click the Format menu, and then click Replace Fonts.

2. Click the Replace drop-down arrow, and then click the font you want.

3. Click the With drop-down arrow, and then click the font you want to substitute.

4. Click Replace.

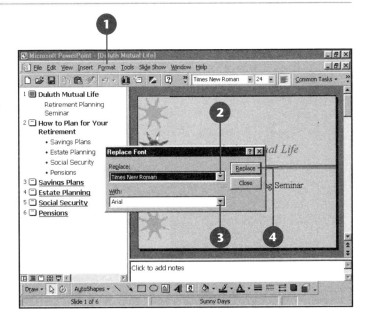

Changing Languages

If your text is written in more than one language, you can designate the language of selected text so the spelling checker uses the right dictionary. For international Microsoft Office users, you can change the language that appears on their screens by enabling different languages. Users around the world can enter, display, and edit text in all supported languages. You'll probably be able to use PowerPoint in your native language.

Mark Text as a Language

1. Select the text you want to mark.

2. Click the Tools menu, and then click Language.

3. Click the language you want to assign to the selected text.

4. Click OK.

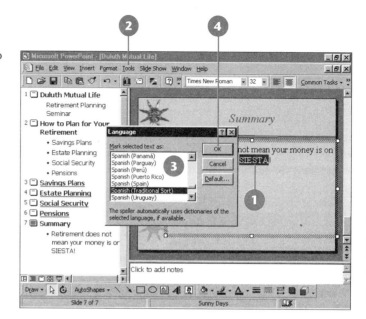

Enable a Language

1. Click the Start button, point to Programs, point to Microsoft Office Tools, and then click Microsoft Office Language Settings.

2. Click to select the check box for the language you want enabled.

3. Click OK.

4. Click Yes to make the change.

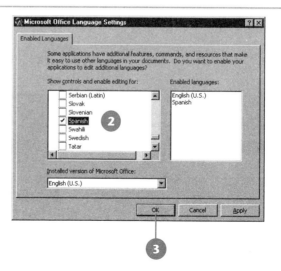

Changing Page Setup Options

Before you print a presentation, you can use the Page Setup dialog box to set the proportions of your presentation slides and their orientation on the page. You can also control slide numbering from the Page Setup dialog box.

TIP

Change the slide start number. *To start numbering at a number other than 1, click the File menu, click Page Setup, and enter the number you want to start with in the Number Slides From box.*

SEE ALSO

See "Creating a Web Page" on page 188 for information on creating Web pages with PowerPoint.

Control Slide Size

1 Click the File menu, and then click Page Setup.

2 Click the Slides Sized For drop-down arrow.

3 Click the size you want.

- Click On-Screen Show for 10-by-7.5-inch slides that fit a computer monitor.

- Click Letter Paper for slides that fit on an 8.5-by-11-inch sheet of paper.

- Click A4 Paper for slides that fit on a 210mm-by-297mm sheet of paper.

- Click 35mm Slides for 11.25-by-7.5-inch slides that fit the proportions of 35mm slide cases.

- Click Overhead for 10-by-7.5-inch slides that fit transparencies.

- Click Banner for 8-by-1-inch slides that are typically used as advertisements on a Web page.

- Click Custom to have PowerPoint set the width and height to fill the printing area for the active printer.

4 Click OK.

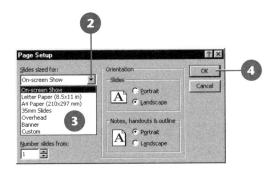

Customize Slide Proportions

1. Click the File menu, and then click Page Setup.

2. Enter a specific width in inches.

3. Enter a specific height in inches.

4. Click OK.

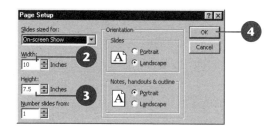

Change Slide Orientation

1. Click the File menu, and then click Page Setup.

2. To orient your slides, click the Portrait or Landscape option button.

3. To orient your notes, handouts, and outline, click the Portrait or Landscape option button in the Notes, Handouts & Outline area.

4. Click OK.

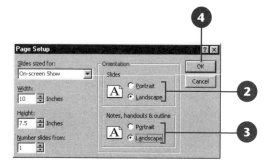

9

Printing a Presentation

You can print all the elements of your presentation—the slides, outline, notes, and handouts—in either color or black and white. The Print dialog box offers standard Windows features, giving you the option to print multiple copies, specify ranges, access printer properties, and print to a file.

When you print an outline, PowerPoint prints the presentation outline as shown in Outline view.

TIP

Print a presentation quickly. *Use the Print button on the Standard toolbar only when you want to bypass the Print dialog box. If you need to make selections in the Print dialog box, use the Print command on the File menu.*

Print a Presentation

1. Click the File menu, and then click Print.
2. Click the Print What drop-down arrow, and then click what you want to print.
3. Change settings in the Print dialog box as necessary.
4. Click OK.

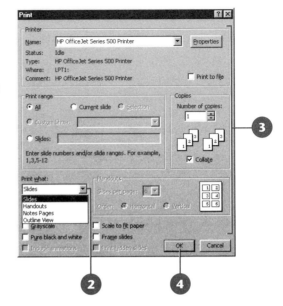

Print a Custom Show

1. Click the File menu, and then click Print.
2. Click the Custom Show drop-down arrow.
3. Click the custom show you want to print.
4. Change settings in the Print dialog box as necessary.
5. Click OK.

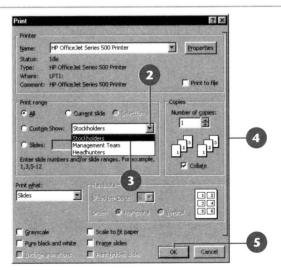

TIP

Scale slides to fit your paper when you print. *Click the File menu, click Print, click to select the Scale To Fit Paper check box, and then click OK.*

TIP

Print in grayscale or pure black and white. *Click the File menu, click Print, click to select the Grayscale or Pure Black And White check box, and then click OK.*

SEE ALSO

See "Creating a Custom Slide Show" on page 200 for information on creating a custom slide show.

SEE ALSO

See "Developing an Outline" on page 34 for information on creating and displaying an outline.

Print a Single Slide or a Range of Slides

1. Click the File menu, and then click Print.

2. If necessary, click the Print What drop-down arrow, and then click Slides.

3. Select the range of slides you want to print.

4. Click OK.

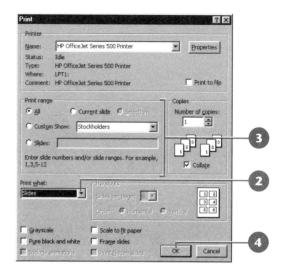

Print an Outline

1. In Outline view, display your outline the way you want it to be printed.

   ◆ Display only slide titles or all text levels

   ◆ Display with or without formatting

   ◆ Display with a small or large view percentage

2. Click the File menu, and then click Print.

3. Click the Print What drop-down arrow, and then click Outline View.

4. Click OK.

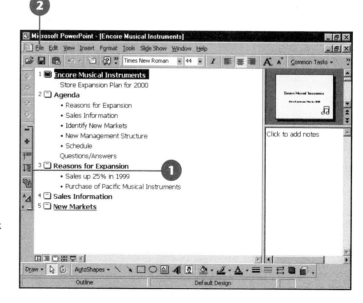

Preparing Handouts

Prepare your handouts in the Print dialog box, where you specify what to print. You can customize your handouts by formatting them in the handout master first. You can also add a header and footer to include the date, slide number, and page number, for example.

TIP

What are the dotted rectangles in the handout master? *The dotted rectangles are placeholders for slides and for header and footer information.*

TIP

Add headers and footer to create consistent handouts. *Headers and footers you add to the handout master are also added to notes pages and the printed outline.*

Format the Handout Master

1. Click the View menu, point to Master, and then click Handout Master.

2. Click one of the buttons on the Handout Master toolbar to specify how many slides you want per page.

3. Use the Formatting and Drawing toolbar buttons to format the handout master.

4. If you want, add a header, footer, date, and page numbering.

5. Click the Close button on the Master toolbar.

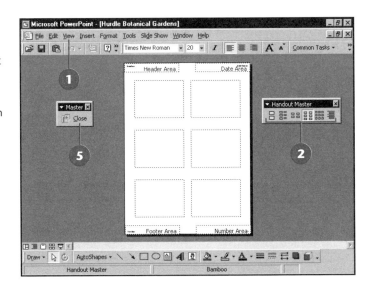

Add Headers and Footers to Handouts

1. Click the View menu, and then click Header And Footer.

2. Click the Notes And Handouts tab.

3. Enter the information you want to appear on your handouts.

4. Click Apply To All.

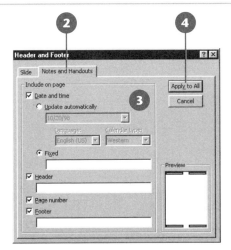

TIP

Print different kinds of handouts. *Use the Print dialog box to print handouts that display only the slides—one, two, three, four, six, or nine to a page. If you want handouts with blank lines for taking notes, export your slides to Word first.*

"I want to print my slides for my audience—two slides per page."

TIP

Add a frame around printed slides. *Click the File menu, click Print, click to select the Frame Slides check box, and then click OK.*

SEE ALSO

See "Exporting Notes and Slides to Word" on page 176 for information on sending slides to Word for creating handouts.

Print Handouts

1 Click the File menu, and then click Print.

2 Click the Print What drop-down arrow, and then click the option you want.

- ◆ Click Slides to print one slide per page.

- ◆ Click Handouts and then click the Slides Per Page drop-down arrow to select one of the five Handouts options.

3 Click an Order option button.

4 Click OK.

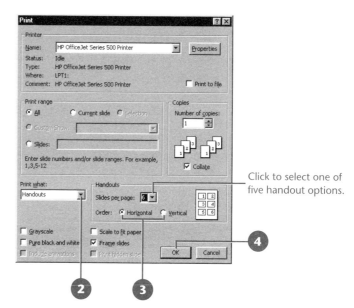

Click to select one of five handout options.

Preparing Speaker Notes

You can add speaker notes to a slide in Normal view using the notes pane. Also, every slide has a corresponding *notes page* that displays a reduced image of the slide and a text placeholder where you can enter speaker's notes. Once you have created speaker's notes, you can reference them as you give your presentation, either from a printed copy or from your computer. You can enhance your notes by including objects on the notes master.

Enter Notes in Normal View

1. Switch to the slide for which you want to enter notes.

2. Click to place the insertion point in the notes pane and type your notes.

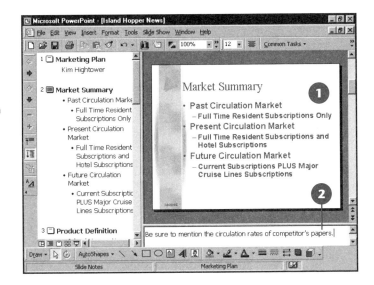

Enter Notes in Notes Page View

1. Switch to the slide for which you want to enter notes.

2. Click the View menu, and then click Notes Page.

3. If necessary, click the Zoom drop-down arrow, and then increase the zoom percentage to better see the text you type.

4. Click the text placeholder.

5. Type your notes.

Reduced image of slide

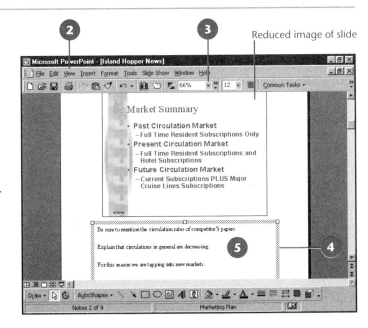

Format the Notes Master

1. Click the View menu, point to Master, and then click Notes Master.

2. Make the format changes you want.

   ◆ You can add objects to the notes master that you want to appear on every page, such as a picture or a text object.

   ◆ You can add a header and footer by clicking the View menu and then clicking Header And Footer.

   ◆ You can add the date, time, or page number to your notes pages.

3. Click the Close button on the Master toolbar.

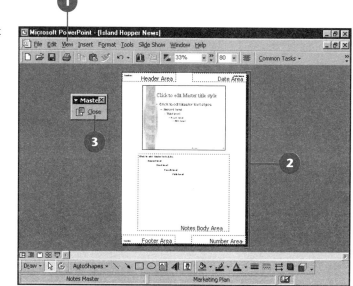

Customizing Notes Pages

You can add dates, numbering, and header and footer text to your notes pages just as you do to your slides. If you have removed objects from the master and decide you want to restore them, you can reapply any of the master placeholders (the slide image, the date, header, and so on) without affecting objects and text outside the placeholders. Moreover, if you delete the slide placeholder or text placeholder from a notes page, for example, you can easily reinsert it.

SEE ALSO

See "Adding a Header and Footer" on page 58 for information on adding header and footer information to your presentation.

Add a Header and Footer to Notes Pages

1. Click the View menu, and then click Header And Footer.

2. Click the Notes And Handouts tab.

3. Add the header and footer information you want.

4. Click Apply To All.

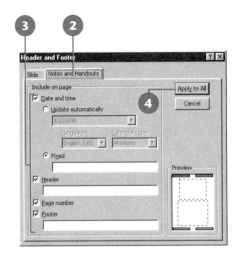

Reinsert Notes Placeholders on the Notes Master

1. Click the View menu, point to Master, and then click Notes Master.

2. Click the Format menu, and then click Notes Master Layout.

3. Click to select the check boxes corresponding to the placeholders you want to reinsert.

4. Click OK.

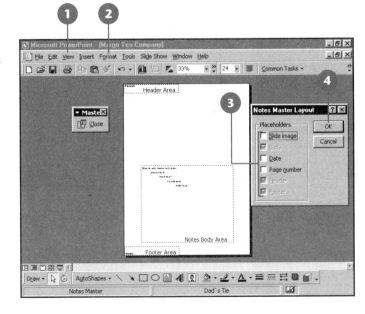

SEE ALSO

See "Exporting Notes and Slides to Word" on page 176 for information on sending notes to Microsoft Word.

SEE ALSO

See "Taking Notes" on page 222 for information on viewing speaker notes on your computer as you give a presentation.

"How can I format my notes pages so they are more attractive?"

Reinsert Placeholders on an Individual Slide

1. In Notes Page view, switch to the slide whose placeholders you want to restore.

2. Click the Format menu, and then click Notes Layout.

3. Click to select the check boxes corresponding to the placeholders you want to reapply.

4. Click OK.

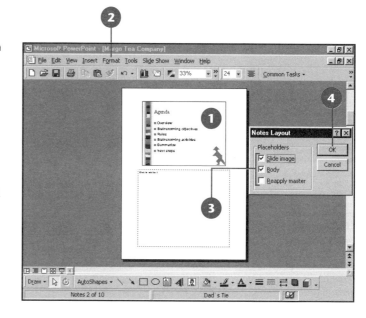

Customize Notes Pages

1. In Notes Page view, right-click a blank area in the notes pane.

2. Click the item you want to format.

   ◆ Click Notes Color Scheme to open the Notes Color Scheme dialog box.

   ◆ Click Notes Background to open the Notes Background dialog box.

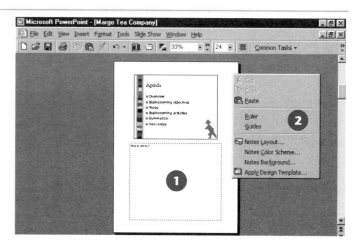

Documenting Presentation Properties

You can get feedback on your presentation before you present it by using PowerPoint's *File Properties* feature. PowerPoint allows you to document your presentation by entering information about the presentation and describing its contents so your feedback team has all the information it needs to evaluate it.

SEE ALSO

See "Opening a Presentation" on page 11 for information on using presentation properties to search for files.

TIP

Automatically display the Properties dialog when saving for the first time.
Click the Tools menu, click Options, click the Save tab, click to select the Prompt For File Properties check box, and then click OK.

Enter Information About a Presentation

1. Click the File menu, and then click Properties.

2. Click the Summary tab.

3. Enter information about the presentation that will help others identify it.

4. Click OK.

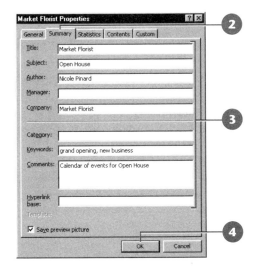

Check Presentation Contents

1. Click the File menu, and then click Properties.

2. Click the Contents tab to review the contents of the presentation.

3. Click OK.

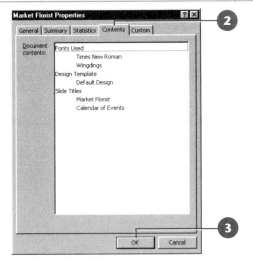

E-Mailing a Presentation

PowerPoint makes it easy to send the presentation to your colleagues directly from PowerPoint if you have installed Microsoft Outlook or Outlook Express. You can send the contents of one slide using the Mail Recipient option, or you can send the entire presentation as an attachment using the Mail Recipient (As Attachment) option. When you send a copy of a slide, the slide is sent in HTML format as the body of the message.

TIP

Close an e-mail message without sending it. *If you decide not to send a slide in an e-mail message, click the E-Mail button on the Standard toolbar to remove the e-mail program toolbar.*

SEE ALSO

See "Holding an Online Meeting" on page 230 for information on discussing a presentation during an online meeting.

Send a Slide in an E-Mail Message

1. Open the presentation and display the slide you want to send.

2. Click the E-Mail button on the Standard toolbar.

3. Click the option to send the current slide.

4. Click the To or Cc button. Select the contacts you want, and then click OK.

5. Click the Send This Slide button on the toolbar.

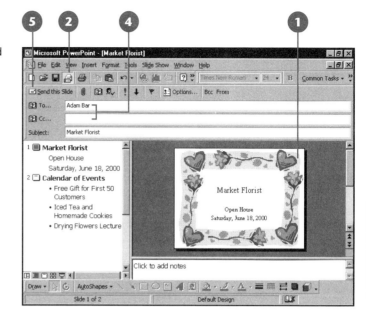

Send a Presentation in an E-Mail Message

1. Open the presentation you want to send.

2. Click the File menu, point to Send To, and then click Mail Recipient (As Attachment).

   Your default e-mail program opens.

3. Fill in the new message form that opens.

4. Click the Send button on the toolbar.

Icons representing attached documents appear here.

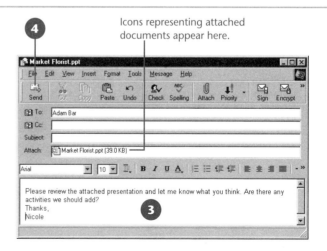

Exporting Notes and Slides to Word

You can send both your notes and slides to Word so that you can use a full array of word processing tools. This is especially handy when you are developing more detailed materials, such as training presentations and manuals.

TIP

Settings to send notes to Word. *By default, PowerPoint pastes your presentation into a Word document. If you change the presentation after sending it to Word, the changes you make to the presentation are not reflected in the Word document. If you click the Paste Link option button in the Write-Up dialog box, however, you create a link between the Word document and the presentation, and changes you make in one are reflected in the other.*

Create Handouts in Word

1 Click the File menu, point to Send To, and then click Microsoft Word.

2 Click the page layout option you want for handouts.

3 To create a link to the presentation, click the Paste Link option button.

4 Click OK.

Word starts, creates a new document, and inserts your presentation with the page layout you selected.

5 Print the document in Word, editing and saving it as necessary.

6 When you're done, click the Close button to quit Word.

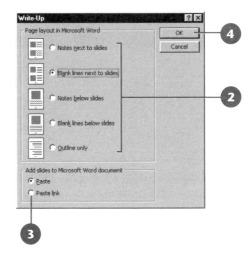

Saving Slides in Different Formats

You can save PowerPoint presentations in a number of formats so that many different programs can access them. For example, you might want to save your presentation as a Web page that you can view in a Web browser. Or you can save a presentation in an earlier version of PowerPoint in case the people you work with have not upgraded to PowerPoint 2000. You can also save an individual slide as a graphic image that you can open in a graphics editor.

SEE ALSO

See "Creating a Web Page" on page 188 for more information on saving your presentation as a Web page.

Save a Presentation in a Different File Type

1. Click the File menu, and then click Save As.

2. Click the Save As Type drop-down arrow, and then click the format you want, such as a Web page, a previous version of PowerPoint, or an RTF (Rich Text Format) outline.

    Many software program can read RTF files.

3. Type a filename.

4. Click Save.

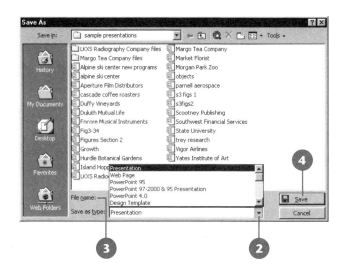

Save a Slide as a Graphic Image

1. Click the File menu, and then click Save As.

2. Click the Save As Type drop-down arrow, and then click the graphics format you want to use, such as JPEG or GIF.

3. Type a filename.

4. Click Save.

5. Click Yes to save all slides as separate graphic image files, or click No to save just the current slide as a graphic image file.

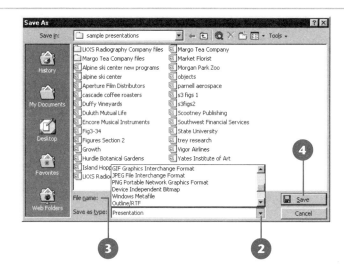

Creating 35mm Slides

A PowerPoint presentation is most effective when you show it electronically because you can use animations, transitions, and multimedia special effects. However, there are times when you need to convert an electronic presentation to physical 35mm slides—perhaps your auditorium doesn't have the hardware necessary to display a computer presentation. PowerPoint offers an online service through a company called Genigraphics that downloads your presentation, prepares the physical medium you need, and ships it back to you.

Start the Genigraphics Wizard and Order Services

1. Open the presentation from which you want to create 35mm slides.

2. Click the File menu, point to Send To, and then click Genigraphics.

3. Click the option button for the type of product or service you want.

4. Click Next to continue.

5. Click the services you want, from 35mm slides to prints or posters.

6. Click Next to continue.

7. Click to select presentation and processing options you want. Click Next to continue.

8. Schedule the date when you need your materials, and enter delivery and billing information. Click Next to continue.

9. Click Finish.

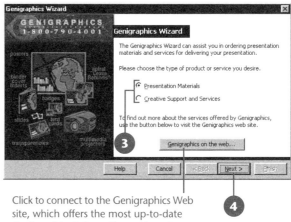

Click to connect to the Genigraphics Web site, which offers the most up-to-date Genigraphics information and services.

10

Creating a Web Presentation

Microsoft PowerPoint 2000 provides you with the tools you need to create and save your presentation as a Web page and to publish it on the World Wide Web. The Save As Web Page feature formats your presentation in *Hypertext Markup Language* (HTML), a simple coding system used to format documents for an intranet or the Internet. Saving your presentation in HTML format means you can use most Web browsers to view your presentation. Any presentation can easily be saved as a Web document and viewed in a Web browser. By saving your PowerPoint presentations as Web pages, you can share your data with others via the Web.

To assist you in creating Web pages, PowerPoint includes several Web templates that you can edit to fit your needs. Incorporating action buttons and hyperlinks within your presentation adds an element of connectivity to your work. If you add action buttons to your slides, you can click a button in slide show to jump instantly to another slide, presentation, or program file. If you add hyperlinks to objects, you can jump to Internet and intranet locations. In addition, Microsoft offers tips, software updates, tools, and general information through its Office Web site.

Using Web Templates

If you intend to use PowerPoint to create Web pages, you might want to take advantage of PowerPoint's specially designed Internet templates. The AutoContent Wizard lets you add hyperlinks between the slides in your presentation or hyperlinks to your e-mail address. The Group Home Page template helps you create a customized home page for your corporate or personal Web site. You can also save any page you design to an FTP server or HTML server using PowerPoint's Save As command.

SEE ALSO

See "Creating a Web Page" on page 188 for information on saving a presentation as a Web page in the HTML file format.

Create a Web Presentation with the AutoContent Wizard

① Click the File menu, and then click New.

② Click the General tab, and then double-click the AutoContent Wizard icon.

③ Click Next to continue.

④ Click the button with the type of presentation you want.

⑤ Click a presentation. Click Next to continue.

⑥ Click the Web Presentation option button to specify how the presentation will be used. Click Next to continue.

⑦ Enter the presentation title and any footer information. Click Next to continue.

⑧ If necessary, enter your e-mail address in the E-mail Hyperlink box and any other information requested.

⑨ Click Finish.

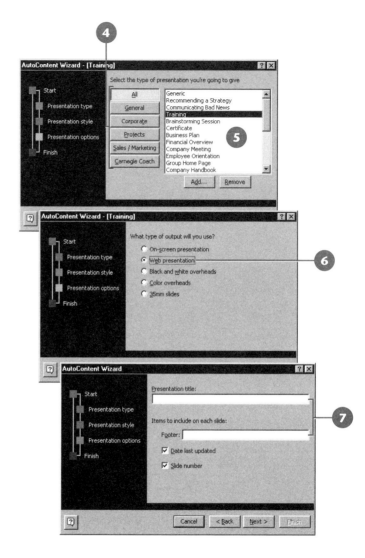

Use the Animation Player to display slide show effects via the Internet. *If you use animation effects in your Web presentations, be sure that your clients have added the PowerPoint Animation Player to their Web browser.*

Design templates based on themes. *Themes have been created and coordinated between some of the Office 2000 programs and FrontPage 2000 to make it easier to create consistent-looking Web pages. PowerPoint 2000 includes design templates consistent with the themes.*

Insert Web elements from the Clip Gallery. *You can insert Web backgrounds, Web banners, Web bullets and buttons, Web dividers, and other Web elements into your presentation from the Clip Gallery. Click the Insert Clip Art button on the Drawing toolbar, click the Web category you want, click the picture you want, and then click Insert Clip. When you're done, click the Close button.*

Create a Home Page

1. Click the File menu, and then click New.

2. Click the Presentations tab.

3. Click the Group Home Page icon.

4. Click OK.

5. Edit the presentation.

6. Click the File menu, click Save As Web Page, specify a filename and location, and then click Save.

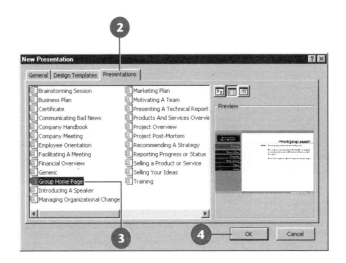

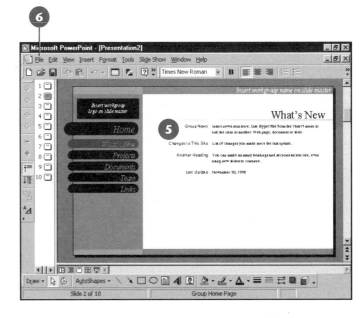

Adding Action Buttons

When you create a self-running presentation to show at a kiosk, you might want a user to be able to move easily to specific slides or to a different presentation altogether. To give an audience this capability, insert *action buttons*, which a user can click to jump to a different slide or presentation. Clicking an action button activates a *hyperlink*, a connection between two locations in the same document or in different documents.

Insert an action button.
Click the AutoShapes button on the Drawing toolbar, point to Action Buttons, and then click the action button you want to insert on your slide.

Insert an Action Button

1. Click the Slide Show menu.

2. Point to Action Buttons, and then choose the action button you want.

3. Drag the pointer to insert the action button, and then release the mouse button when the action button is the size you want.

4. Fill in the action settings you want, and then click OK.

Test an Action Button

1. Click the Slide Show View button.

2. Display the slide containing the action button.

3. Click the action button.

Create an Action Button to Go to a Specific Slide

① Click the Slide Show menu, point to Action Buttons, click the Custom Action button.

② Drag the pointer to insert the action button on the slide.

③ Click the Hyperlink To option button, click the drop-down arrow, and then click Slide from the list of hyperlink destinations.

④ Select the slide you want the action button to jump to.

⑤ Click OK.

⑥ Click OK.

⑦ Right-click the action button, and click Add Text.

⑧ Type the name of the slide the action button points to.

⑨ Click outside the action button to deselect it.

⑩ Run the slide show and test the action button.

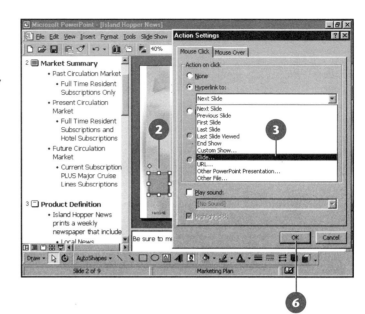

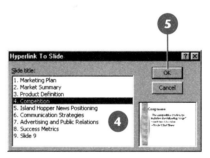

Adding Hyperlinks to Objects

You can turn one of the objects on your slide into an action button so that when you click or move over it, you activate a hyperlink and jump to the new location. You can point hyperlinks to almost any destination, including slides in a presentation and Web pages on the World Wide Web.

TIP

Edit a hyperlink quickly.
Right-click the object with the hyperlink, point to Hyperlink, and then click Edit Hyperlink.

SEE ALSO

See "Creating Hyperlinks to External Objects" on page 186 for more information on creating hyperlinks to objects.

Add a Hyperlink to a Slide Object

1. Right-click an object on the slide, and then click Action Settings.

2. Click the Mouse Click or Mouse Over tab.

3. Click the Hyperlink To option button.

4. Click the Hyperlink To drop-down arrow.

5. Click a destination for the hyperlink.

6. Click OK.

7. Run the slide show and test the hyperlink by clicking the object in the slide show.

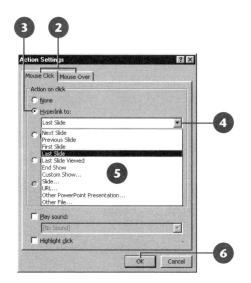

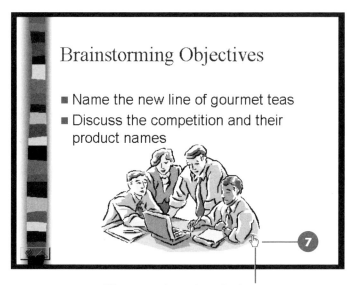

When you point to the action button, the pointer changes shape.

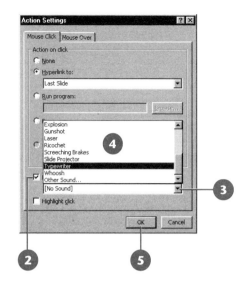

TIP

Highlight a click or mouse over. *When you click or move over a hyperlink, you can highlight the object. In the Actions Settings dialog box, click to select the Highlight Click or Highlight When Mouse Over check box.*

"I'd like a sound to play when I click a hyperlink."

TIP

Create an action button to a sound. *Click the Slide Show menu, point to Action Buttons, click the Sound action button, drag to create the sound action button, click the Play Sound drop-down arrow, select the sound you want, and then click OK.*

Add a Default Sound to a Hyperlink

1 In Normal or Slide view, right-click the object with the hyperlink, and then click Action Settings.

2 Click to select the Play Sound check box.

3 Click the Play Sound drop-down arrow.

4 Click the sound you want to play when the object is clicked during the show.

5 Click OK.

Add a Custom Sound to a Hyperlink

1 Right-click the hyperlinked object, and then click Action Settings.

2 Click to select the Play Sound check box, and then click the Play Sound drop-down arrow.

3 Scroll to the bottom of the Play Sound list, and then click Other Sound.

4 Locate and select the sound you want to use.

5 Click OK, and then click OK again.

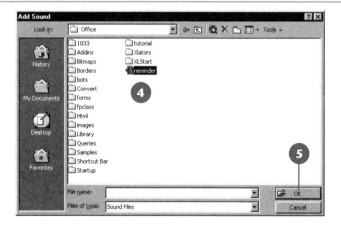

10

Creating Hyperlinks to External Objects

You can create hyperlinks in your presentation that access other sources, such as another presentation, a file, a Web site, or even a program. This feature is especially useful for kiosk presentations, where you want to make information available to your audience, even if you can't be there to provide it.

Create a Hyperlink to Another Presentation

1. Right-click an object on your slide, and then click Action Settings.

2. Click the Hyperlink To option button, and then click Other PowerPoint Presentation from the list of hyperlinks.

3. Locate and select the presentation you want, and then click OK.

4. Select the slide that you want to link to.

5. Click OK.

6. Click OK again to save the hyperlink.

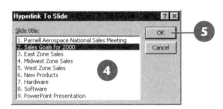

Create a Hyperlink to an External File

1. Right-click an object on your slide, click Action Settings, and then click the Hyperlink To option button.

2. Click Other File in the list of hyperlinks.

3. Locate and select the file on your computer.

4. Click OK, and then click OK again.

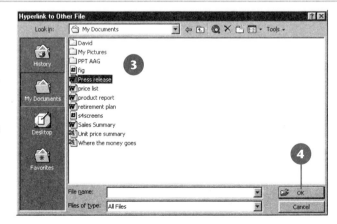

Create a Hyperlink to a Web Page

1. Right-click an object on your slide, click Action Settings, and then click the Hyperlink To option button.

2. Click URL in the list of hyperlinks.

3. Enter the URL of the Web page.

4. Click OK.

5. Click OK again to save the hyperlink.

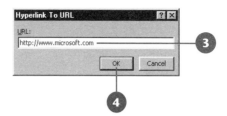

Create a Hyperlink to a Program

1. Right-click an object on your slide, and click Action Settings.

2. Click the Run Program option button.

3. Click the Browse button and then locate and select the program on your computer or network.

4. Click OK.

5. Click OK to save the hyperlink that runs the program.

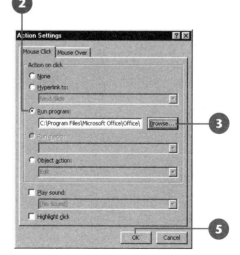

10

Creating a Web Page

PowerPoint allows you to save any presentation as a Web page, written in HTML, the language used by Internet browsers to interpret and display Web pages. You can save a file as an HTML file by using the Save As command or the Save As Web Page command. Once you save the file in HTML format, you can preview and then publish the Web page. To publish a Web page means to place a copy of the presentation in HTML format on the Web. You can publish a complete presentation, a custom show, a single slide, or a range of slides.

TIP

Create a Web folder. *In the Save As dialog box, click the Web Folders icon on the Places bar, click the New Folder button, type the Web address of the Web folder you want to add, click Next, and then follow any remaining wizard instructions.*

Save a Presentation as a Web Page

1. Click the File menu, and then click Save As Web Page.

2. Click one of the icons on the Places bar for quick access to frequently used folders.

3. If you want to save the file in another folder, click the Save In drop-down arrow, and then select a location for your Web page.

4. Click Change Title to change the title of your Web page.

5. Type the new title in the Page Title box.

6. Click OK.

7. Click Save.

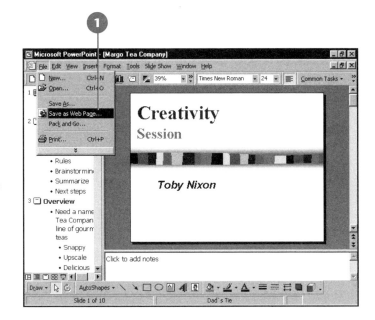

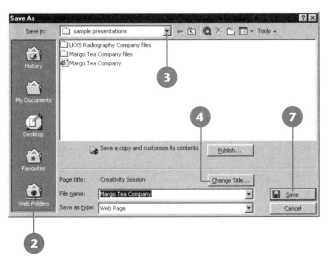

TIP

Save a presentation to an FTP server. *Click the File menu, and then click Save As. Click the Save In drop-down arrow, and then click FTP Locations. Double-click Add/Modify FTP locations. Type the address of the FTP server and any user information, and then click Add. Click OK. Choose the FTP server from the list in the Save As dialog box, and click Open.*

TIP

What is a Web server? *A Web server is a computer on the Internet or intranet that stores Web pages.*

SEE ALSO

See "Understanding Office Server Extensions" on page 234 for information on publishing and viewing Office documents directly from a Web server with Office Server Extensions.

Save and Publish a Presentation as a Web Page

1. Click the File menu, and then click Save As Web Page.

2. Click one of the icons on the Places bar for quick access to frequently used folders.

   If you're connected to a Web server with Office Server Extensions, click the Web Folders icon to select a location on the Internet or intranet.

3. If you want to save the file in another folder, click the Save In drop-down arrow, and then select a location for your Web page.

4. Click Change Title to change the title of your Web page.

5. Type the new title in the Page Title box.

6. Click Publish.

7. Make your selections in the Publish As Web Page dialog box.

8. Click to select the Open Published Web Page In Browser check box.

9. Click Publish.

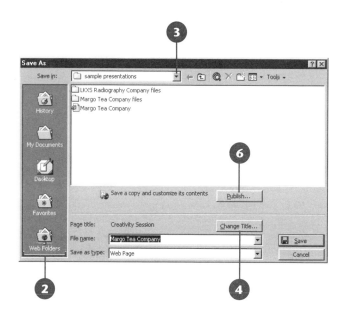

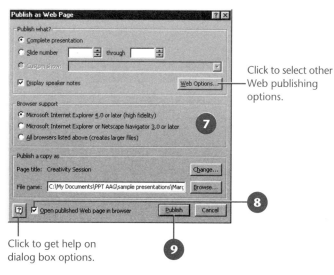

Click to select other Web publishing options.

Click to get help on dialog box options.

Changing Web Page Options

When you save or publish a presentation as a Web page, you can change the appearance of the Web page by changing PowerPoint's Web options. You can set Web options to add slide navigation buttons, change Web page colors, show slide transitions and animations in the browser window, and resize graphics to fit the display of the browser window.

SEE ALSO

See "Creating a Web Page" on page 188 for information on accessing the Web Options dialog box from the Publish As A Web Page dialog box.

TIP

International Web pages.
PowerPoint saves Web pages by using the appropriate international text encoding so that users on any language system are able to view the correct characters.

Change Web Page Options

1. Click the Tools menu, and then click Options.

2. Click the General tab.

3. Click Web Options.

4. Click the General tab.

5. Click the options you want to use when you save or publish a Web page.

   ◆ To add slide navigation controls and change the Web page colors, click to select the Add Slide Navigation Controls check box, and then click the Colors drop-down arrow and select a color scheme.

   ◆ To show slide transitions and animations, click to select the Show Slide Animation While Browsing check box.

   ◆ To allow graphics to fit in different size browser windows, click to select the Resize Graphics To Fit Browser Window check box.

6. Click OK.

7. Click OK.

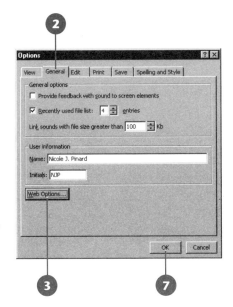

Opening a Web Page

After saving a presentation as a Web page, you can open the Web page, an HTML file, in PowerPoint. This allows you to quickly and easily switch from HTML to the standard PowerPoint format and back again without losing any formatting or functionality. For example, if you create a formatted chart in a PowerPoint presentation, save the presentation file as a Web page, and then reopen the Web page in PowerPoint, the chart will look the same as the original chart in PowerPoint. PowerPoint preserves the original formatting and functionality of the presentation.

Open button

Open a Presentation as a Web Page in PowerPoint

1. Click the Open button on the Standard toolbar.

2. Click the Files Of Type drop-down arrow, and then click Web Pages.

3. Click one of the icons on the Places bar for quick access to often-used folders.

4. If the file is located in another folder, click the Look In drop-down arrow, and select the folder where the file is located.

5. Click the name of the presentation file.

6. Click Open.

To open the Web page in your browser, click the Open button drop-down arrow, and then click Open In Browser.

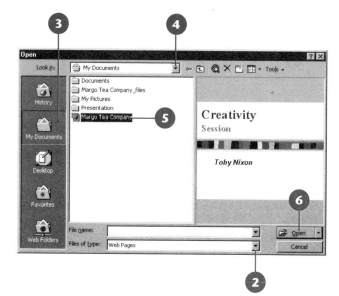

10

Previewing a Web Page

Once you've created a presentation and saved it as a Web page, you can see how it looks in your browser—Microsoft Internet Explorer or another browser. It is a good idea to preview your page before you publish it to the Web just as you would preview a document before you print it. Previewing a Web page shows you what the page will look like once it's posted on the Internet. When you display a Web presentation in a Web browser, a *navigation bar* appears with toolbar buttons to make it easy to navigate through the Web presentation. You can also view your presentation as a Web page one slide at a time, in full-screen mode, as an outline, or as the slide master.

Preview a Web Page

1. Open the presentation file you want to view as a Web page.

2. Click the File menu, and then click Web Page Preview.

   Your Web browser opens, displaying your Web page.

3. Click the Next Slide or Previous Slide button on the navigation bar to move from slide to slide.

4. Click the Full Screen Slide Show button on the navigation bar to display the presentation in slide show.

5. Click the Expand/Collapse Outline button on the navigation bar to display more or less outline detail.

6. Click the Close button to quit the browser and return to PowerPoint.

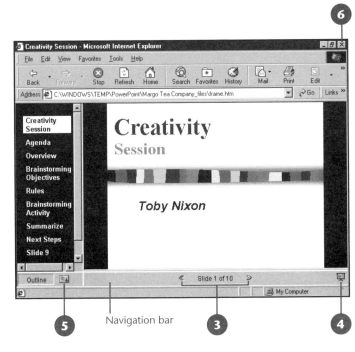

Navigation bar

TIP

View a Web presentation outline in a browser. *Start your Web browser, click the File menu, click Open, locate and open the folder containing your Web presentation, and then double-click the file OUTLINE.HTM.*

TIP

Show animation and transition effects while viewing your presentation in a browser. *Click the Tools menu, click Options, and then click the General tab. Click Web Options, click the Show Slide Animation While Browsing check box, and then click OK. Click OK again to close the Options dialog box.*

TIP

Specify text to be displayed during Web presentations. *If you use an object in a presentation that you plan to present on the Web, you can enter text that is displayed while the page loads. Select the object, click the Format menu, click AutoShape, click the Web tab, enter the text, and then click OK.*

View an Individual Slide

1. Start your Web browser.

2. Click the File menu, and then click Open.

   If necessary, click Browse to help you locate your Web presentation.

3. Locate and open the folder containing your Web presentation.

4. Double-click the file SLIDE000X.HTM, where "X" is the number of the slide.

5. Click OK.

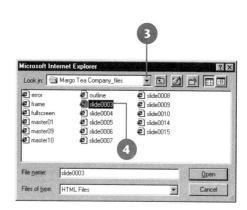

View a Presentation in Full-Screen Mode

1. Start your Web browser.

2. Click the File menu, and then click Open.

   If necessary, click Browse to help you locate your Web presentation.

3. Locate and open the folder containing your Web presentation.

4. Double-click the file FULLSCREEN.HTM.

5. Click OK.

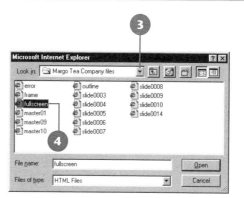

10

Using the Web Toolbar

With the Web toolbar, you are one click away from accessing the features of your Web browser. You can use the Web toolbar to go to your start page (also known as a home page), access a Web search page, or open a specific Web page.

Show Only Web Toolbar button

Start Page button

Display and Hide the Web Toolbar

1. Click the View menu, point to Toolbars, and then click Web.

2. Click the Show Only Web Toolbar button on the Web toolbar to hide the rest of the toolbars.

3. Click the Show Only Web Toolbar button on the Web toolbar again to restore the hidden toolbars.

4. Click the View menu, point to Toolbars, and then click Web again to hide the Web toolbar.

View Your Start Page

1. Display the Web toolbar.

2. Click the Start Page button on the Web toolbar.

3. Establish an Internet connection if prompted.

   Your browser opens, displaying your start or home page.

Web toolbar

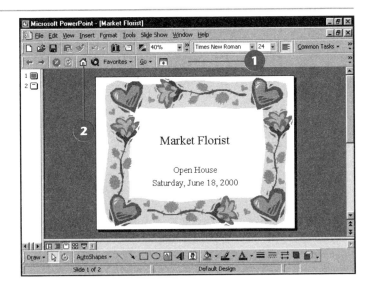

TIP

Web addresses and URLs.
*Every Web page has a uniform resource locator (URL), a Web address in a form your browser program can decipher. Like postal addresses and e-mail addresses, each URL contains specific parts that identify where a Web page is located. For example, the URL for Microsoft's Web page is **http:// www.microsoft.com/** where "http://" shows the address is on the Web and "www.microsoft.com" shows the computer that stores the Web page. As you browse various pages, the URL includes their folders and filenames.*

Search The
Web button

Open a Specific Web Page or File

1. Display the Web toolbar.

2. Click the Go button on the Web toolbar, and then click Open.

3. Type the URL of the Web page or location of the file that you want to open.

4. Click to select the Open In New Window check box.

5. Click OK.

   Your browser opens, displaying your Web page or file.

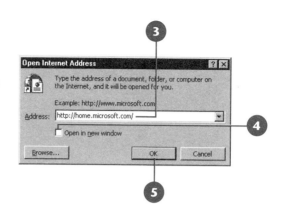

Search the Web

1. Display the Web toolbar.

2. Click the Search The Web button on the Web toolbar.

   Your browser opens, displaying your Web search page.

3. Click a hyperlink to a search engine, and then follow the directions to search the Web for information.

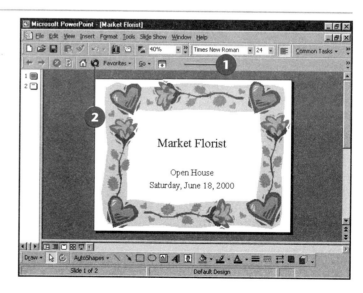

Accessing Office Information on the Web

New information about programs comes out with great frequency. You have access to an abundance of information about Power-Point and other programs in the Office suite from Microsoft. This information is constantly being updated. Answers to frequently asked questions, user forums, and update offers are some of the types of information you can find about Microsoft Office. You can also find out about conferences, books, and other products that help you learn just how much you can do with your Office software.

TRY THIS

Join a newsgroup. *If you have a USENET newsreader, you might also consider accessing the newsgroup microsoft.public.powerpoint to meet and share ideas with other PowerPoint users.*

Find Online Office Information

1. Click the Help menu, and then click Office On The Web.

2. Establish an Internet connection if prompted.

   Your Web browser opens, displaying the Microsoft Office Update Web page.

3. Click a hyperlink of interest.

4. Click the Close button to quit the browser and return to PowerPoint.

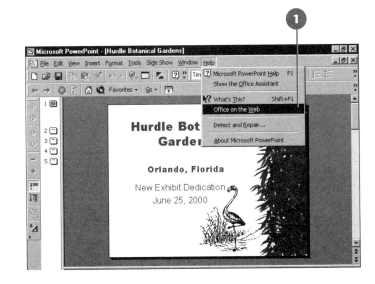

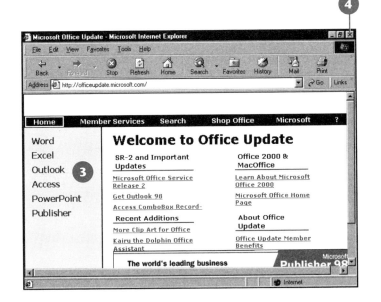

Preparing a Slide Show

Microsoft PowerPoint 2000 provides many tools to help you coordinate your slide show as a complete multimedia production.

Before you can deliver a slide show, you need to set up for the type of show you want. Some presentations include slides that are appropriate for one audience but not for another. PowerPoint lets you create custom slide shows that include only a selection of slides, in whatever order you want, intended for a given audience. If you are presenting a slide show using a second monitor or projection screen, PowerPoint includes the tools you need to get the job done without the hassle.

A slide show can feature special visual, sound, and animation effects. For example, you can include special *transitions* or actions between slides. Using *animations*, effects that animate your slide elements such as text flying in from the right, you can also control how the audience first sees each element of the slide.

PowerPoint includes tools that let you time your presentation to make sure that it is neither too long nor too short. You can also make a PowerPoint presentation come alive with the proper use of narration and music. You can record a narration or music and insert it directly into your slide show.

Setting Up a Slide Show

PowerPoint offers several types of slide shows appropriate for a variety of presentation situations, from a traditional big-screen slide show to a show that runs automatically on a computer screen at a conference kiosk. When you don't want to show all of the slides in a PowerPoint presentation to a particular audience, you can specify only a range of slides to show, or you can hide individual slides.

SEE ALSO

See "Timing a Presentation" on page 212 for information on using rehearsed timings.

SEE ALSO

See "Recording a Narration" on page 214 for more information on narrations.

Set Up a Show

1. Click the Slide Show menu, and then click Set Up Show.

2. Choose the show type you want.

   ◆ Click the Presented By A Speaker option button to run a traditional full screen slide show, where you can advance the slides manually or automatically.

   ◆ Click the Browsed By An Individual option button to run a slide show in a window and allow access to some PowerPoint commands.

   ◆ Click the Browsed At A Kiosk option button to create a self-running, unattended slide show for a booth or kiosk. The slides will advance automatically, or a user can advance the slides or activate hyperlinks.

3. Click to select additional show setting check boxes as appropriate.

4. Click OK.

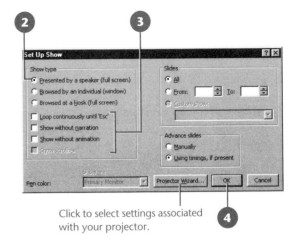

Click to select settings associated with your projector.

Open a presentation in Slide Show view. *If you want a presentation file to open directly to a slide show rather than in a document window, click the File menu, click Save As, click the Save As Type drop-down arrow, and click PowerPoint Show.*

Hide slides in Normal or Slide view. *Display the slide you want to hide in Normal or Slide view, click the Slide Show menu, and then click Hide Slide. To show a hidden slide, click it, click the Slide Show menu, and then click Hide Slide again.*

Run a slide show continuously. *Open the presentation you want to run, click the Slide Show menu, click Set Up Show, click to select the Look Continuously Until 'Esc' check box, and then click OK.*

Show a Range of Slides

1 Click the Slide Show menu, and then click Set Up Show.

2 Click the From option button.

3 Enter the first and last slide numbers of the range you want to show.

4 Click OK.

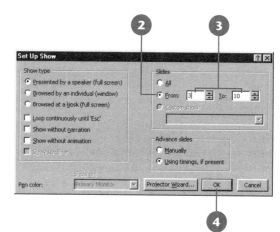

Hide Slides

1 In Slide Sorter view, click the slide you want to hide.

2 Click the Hide Slide button on the Slide Sorter toolbar.

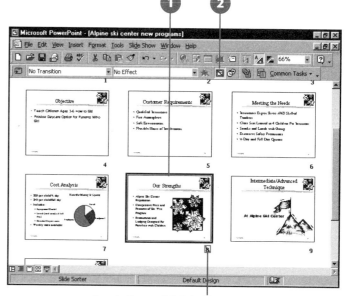

Icon indicates slide is hidden

11

Creating a Custom Slide Show

If you plan to present a slide show to more than one audience, you don't have to create a separate slide show for each audience. Instead, you can create a *custom slide show* that allows you to specify which slides from the presentation you will use and the order in which they will appear.

TIP

Use the Set Up Show command to display a custom slide show. *Click the Slide Show menu, click Set Up Show, click the Custom Show option button, click the Custom Show drop-down arrow, select the custom slide show, and then click OK.*

Create a Custom Slide Show

1. Click the Slide Show menu, and then click Custom Shows.

2. Click New.

3. Type a name for the show.

4. Double-click the slides you want to include in the show in the order you want to present them.

5. Click OK.

6. Click Close.

List of custom slide shows for this presentation

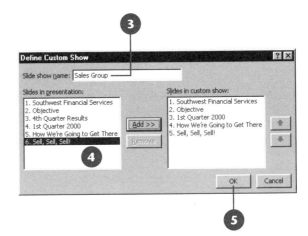

Show a Custom Slide Show

1. Click the Slide Show menu, and then click Custom Shows.

2. Click the custom slide show you want to run.

3. Click Show.

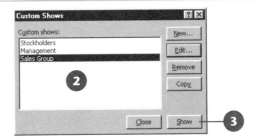

Delete a custom slide show. *Click the Slide Show menu, click Custom Shows, click the show you want to delete, click Remove, and then click Close.*

Create as many custom slide shows as you want within a presentation. *To create a new custom slide show from an existing one, click Edit in the Custom Shows dialog box, add and remove the slides you want, rename the slide show, and then click OK.*

Create a custom slide show from an existing one. *To create a custom slide show similar to an existing custom show, click the existing custom show in the Custom Shows dialog box, and then click the Copy button. This creates a new custom show named Copy Of Existing Show. Click the Edit button to edit the copy, and give the new custom slide show its own name.*

Edit a Custom Slide Show

1. Click the Slide Show menu, and then click Custom Shows.

2. Click the show you want to edit.

3. Click Edit.

4. To add a slide, click the slide in the Slides In Presentation list and then click the Add button. The slide appears at the end of the Slides In Custom Show list.

5. To remove a slide from the show, click the slide in the Slides In Custom Show list, and then click Remove.

6. To move a slide up or down in the show, click the slide in the Slides In Custom Show list, and then click the up or down arrow button.

7. Click OK.

8. Click Close.

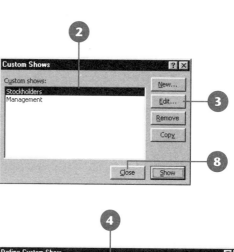

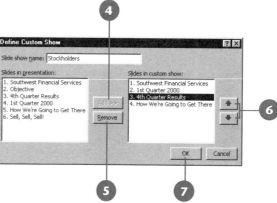

Setting Up a Slide Show Screen

If you present a slide show on a second monitor, projection system, or laptop, PowerPoint provides the tools you need to help set up your computer for the presentation. You can run a slide show on a secondary monitor while you use the first monitor to preview the next slide, view the speaker's notes, or even edit slides before displaying them to the audience. If you use a projection system to run a slide show, the Projector Wizard helps you establish a connection to the projector. If you use a laptop computer, PowerPoint disables screensavers and low-power screen mode to prevent interruptions during a presentation.

Set Up a Slide Show to Run on a Secondary Monitor

1. Connect the secondary monitor to your computer.

2. Click the Slide Show menu, and then click Set Up Show.

3. Click the Show On drop-down arrow, and then select Primary Monitor or Secondary Monitor (the monitor in which you want to show the presentation).

4. Click OK.

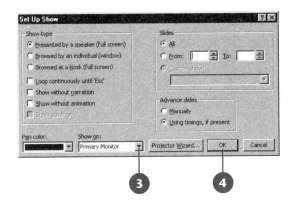

TIP

What you need to run on a second monitor. *You must be running Microsoft Windows 98 or later or Microsoft Windows NT 5.0 or later, and have dual-monitor hardware.*

SEE ALSO

See "Setting Up a Slide Show" on page 198 for more information on selecting other slide show options.

Set Up a Slide Show to Run on a Projection System

1. Connect the projection system to your computer.

2. Click the Slide Show menu, and then click Set Up Show.

3. Click Projector Wizard.

4. Click the Yes or No option button.

5. Click Next to continue.

6. Click the Projector drop-down arrow, and then select the projector.

7. Click Next to continue.

   The wizard adjusts your computer to the projector you have chosen.

8. Click Finish.

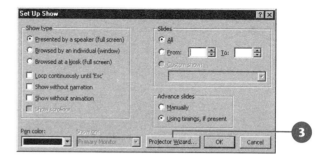

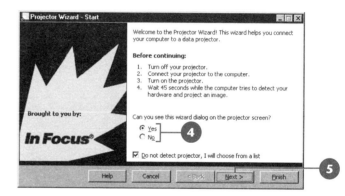

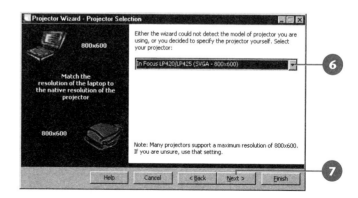

Creating Slide Transitions

If you want to give your presentation more visual interest, you can add transitions between slides. For example, you can create a *fading out* effect so that one slide fades out as it is replaced by a new slide, or you can have one slide appear to push another slide out of the way. You can also add sound effects to your transitions, though you need a sound card and speakers to play them.

TIP

When does a transition take effect? *When you add a transition effect to a slide, the effect takes place between the previous slide and the selected slide.*

Specify a Transition

1. Click the Slide Sorter View button.

2. Click the slide to which you want to add a transition effect.

3. Click the Slide Transition Effects drop-down arrow.

4. Click the transition effect you want.

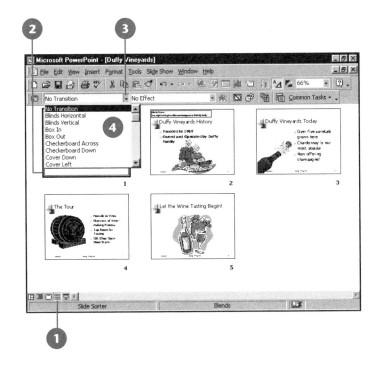

Apply a Transition to All Slides in a Presentation

1. Click the Slide Show menu, and then click Slide Transition.

2. Click the Effect drop-down arrow, and then click the transition you want.

3. Click Apply To All.

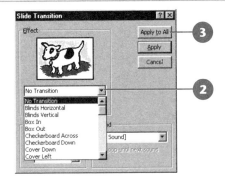

View a slide's transition quickly in Slide Sorter view. *In Slide Sorter view, click a slide's transition icon to view the transition's effect.*

Use the Slide Transition button in Slide Sorter view. *In Slide Sorter view, click the Slide Transition button on the Slide Sorter toolbar to quickly open the Slide Transition dialog box.*

Record your own sounds and use them as slide transitions. *If you have a microphone, use the Sound Recorder accessory that comes with Windows to record and save a sound. In the Slide Transition dialog box, click the Sound drop-down arrow, click Other Sound, locate and select the sound you created in the Add Sound dialog box, and then click OK.*

Set Transition Effect Speeds

1. In Normal, Slide, or Slide Sorter view, click or display the slide whose transition effect you want to edit.

2. Click the Slide Show menu, and then click Slide Transition.

3. Click the Slow, Medium, or Fast option button.

4. Click Apply.

Icon indicates slide has a transition

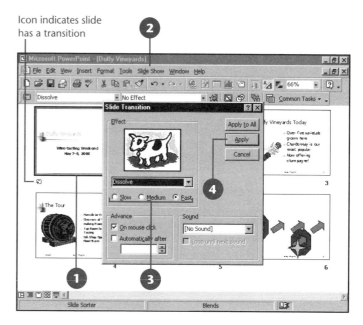

Add Sound to a Transition

1. In Normal, Slide, or Slide Sorter view, click or display the slide to which you want to add a transition sound.

2. Click the Slide Show menu, and then click Slide Transition.

3. Click the Sound drop-down arrow, and then click the sound you want.

4. Click Apply.

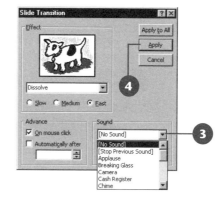

Adding Animation

You can use animation to introduce objects onto a slide one at a time or with special animation effects. For example, a bulleted list can appear one bulleted item at a time, or a picture or chart can fade gradually into the slide's foreground. You can use many kinds of animations with PowerPoint. Some are called *preset animations*—effects that PowerPoint has designed for you. Many of the preset animations contain sounds. You can also design your own *customized animations*, including those with your own special effects and sound elements.

TIP

View a slide's animation quickly in Slide Sorter view. *In Slide Sorter view, click a slide's animation icon to view the animation.*

Use Preset Animation

1. Select the slide or object you want to animate.

2. Click the Slide Show menu, and then point to Preset Animation.

3. Click the animation you want.

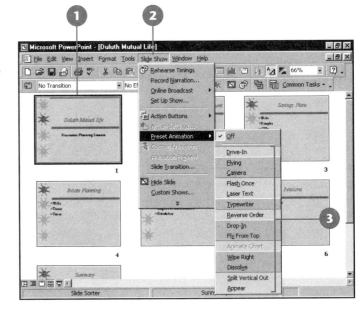

Preview an Animation

1. Click the Normal View or Slide View button, and then display the slide containing the animation you want to preview.

2. Click the Slide Show menu, and then click Animation Preview.

3. Click the Close button.

The animation plays in the window.

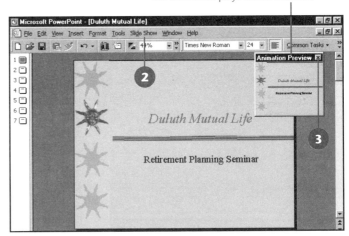

"How can I animate an object on my slide?"

Apply a Customized Animation

1 In Normal or Slide view, right-click the object, and then click Custom Animation.

2 On the Effects tab, click the Entry Animation And Sound drop-down arrow, and then click the effect you want.

3 Click the Entry Animation From drop-down arrow, and then click the effect you want.

4 Click Preview to see the animation effect.

5 Click OK.

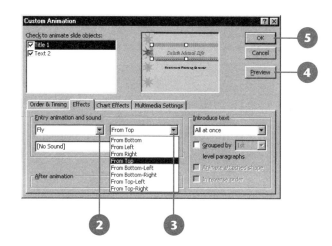

Add Sound to an Animation

1 In Normal or Slide view, right-click the object, and then click Custom Animation.

2 On the Effects tab, choose an effect from the list of animation effects.

3 Click the Sound drop-down arrow, and then click the sound effect you want.

4 Click Preview to see the animation effect.

5 Click OK.

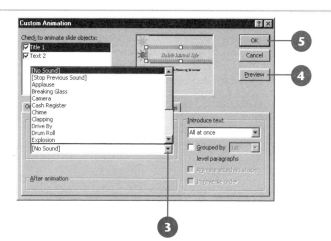

11

Using Specialized Animations

Using specialized animations, you can apply animations specific to certain objects. For example, for a text object, you can introduce the text on your slide all at once or by word or letter. Similarly, you can introduce bulleted lists one bullet item at a time and apply different effects to older items, such as graying the items out as they are replaced by new ones. You can animate charts by introducing chart series or chart categories one at a time.

TIP

Animate the attached shape with text. *In the Custom Animation dialog box, select the text object you want to animate, click the Effects tab, and click to select the Animate Attached Shape check box.*

Animate Text

1. In Normal or Slide view, right-click the selected text object, and then click Custom Animation.

2. On the Effects tab, choose an effect from the list of animation effects.

3. Click the Introduce Text drop-down arrow, and click the effect you want.

4. Click Preview to see the animation effect.

5. Click OK.

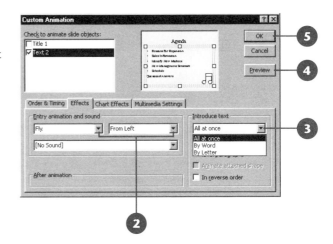

Animate Bulleted Lists

1. In Normal or Slide view, right-click the bulleted text, and then click Custom Animation.

2. On the Effects tab, choose an effect from the list of animation effects.

3. Click to select the Grouped By check box.

4. Click the Grouped By drop-down arrow, and then click at what paragraph level bulleted text will be animated.

5. Click Preview to see the animation effect.

6. Click OK.

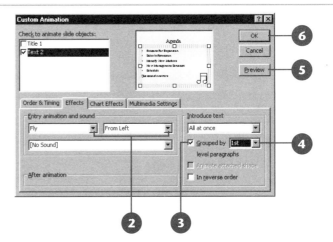

"How can I make the bars on my bar chart appear one at a time with a neat animation effect?"

Dim Text After It Is Animated

1. In Normal or Slide view, right-click the text, and then click Custom Animation.

2. On the Effects tab, choose an effect from the list of animation effects.

3. Click the After Animation drop-down arrow, and then click the dim text color or option you want.

4. Click Preview to see the animation effect.

5. Click OK.

Animate Chart Elements

1. In Normal or Slide view, right-click the chart, and then click Custom Animation.

2. On the Chart Effects tab, click the Introduce Chart Elements drop-down arrow.

3. Click the order in which chart elements should be introduced.

4. Click Preview to see the animation effect.

5. Click OK.

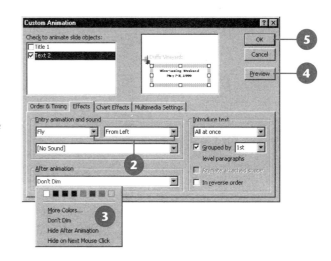

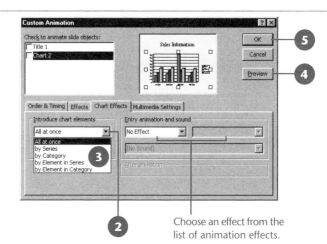

Choose an effect from the list of animation effects.

Coordinating Multiple Animations

The Custom Animation dialog box helps you keep track of your presentation's animations by listing all animated and unanimated objects in a single location. Use these lists if your slides contain more than one animation, because they help you determine how the animations will work together. For example, you can control the animation of each object, in what order each object appears, and how long to wait between animation effects. As you build up your animations, you can preview them to make sure that the combined effect is what you want.

Add Animation to Unanimated Slide Objects

1. In Normal or Slide view, click the Slide Show menu, and then click Custom Animation.

2. Click to select the check box for the slide object that you want to animate.

3. On the Effects tab, choose an animation effect and any additional animation options.

4. Click Preview to see the animation effect.

5. Click OK.

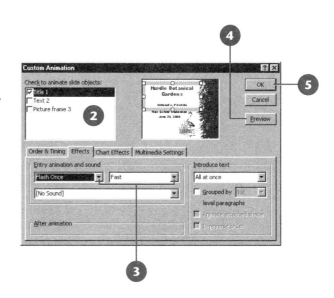

Modify the Animation Order

1. In Normal or Slide view, click the Slide Show menu, and then click Custom Animation.

2. Click the Order & Timing tab.

3. Click the slide object whose animation order you want to change.

4. Click the Move Up or Down arrow button.

5. Click OK.

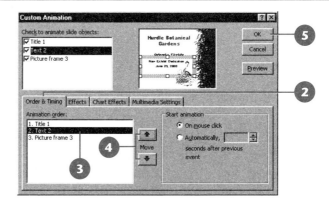

TIP

Play a sound or video using animation order. *In the Custom Animation dialog box, select the media object you want to play, click the Multimedia Settings tab, click to select the Play Using Animation Order check box, and then click the start or stop option button you want.*

"How can I set a two-minute lag between animations?"

SEE ALSO

See "Adding Animation" on page 206 and "Using Specialized Animations" on page 208 for information on creating animations.

SEE ALSO

See "Setting Up a Slide Show" on page 198 for information on running a slide show without animation.

Set Time Between Animations

1. In Normal or Slide view, click the Slide Show menu, and then click Custom Animation.

2. Click the Order & Timing tab.

3. Choose one of the animations from the Animation Order list.

4. Click the Automatically option button.

5. Enter the number of seconds between this animation and the previous event.

6. Click OK.

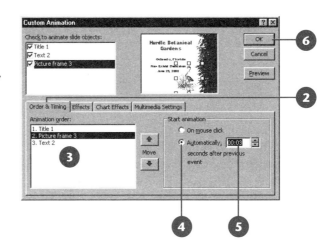

Remove an Animation

1. In Normal or Slide view, click the Slide Show menu, and then click Custom Animation.

2. Click to clear the check box for the animation you want to remove from the list.

3. Click OK.

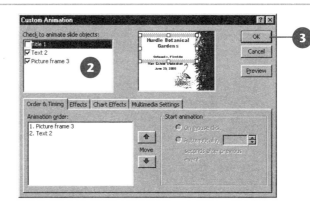

Timing a Presentation

If you have a time limit for presenting your slide show, you can use PowerPoint's timing features to make sure that your presentation is not taking too long or going too fast. You can specify the amount of time given to each slide and test yourself during rehearsal using the *slide meter*, which ensures that your timings are legitimate and workable. By rehearsing timings, you can vary the amount of time each slide appears on the screen. If you want the timings to take effect, make sure the show is set to use timings in the Set Up Show dialog box.

TIP

Clear slide timings. *Before you rehearse timings, clear any timings you have set in the Slide Transition dialog box, which assigns the same amount of time to each slide.*

Set Timings Between Slides

1. Click the Slide Show menu, and then click Slide Transition.

2. Click to select the Automatically After check box.

3. Enter the time (in seconds) before the presentation automatically advances to the next slide after displaying the entire slide.

4. Click Apply To All.

Create Timings Through Rehearsal

1. Click the Slide Show menu, and then click Rehearse Timings.

2. As the slide show runs, rehearse your presentation by pressing Enter to go the next slide.

3. Click Yes to accept the timings you just recorded.

4. Review the timings in Slide Sorter view.

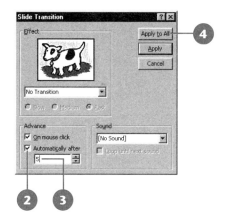

Time, in seconds, spent on this slide

Time for the entire presentation

Morgan Park Zoo

Grand Opening
Nashua, New Hampshire
May 9, 2000

Control slide show timings. *To control whether your presentation uses timings you set or advances manually, click the Slide Show menu, click Set Up Show, click the Manually or Using Timings, If Present option button, and then click OK.*

See "Creating Slide Transitions" on page 204 for more information on creating transitions between slides.

"How can I set a particular slide so I have more time to talk?"

Test Timings

1. Start the slide show presentation.

2. Rehearse your presentation, and note when the slides advance too quickly or too slowly.

Edit Timings

1. Click the Slide Sorter View button.

2. Click the slide whose timing you want to change.

3. Click the Slide Show menu, and then click Slide Transition.

4. Enter a new value in the Seconds box.

5. Click Apply to save the new timing.

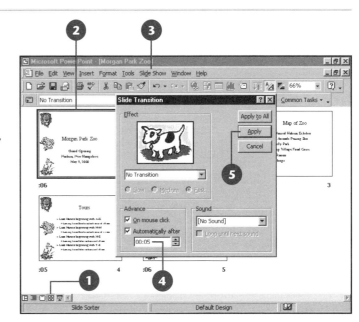

Recording a Narration

If you are creating a self-running presentation, you might want to add a narration to emphasize the points you make. PowerPoint lets you record your own narration as you rehearse your slide show. You will need a microphone and a computer with a sound card to record the narration. When you play back a narration, the recording is synchronized with the presentation, including all slide transitions and animations.

Record a Narration

1. Click the Slide Show menu, and then click Record Narration.

2. Click Set Microphone Level and set the microphone level you want.

3. Click Change Quality.

4. Click the Name drop-down arrow, and then click the recording quality you want.

5. Click OK.

6. Click to select the Link Narrations In check box to insert the narration as a linked object if necessary.

7. Click OK.

8. If necessary, click Current Slide or First Slide.

9. Speak clearly into the microphone attached to your computer and record your narration for each slide.

10. Click Yes when prompted to save slide timings along with your narration.

11. Rerun the slide show and verify that your narration has been recorded along with the automatic timings.

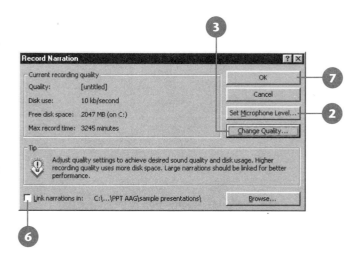

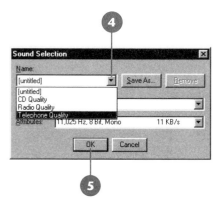

Presenting a Slide Show

When you're ready to give a slide show, you'll find that Microsoft PowerPoint 2000 provides many tools for presenting your show to audiences everywhere. PowerPoint accommodates the following situations:

◆ Presenting to a live audience in a conference room or auditorium

◆ Showing your presentation on a computer that doesn't necessarily have PowerPoint installed

◆ Broadcasting your presentation over an intranet or the Internet

◆ Meeting with a remote audience over the Internet in "real time"

◆ Participating in a Web discussion about your presentation

In all these situations, PowerPoint not only gives you flexibility in controlling how you run your show, but also helps you keep track of the ideas you and others have during your presentation. Finally, PowerPoint helps you use the World Wide Web to your advantage—an increasingly important consideration in today's information-oriented world.

Presenting a Show

Once your slide show is in its final state, it's time to consider how to show it to the world. PowerPoint gives you several stand alone and Web-based ways to give and share your presentation.

Presenting to a Live Audience

When you are giving the show in person, you can use PowerPoint's slide navigation tools to move around your presentation. You can move forward and backward or move to a specific slide. If you have set up custom slide shows, you can easily jump to one of those shows in the middle of your presentation. As you're presenting your slide show, you can highlight key ideas by using the mouse as a pointer or light pen.

PowerPoint also lets you record ideas that come up during the presentation by using Meeting Minder, exporting ideas to a Word document file, or inserting them into your own personal calendar.

Presenting on the Road

If you are taking your presentation to another site, you might not need the entire PowerPoint package. Rather than installing PowerPoint on the site's computers, you can pack your presentation into one compressed file, storing it on a portable disk. Once you reach your destination, you can expand the compressed file onto your client's computer and play it, regardless of whether that computer has PowerPoint installed.

Broadcasting to an Online Audience

When you are giving a presentation to an online audience at remote locations, you can use PowerPoint to broadcast the presentation, including video and audio, over the Internet or intranet. PowerPoint uses Microsoft NetShow to broadcast the presentation. By using Microsoft Outlook or any other e-mail program, you can schedule the broadcast like any other online meeting. The presentation is saved as a Web page in HTML format, so all that your audience needs in order to view the presentation is a Web browser. If an audience member misses a broadcast, the broadcast can be recorded and saved on a Web server for playback at a later time.

Collaborating with an Online Audience

When you want to collaborate on a presentation over the Internet, you can use a tool that comes with PowerPoint called NetMeeting. You can share and exchange information with people at different sites in real time as if everyone were in the same room. As host for the meeting, you can let participants change the presentation by turning on collaboration. You can also turn it off at anytime.

With PowerPoint, you can also participate in a Web discussion. This is a useful feature when you want to get feedback on your presentation. People involved in the online collaboration can add, reply to, edit, print, and filter discussion text using the Discussion pane.

Starting a Slide Show

Once you have set up your slide show, you can start the show at any time. As you run your slide show, you can use the Slide Show view popup menu to access certain PowerPoint commands without leaving Slide Show view. If your show is running at a kiosk, you might want to disable this feature.

TIP

Start a slide show quickly from the current slide. *Click the Slide Show button located in the lower-left corner of the presentation window.*

TIP

Open the popup menu quickly. *In Slide Show view, right-click the screen.*

SEE ALSO

See "Setting Up a Slide Show" on page 198 for information on setting up a slide show.

Start a Slide Show and Display the Popup Menu

1. Click the Slide Show menu, and then click View Show.

2. Move the mouse pointer to display the popup menu button.

3. Click the popup menu button in the lower-left corner of the slide to display the popup menu.

Set Popup Menu Options

1. Click the Tools menu, and then click Options.

2. Click the View tab.

3. Click to select the popup menu options you want.

4. Click OK.

12

Navigating a Slide Show

In Slide Show view, you advance to the next slide by clicking the mouse button or pressing the Enter key. In addition to those basic navigational techniques, PowerPoint provides keyboard shortcuts that can take you to the beginning, end, or any particular slide in your presentation. You can also use the navigation commands on the shortcut menu to access slides in custom slide shows.

PowerPoint automatically hides the pointer. *After a period of inactivity during a normal full-screen slide show, PowerPoint automatically hides the pointer and slide show icon. In addition, minor mouse jiggles don't cause the pointer to appear.*

Use Slide Show View Navigation Shortcuts

Refer to the adjacent table for information on Slide Show view navigation shortcuts.

SLIDE SHOW VIEW SHORTCUTS	
Action	**Result**
Mouse click	Moves to the next slide
Right-mouse click	Moves to previous the slide (only if the Shortcut Menu On Right-Click option is disabled)
Press Enter	Moves to the next slide
Press Home	Moves to the first slide in the show
Press End	Moves to the last slide in the show
Press Page Up	Moves to the previous slide
Press Page Down	Moves to the next slide
Press a slide number, and then press Enter	Moves to the slide number you specified
Press Esc	Exits Slide Show view

Go to a Specific Slide

1. In Slide Show view, right-click a slide.

2. Point to Go, and then point to By Title.

3. Click the title of the slide you want to go to.

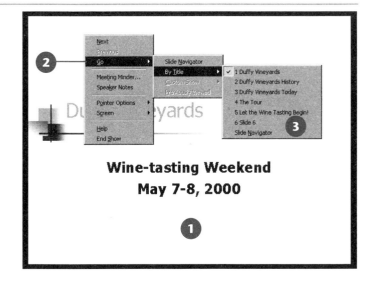

End a slide show with a black slide. *You can select an option to end a slide show with a black slide. Click the Tools menu, click Options, click the View menu, click to select the End With Black Slide check box, and then click OK.*

"How can I move easily through my slide show?"

See "Creating a Custom Slide Show" on page 200 for information on creating, viewing, and editing custom slide shows.

Use Slide Navigator

1. In Slide Show view, right-click a slide.

2. Point to Go, and then click Slide Navigator.

3. If the slide you want to view is in a custom slide show, click the Show drop-down arrow, and then click the custom slide show you want.

4. Click the slide title for the slide you want to display.

5. Click Go To.

The slide you displayed most recently appears here.

Go to a Custom Slide Show

1. In Slide Show view, right-click a slide.

2. Point to Go, and then point to Custom Show.

3. Click the custom slide show that you want to go to.

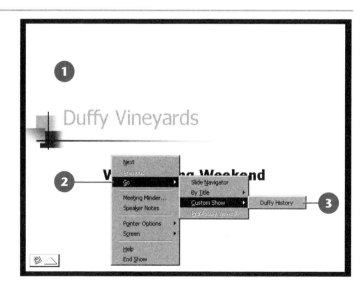

12

Emphasizing Points

When you are presenting your slide show, you can turn your mouse pointer into a light pen to highlight and circle your key points. If you decide to use a light pen, you might want to set its colors to match the colors in your presentation. Marks you make on a slide with the light pen during a slide show are not permanent.

SEE ALSO

See "Starting a Slide Show" on page 217 for information on starting a slide show and displaying the popup menu.

Change Pointer Options

1. In Slide Show view, right-click the slide.

2. Point to Pointer Options.

3. Click a pointer option.

   ◆ Automatic hides the pointer until you move the mouse.

   ◆ Hidden makes the pointer invisible throughout the presentation.

   ◆ Arrow turns the pointer into an arrow shape.

   ◆ Pen turns the pointer into a pen shape.

Use a Light Pen During a Slide Show

1. In Slide Show view, right-click an empty spot on the slide.

2. Point to Pointer Options.

3. Click Pen.

   The pointer changes to the shape of a pen.

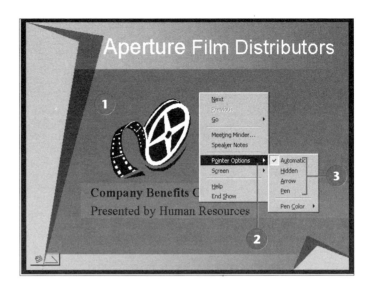

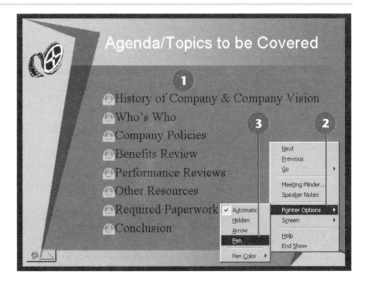

TIP

Turn the pen back to the mouse pointer quickly. *To turn the light pen back to the normal mouse pointer, right-click a slide in slide show, point to Pointer Options, and then click Arrow.*

4 Drag the mouse pointer to draw on your slide presentation with the pen. Use the pen to accentuate points on your slide.

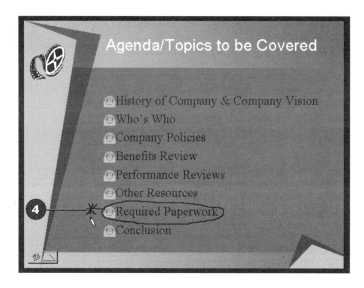

SEE ALSO

See "Navigating a Slide Show" on page 218 for information on moving around in a slide show or custom slide show.

Set the Pen's Color

1 In Slide Show view, right-click a slide.

2 Point to Pointer Options.

3 Point to Pen Color.

4 Click the color you want to use for lines drawn by the pen.

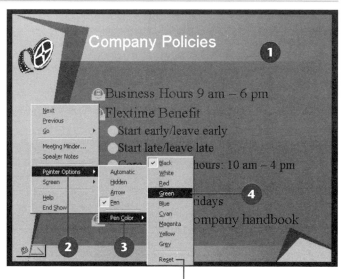

Click to return the pen to its original color.

Taking Notes

When your presentation generates ideas or action items that you want to record, you can keep track of those items using PowerPoint's *Meeting Minder*. You can also use Meeting Minder to export your notes to a Word document or into Office 2000's calendar and schedule program, Microsoft Outlook. Lastly, you can also view and edit your speaker notes while giving your presentation.

TIP

Edit information in Meeting Minder. *You can add or edit information from Meeting Minder even when you are not presenting a slide show. To access Meeting Minder outside of Slide Show view, click the Tools menu and then click Meeting Minder.*

Create an Action Item

1. In Slide Show view, right-click a slide, and then click Meeting Minder.

2. Click the Action Items tab.

3. Type a description of the action you want to record.

4. Type the name of the person assigned to the action.

5. Type the due date of the action.

6. Click Add.

7. Click OK.

Create Meeting Minutes

1. In Slide Show view, right-click a slide and then click Meeting Minder.

2. Click the Meeting Minutes tab.

3. Type your minutes into the Meeting Minutes box.

4. Click OK.

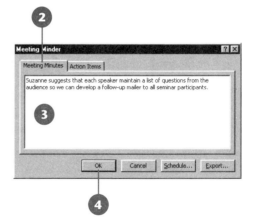

TIP

Start Outlook from Slide Show view. *You can send your meeting minutes to Microsoft Outlook by clicking the Schedule button in the Meeting Minder dialog box. Outlook is a powerful tool that lets you manage your personal schedule, set up minutes for your group, and record notes for yourself.*

TRY THIS

Post action items to Microsoft Outlook. *You can post your action items to Microsoft Outlook to manage the information. Click the Tools menu, click Meeting Minder, click Export, click to select the Post Action Items To Microsoft Outlook check box, and then click Export Now.*

TIP

Take notes during an online meeting. *Participants in an online meeting can use the Meeting Minder dialog box or the Speaker Notes dialog box to take notes. The notes are visible to all participants.*

Export Action Items and Minutes to Word

1. Click the Tools menu, and then click Meeting Minder.

2. Enter your minutes or action items.

3. Click Export.

4. Click to select the Send Meeting Minutes And Action Items To Microsoft Word check box.

5. Click Export Now.

6. Edit the items in Microsoft Word, and then save the document.

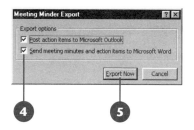

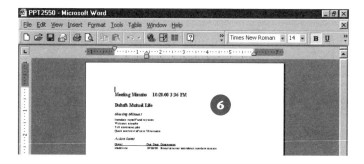

View and Edit Speaker Notes

1. In Slide Show view, right-click a slide, and then click Speaker Notes.

2. Enter new speaker notes or view the current notes.

3. Click Close.

   You can leave the Speaker Notes dialog box open if you want as you go from one slide to another.

12

Taking a Show on the Road

If your audience can't come to you and you can't connect to them over the Internet, you might have to go to them, bringing your presentation with you. You don't need to bring the complete PowerPoint program. Instead, you can bring only those tools needed to present the slide show. PowerPoint provides the *PowerPoint Viewer*, a small program that runs PowerPoint slide shows. You can also use PowerPoint's Pack And Go Wizard to pack your presentation into a single compressed file that will fit on one or two floppy disks.

> **TIP**
>
> **Can't include TrueType fonts with copyright restrictions.** *The Pack And Go Wizard cannot include TrueType fonts that have built-in copyright restrictions.*

Run the Pack And Go Wizard

1. Click the File menu, and then click Pack And Go.

2. Click Next to start the Pack And Go Wizard.

3. Select the presentation you want to pack. Click Next to continue.

4. Select the hard disk where you want to send the packed file. Click Next to continue.

5. Click the Include Linked Files check box to include any files you linked to your presentation, and click the Embed TrueType Fonts check box to ensure that your fonts will appear correctly when you show the presentation. Click Next to continue.

6. If the computer on which you will show your presentation doesn't have PowerPoint installed, click the Viewer For Windows 95 Or NT option button. Click Next to continue.

7. Click Finish to pack your presentation.

8. Click OK.

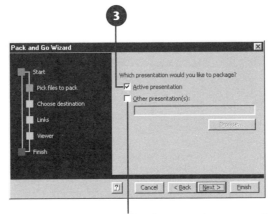

Click to locate another presentation.

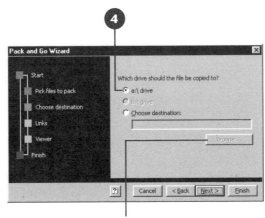

Click to locate the drive on which you want to pack the presentation.

Unpack a Presentation

pngsetup

1 Start Windows Explorer and open the folder containing your packed presentation file.

2 Double-click the PNGSETUP icon.

3 Enter a destination folder.

4 Click OK.

5 Click Yes to view the slide show now, or click No to view it later.

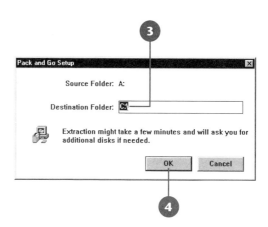

TIP

Use Find to help locate the programs. *In Windows Explorer, click the Tools menu, point to Find, and then click Files And Folders. Enter the name of the program you want to find, and then click Find Now. Double-click the program to start it.*

ppview32

View a Slide Show with the PowerPoint Viewer

1 Start Windows Explorer and open the folder containing the PowerPoint Viewer (PPVIEW32).

2 Double-click PPVIEW32 to start the PowerPoint Viewer.

3 Click the Look In drop-down arrow, and then locate the folder containing your unpackaged presentation.

4 Click the name of your slide show.

5 Click Show.

6 Click Exit.

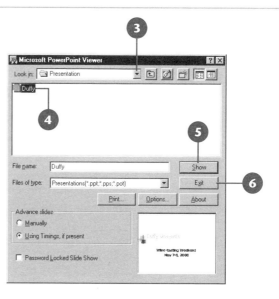

12

Setting Up And Scheduling a Broadcast

You can broadcast a presentation over an intranet or the Internet. Broadcasting is useful when your audience is large or at remote locations. Using an e-mail program, such as Microsoft Outlook 2000, you can schedule the broadcast just like any other meeting. The presentation is saved as a Web page in HTML format, so all that your audience needs is a Web browser to see the presentation. If an audience member misses a broadcast or if you want to archive it, the broadcast can be recorded and saved on a Web server so that it is available for playback at any time.

SEE ALSO

See "Starting and Viewing a Broadcast" on page 228 for more information on starting or viewing a presentation broadcast.

Set Up and Schedule a New Broadcast

1 Open the presentation you want to broadcast.

2 Click the Slide Show menu, point to Online Broadcast, and then click Set Up And Schedule.

3 Click the Set Up And Schedule A New Broadcast option button.

4 Click OK.

5 Click the Description tab, and then enter the information you want displayed on the lobby page for the broadcast.

6 If you need to set options for broadcasting, click the Broadcast Settings tab.

7 Click to select the audio and video options you want.

8 Click to select the audience feedback options you want.

9 If you want, click to select the Record The Broadcast And Save It In This Location check box. Click Browse to select the location where you want to save the broadcast.

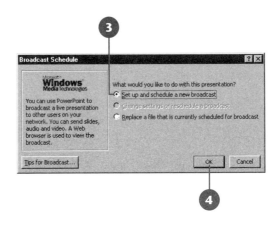

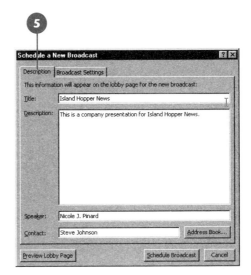

TIP

Setup requirements for video and audiences of more than 15 people. *You must specify either a NetShow server on a LAN or a third-party NetShow service provider in the Server Options dialog box.*

TIP

What is NetShow?
PowerPoint 2000 uses Microsoft NetShow technology to enable broadcasting of presentations to a wide audience over an intranet or network.

TIP

Reschedule or delete a broadcast. *Click the Slide Show menu, point to Online Broadcast, click Set Up And Schedule, click the Change Settings Or Reschedule A Broadcast option button, click OK, click the broadcast you want to reschedule or delete, click Reschedule or Delete, and then use your e-mail program to inform audience members.*

SEE ALSO

See "Holding an Online Meeting" on page 230 for more information on using an e-mail program to schedule a broadcast.

10 Click Server Options, specify a share location and a NetShow server location if necessary, and then click OK.

11 Click Schedule Broadcast, select a MS Exchange profile if necessary, and then click Yes or No to continue with or without a NetShow server.

12 Click the To button. Select the attendees to whom you want the message sent, and then click OK.

13 Click to select the e-mail options you want.

14 Click the Send button on the toolbar.

15 Click OK to confirm your broadcast has been successfully scheduled.

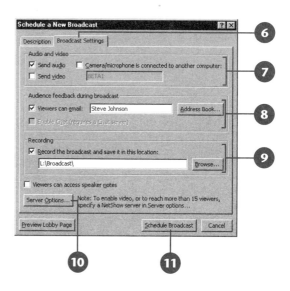

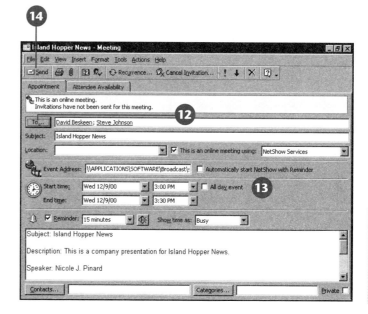

Starting and Viewing a Broadcast

Before you start a presentation broadcast, you must have already set up and scheduled the broadcast. To view a presentation broadcast, you need to have Internet Explorer 4 or later. It is a good idea to join a broadcast about 15 minutes early just in case the presenter has last-minute information for you. You'll see a *lobby page*—a page that contains information about the broadcast and lets you know how much time is left before the broadcast begins. If there is a delay in the start of the broadcast, the presenter can send a message that will be displayed on the lobby page.

TIP

Join a presentation broadcast late? *During the broadcast, click View Previous Slides to view the slides you missed.*

Start a Broadcast

1. Open and save the presentation that you want to broadcast.

2. Click the Slide Show menu, point to Online Broadcast, and then click Begin Broadcast.

   Your presentation is saved as a Web page in HTML format at the server location you designated. PowerPoint checks audio and video to make sure they are working.

3. If you have any information you want to send to your audience, click Audience Message, type the message, and then click Update.

4. If you want, click Preview Lobby Page to view the lobby page.

5. When you're ready to begin, click Start.

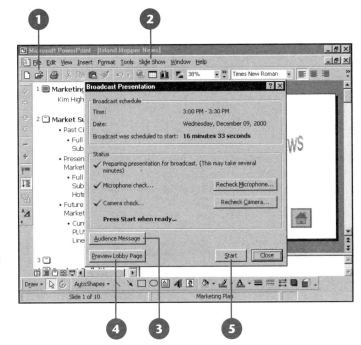

View a broadcast for the first time. *You might be asked to download some ActiveX controls for Internet Explorer 4.*

View a broadcast on different computers. *Since the presentation is broadcasted as a Web page in HTML format, the audience can view it on personal computers, UNIX, and Macintosh computers.*

View a broadcast using Microsoft Outlook. *If you are using Outlook and you accept the invitation, you will be sent a reminder 15 minutes before the broadcast begins. When the reminder message appears, click View NetShow.*

Waiting for a broadcast to begin? *You can minimize the lobby page and continue working while you wait for the broadcast to begin. The broadcast will automatically begin.*

View a Broadcast

1. Open the e-mail message that contains the broadcast invitation.

2. Click the URL for the broadcast.

Internet Explorer opens to a lobby page that contains information about the broadcast. When the broadcast starts, it will be shown in your Web browser.

Depending on the options set by the presenter, you might be able to chat with others viewing the broadcast and send e-mail messages to the presenter.

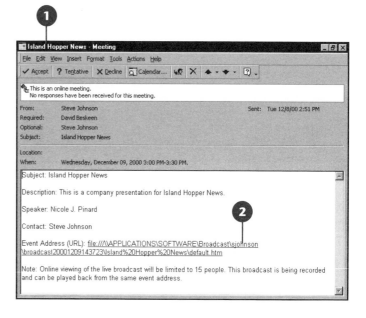

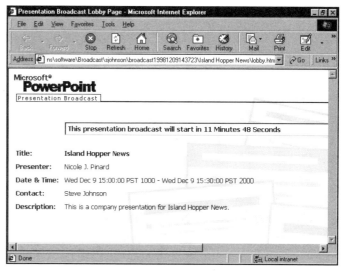

Holding an Online Meeting

Microsoft NetMeeting is a program that comes with PowerPoint 2000. It allows you to host, participate, and collaborate in an online meeting over the Internet or intranet. You can share and exchange information as if everyone were in the same room. As a host for an online meeting you start the meeting and control the presentation. You can allow participants to make changes to the presentation. Each person in the online meeting can then take turns editing and controlling the presentation. As a participant and collaborator, you can share applications and documents, send text messages in Chat, transfer files, and work on the Whiteboard.

TIP

Receive an online meeting call. *You must have NetMeeting running on your computer to receive an online meeting call.*

Hold an Online Meeting

1. Open the presentation you want to share.

2. Click the Tools menu, point to Online Collaboration, and then click Meet Now.

3. If this is your first meeting, the Microsoft NetMeeting dialog box appears. Fill out the information in the My Information and Directory boxes as instructed.

4. In the Place A Call dialog box, do one of the following.

   ◆ Type or select the people you want to invite to the online meeting, and then click Call. To invite additional people, click Call Participant on the Online Meeting toolbar to display the Place A Call dialog box again.

   ◆ If you know the computer name or network Internet protocol address of the person you want to invite, click Advanced.

   ◆ Click Cancel to start NetMeeting so it runs in the background on your computer.

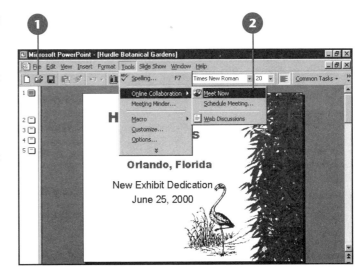

Enter the names of the people you want to invite to the meeting.

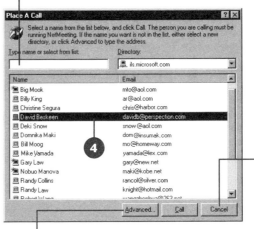

Click to start NetMeeting running in the background.

Click to enter the computer name or protocol address of the person you want to invite.

TIP

Start NetMeeting using the Start menu. *Click the Start menu, point to Programs, and then click NetMeeting.*

TIP

Schedule a Microsoft Outlook online meeting. *Click the Tools menu, point to Online Collaboration, click Schedule Meeting, select the mail options you want, and then click the Send button.*

SEE ALSO

See "Setting Up and Scheduling a Broadcast" on page 226 for information on scheduling events using Microsoft Outlook.

TIP

Join an online meeting. *If you receive an online meeting call, click Accept in the Join Meeting dialog box. If you receive an Outlook reminder for the meeting, click Start This NetMeeting (host), or Join This NetMeeting (participant). To receive an Outlook reminder to join a meeting, you need to have accepted the meeting from an e-mail message.*

Collaborate in an Online Meeting

1. As the host, click the Allow Others To Edit button on the Online Meeting toolbar.

2. When collaboration is turned on, click anywhere in the presentation to gain control. Double-click anywhere in the presentation to gain control if you are not the host.

3. Click the Allow Others To Edit button again to turn off collaboration, or press Esc if you don't have control of the presentation.

Participate in an Online Meeting

◆ Use the buttons on the Online Meeting toolbar to participate in an online meeting.

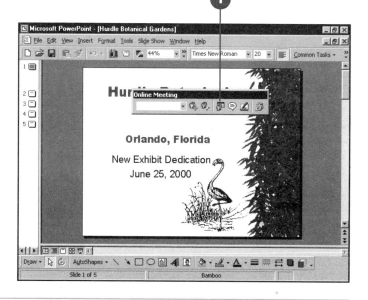

ONLINE MEETING TOOLBAR	
Button	**Description**
	Allows the host to invite additional participants to the online meeting
	Allows the host to remove a participant from the online meeting
	Allows participants to edit and control the presentation during the online meeting
	Allows participants to send messages in a Chat session during the online meeting
	Allows participants to draw or type on the Whiteboard during the online meeting
	Allows the host to end the online meeting for the entire group or a participant to disconnect

12

Participating in a Web Discussion

You can discuss a presentation with other people using the Internet or a corporate intranet using an online collaborative feature, called *Web discussion*. To take advantage of this online feature, you need to first select a discussion server. Once you've set up the server, you can start a discussion, reply to discussion remarks, print a discussion, and filter discussions to see remarks from a certain person or from a particular time period.

SEE ALSO

See "Understanding Office Server Extensions" on page 234 for information on setting up a server for a Web discussion.

TIP

Print discussions. *Start a discussion, click the Discussions button on the Discussions toolbar, click Print Discussions, select the print options you want, and then click OK.*

Select a Web Discussion Server

1. Open the presentation about which you want to have a discussion.

2. Click the Tools menu, point to Online Collaboration, and then click Web Discussions.

   If you are selecting a discussion server for the first time, skip to step 5.

3. On the Discussions toolbar, click the Discussions button, and then click Discussion Options.

4. Click Add.

5. Type the name of a discussion server provided by your administrator.

   The discussion server needs to have Office Server Extensions to hold a Web discussion.

6. If your administrator has set up security by using the Secure Sockets Layer (SSL) message protocol, click to select the Secure Connection Required (SSL) check box.

7. Type the name you want to use for the server.

8. Click OK.

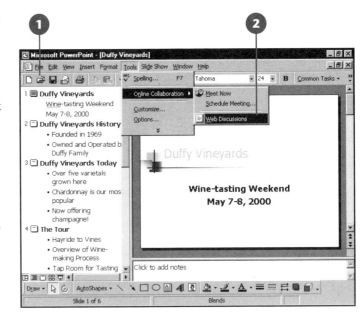

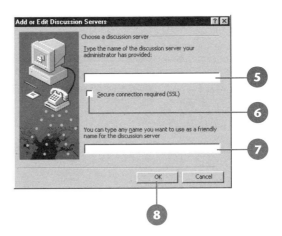

Start and Close a Web Discussion

1. Open the presentation for which you want to start a discussion.

2. Click the Tools menu, point to Online Collaboration, and then click Web Discussions.

3. Click the Insert About The Presentation button on the Discussions toolbar.

4. Type the subject of the discussion.

5. Type your comments.

6. Click OK.

7. Click the Close button on the Discussions toolbar.

Reply to a Web Discussion Remark

1. Open the presentation that contains the discussion you want to join.

2. Click the Tools menu, point to Online Collaboration, and then click Web Discussions.

3. Click the Show A Menu Of Actions button, and then click Reply.

4. Type your reply, and then click OK.

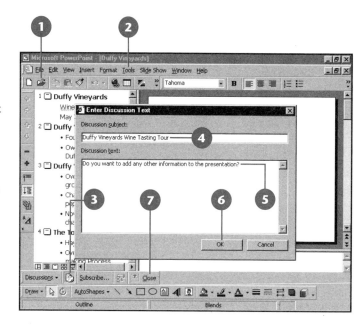

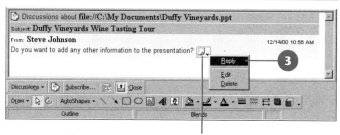

Show A Menu Of Actions button

12

Understanding Office
Server Extensions

Microsoft Office 2000 uses *Office Server Extensions* to provide a bridge between current Web technologies and the functionality needed to make the Web a friendly place to work with people and information. Office Server Extensions are a set of features that makes it easy to work with Office files and collaborate on the Web. Office Server Extensions allow you to publish and view Web documents directly from a Web server—a computer on the Internet that stores Web pages—with Office programs or Internet Explorer; to perform Web discussions and exchange information on documents located on the Web server; and to receive notification when a document on a Web server has been changed, which is known as *Web Subscription* and *Web Notification*.

Office Server Extensions are a superset of Microsoft FrontPage Extensions and other technologies that reside on an Windows NT–based Web servers to provide additional publishing, collaboration, and document management capabilities. Office Server Extensions do not replace existing Web server technologies. Rather, the extensions in Office 2000 are designed to enhance your experience with Office in a Web-based environment.

Office Server Extensions are included with Office 2000 Premium. To set up your computer with Office Server Extensions, you need a computer with Windows NT Workstation 4.0 or later running Personal Web Server 4.0 or later, or Windows NT Server 4.0 or later running Internet Information Server 4.0 or later. With the Server Extensions Configuration Wizard, you can set up and configure an existing Web server to use the Office Server Extensions.

Web File Management

Office Server Extensions make publishing and sharing documents on Web servers as easy as working with documents on file servers. Office 2000 enables you to create folders, view properties, and perform file drag-and-drop operations on Web servers just as you would on normal file servers. You can also perform these same Web server file operations directly from the Windows Explorer. In Internet Explorer, Office Server Extensions enable on-the-fly displays of Web directory listings, files, and HTML views of Web folders.

Web Discussions

With the Office Server Extensions installed on a Web server, you can have online discussions in Web page (HTML) files and Office 2000 documents. A *Web discussion* is an online, interactive conversation that takes place within the Web page or document (also called *in-line*) or that occurs as a general discussion about the Web page or Office document, which is stored in the Discussion pane at the bottom of the page. A Web discussion can occur only through Internet Explorer or an Office program. Using the Discussions toolbar, users can insert new comments, edit and reply to existing comments, subscribe to a particular document, and view or hide the Discussion pane.

Customizing PowerPoint

Although Microsoft PowerPoint 2000 is designed to be flexible and easy to use, you can customize the program to reflect your own preferences and the way you work. Increase your productivity by modifying PowerPoint's toolbars and menus to display the features you use most frequently. You can customize PowerPoint by automating frequent tasks and keystrokes with macros attached to buttons. You can even create your own dialog box that appears when you first start PowerPoint. The purpose of each of these customization features is the same—to make PowerPoint even easier to use and permit you to accomplish more with less effort.

Setting PowerPoint Options

You can also customize the performance of many PowerPoint features including its editing, saving, spelling, viewing, and printing procedures. The initial settings for these procedures are called the *defaults*. If you change a default setting, PowerPoint will use the new setting for all subsequent PowerPoint sessions, until you change the setting again.

Change View Defaults

1. Click the Tools menu, and then click Options.

2. Click the View tab.

3. Change the View settings as necessary.

4. Click OK.

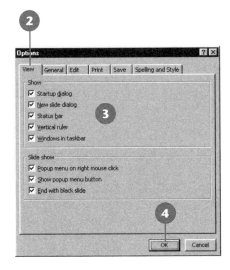

Change General Defaults

1. Click the Tools menu, and then click Options.

2. Click the General tab.

3. Change the General settings as necessary.

4. Click OK.

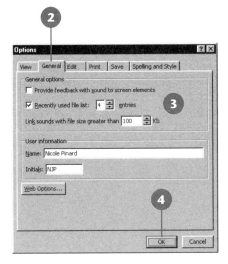

SEE ALSO

See "Documenting Presentation Properties" on page 174 for information on entering file properties.

TIP

Set default print settings for a specific presentation. *Click the Tools menu, click Options, click the Print tab, click the Use The Following Default Print Settings option button, click the print settings you want, and then click OK.*

TIP

Set the default location in which files are saved. *Click the Tools menu, click Options, click the Save tab, type the hard disk or folder location where you want to save files in the Default File Location box, and then click OK.*

Change Edit Defaults

1. Click the Tools menu, and then click Options.

2. Click the Edit tab.

3. Change the Edit settings as necessary.

4. Click OK.

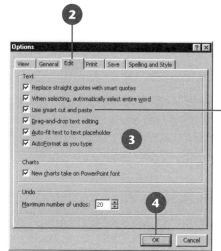

Select to add or remove spaces as needed when you edit text.

Change Spelling and Style Defaults

1. Click the Tools menu, and then click Options.

2. Click the Spelling And Style tab.

3. Change the Spelling and Style settings as necessary.

4. Click OK.

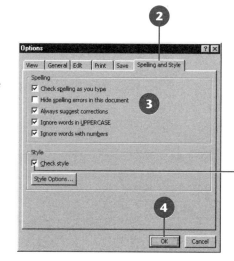

Check to have PowerPoint review the style in your presentation.

Customizing Menus and Toolbars

You can change the default toolbar options, such as having the Standard and Formatting toolbars share one row, or you can create new toolbars and customize the existing ones to maximize your efficiency. When you create a new toolbar and begin filling it with the buttons you use most for a given task, you can place icons on those buttons by either selecting an icon from the set that comes with PowerPoint or creating a new button using the Button Editor.

TIP

Restore a toolbar to its original appearance. *If you have changed one of the default toolbars and you want to restore it to its original appearance, click it on the Toolbars tab in the Customize dialog box, and then click the Reset button.*

Change Menu and Toolbar Options

1. Click the Tools menu, and then click Customize.

2. Click the Options tab.

3. Change the Options settings as necessary.

4. Click Close.

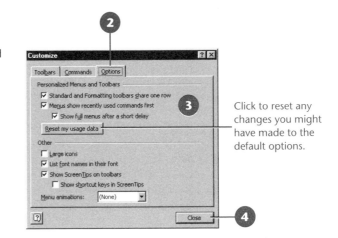

Click to reset any changes you might have made to the default options.

Add a Toolbar

1. Click the Tools menu, and then click Customize.

2. Click the Toolbars tab.

3. Click New.

4. Type a name for your new toolbar.

5. Click OK.

6. Click Close.

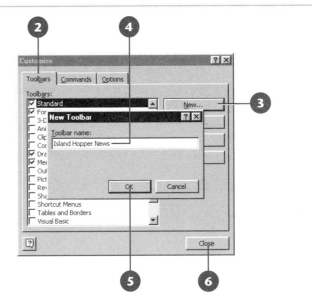

Enlarge a toolbar for easy readability. *If you have limited vision, you might want to create a toolbar with the buttons you use most frequently, and then enlarge those buttons by clicking the Options tab in the Customize dialog box, and then clicking the Large Icons check box.*

Delete a toolbar. *In the Customize dialog box, click the Toolbars tab, click the toolbar you want to delete, and then click the Delete button. You can also open the Customize dialog box, and then simply drag the button off the toolbar in the PowerPoint window.*

Move a toolbar. *A toolbar at the top or edge of a window is* docked; *if it appears somewhere else, it is* floating. *To move a floating toolbar, click its title bar and drag it to a new location.*

Add Buttons to a Toolbar

1. Click the Tools menu, and then click Customize.

2. Click the Toolbars tab, and then double-click the toolbar to which you want to add buttons.

   The toolbar is displayed.

3. Click the Commands tab.

4. Click the category in the Categories list containing the button you want to add to the toolbar.

5. Click the command in the Commands list that you want to add as a button on the toolbar.

6. Drag the command to the toolbar. If the command has a button icon associated with it, that icon appears. If it doesn't, the name of the command appears.

7. Repeat steps 4, 5, and 6 to add all the buttons you want to the toolbar.

8. Click Close.

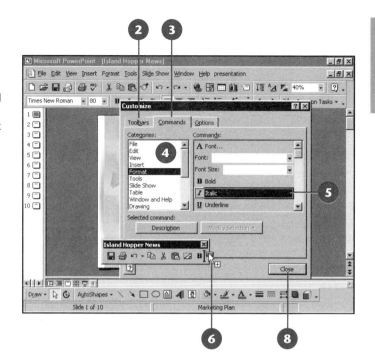

Maximizing Efficiency with Macros

If you find yourself repeating the same set of steps over and over or if you need to add new functionality to PowerPoint, you could create a macro. PowerPoint macros can run several tasks for you at the click of a button. You can easily create your own macros using PowerPoint's Macro Recorder, which records your actions, and then replays them. You can then add the macro to the PowerPoint toolbars or to the PowerPoint menus for easy access.

TRY THIS

Reasons to record a macro. *You might run a macro to speed up editing and formatting tasks, combine multiple commands into one, make a dialog option more accessible, or automate a complex series of tasks.*

Record a Macro

1. Click the Tools menu, point to Macro, and then click Record New Macro.

2. Type a name for the macro.

3. If necessary, type the name of the presentation in which you want to place the macro.

4. If you want, add to the description of the macro in the Description box.

5. Click OK.

6. Perform the actions you intend to place in the macro. Any action you perform in PowerPoint is recorded in the macro.

7. Click the Stop Recording button on the Macro toolbar.

Run a Macro

1. Click the Tools menu, point to Macro, and then click Macros.

2. Click the name of the macro you want to run.

3. Click Run.

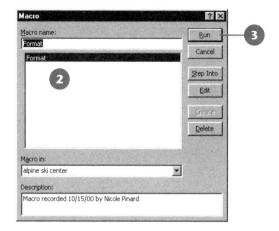

Delete a Macro

1. Click the Tools menu, point to Macro, and then click Macros.

2. Click the macro name.

3. Click Delete.

4. Click Yes to confirm the macro deletion.

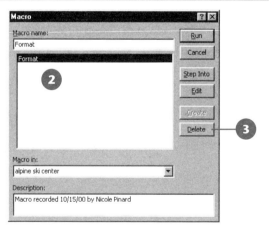

Controlling a Macro

If your macro is not doing what you expect, you might want to run it one step at a time rather than all at once to find out where it is failing. This process is known as *debugging*. When you use the Macro Recorder, you are actually writing a program in a programming language called *Microsoft Visual Basic*. All macros for a particular presentation are stored in a *macro module*, a collection of Visual Basic programming codes that you can copy to other presentation files. You can view and edit your Visual Basic modules using the Visual Basic editor. By learning Visual Basic you can greatly increase the scope and power of your programs.

TIP

Display the Debug toolbar.
Click the View menu, point to Toolbars, and then click Debug.

Run a Macro One Step at a Time

1. Click the Tools menu, point to Macro, and then click Macros.

2. Click the name of the macro you want to run.

3. Click the Step Into button.

4. If necessary, display the Debug toolbar.

5. Click the Step Into button on the Debug toolbar.

6. Continue to click the Step Into button until you have worked through all the steps in the macro.

7. Click the File menu, and then click Close And Return To Microsoft PowerPoint.

Edit a Macro

1. Click the Tools menu, point to Macro, and then click Macros.

2. Click the macro you want to edit, and then click Edit.

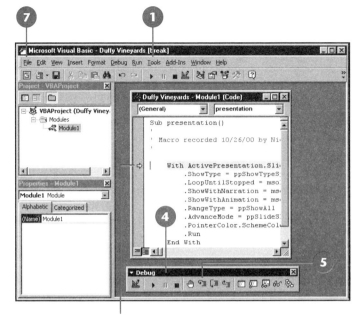

Arrow indicates current step

TIP

Use the Visual Basic editor to help correct macro problems. *If a problem occurs while you step through a macro, you have probably discovered why your macro isn't working. You can correct the problem using the Visual Basic editor.*

TIP

Use the keyboard to access the Visual Basic editor quickly. *To quickly access the Visual Basic editor, press Alt+F11.*

TIP

Get help with Visual Basic. *To learn more about Visual Basic, place your macro in Edit mode, click the Help menu, and then click Microsoft Visual Basic Help.*

③ Click the Module window containing the Visual Basic code for your macro.

④ Type new Visual Basic commands, or edit the commands already present.

⑤ Click the File menu, and then click Close And Return To Microsoft PowerPoint.

③ The Module window contains your Visual Basic macro code.

Copy a Macro Module to Another Presentation

① Open the presentation files you want to copy the macro from and to.

② Click the Tools menu, point to Macro, and then click Visual Basic Editor.

③ Click the View menu, and then click Project Explorer.

④ Drag the module you want to copy from the source presentation to the destination presentation.

⑤ Click the File menu, and then click Close And Return To Microsoft PowerPoint.

Presentation files currently open

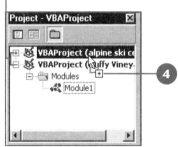

Assigning a Macro to a Toolbar or Menu

Once you create a macro, you can then add the macro to the PowerPoint toolbars or to the PowerPoint menus for easy access.

"I'd like to be able to access my macro from the menu bar."

Assign a Macro to a Toolbar

1. Click the Tools menu, and then click Customize.

2. Click the Commands tab.

3. Click Macros in the Categories box.

4. Click the macro name, and drag it to the toolbar.

5. Click Modify Selection, and then select a style and button image for your macro button.

6. Click Close.

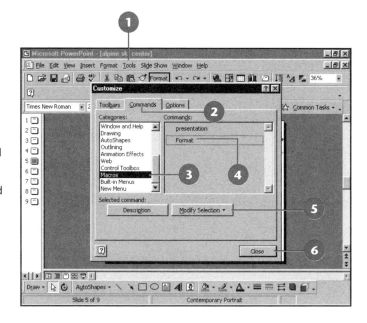

Assign a Macro to a Menu

1. Click the Tools menu, and then click Customize.

2. Click the Commands tab.

3. Click Macros in the Categories box.

4. Click the macro name, and drag it to the menu bar.

5. Click Modify Selection, and then select a style and text for your menu entry.

6. Click Close.

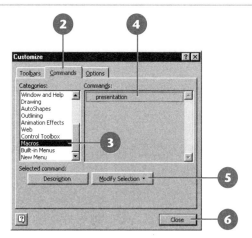

Index

moving, *continued*
    with precision, 81, 90–93
    text, 32
    toolbars, 239
    vertices in freeforms, 78
    WordArt text, 133
    See also navigating; rearranging
moving averages, in Graph
    charts, 154
multimedia objects. *See* clips
multiple animations, coordinating, 210–11

narrations, recording, 214
navigating
    objects, 95
    slide shows, 216, 218–19
    slides in Slide view, 13
navigation bar, 192
navigation controls
    adding to Web pages, 190
    shortcuts in Slide Show view,
      218
NetMeeting (Microsoft), 216
NetShow (Microsoft), 216, 227
networks, inserting slides from,
    159
New Office Document dialog
    box, starting PowerPoint
    from, 6
New Presentation dialog box,
    7, 9
newsgroups, PowerPoint user
    newsgroup, 196
New Slide dialog box, inserting
    clips, 112
Normal view, 12, 28
    entering notes, 170
    entering text, 25, 29, 30–31

manipulating objects, 26–27
notes, 155
    adding to presentations, 12
    editing, 171, 223
    entering, 170
    formatting, 171
    preparing speaker notes,
      170–71
    taking notes during slide
      shows/meetings,
      222–23
    See also comments; notes
      pages
notes master
    displaying slide
      miniatures, 55
    formatting notes, 171
    reinserting placeholders on,
      172
    viewing, 53
notes pages, 170
    adding dates/times/headers/
      footers/numbering to,
      171, 172
    customizing, 172–73
    headers and footers as added
      to, 168
    printing, 165, 168
    sending to Word, 176
Notes Page view, entering notes,
    170
notes pane (Normal view), 12,
    171
    resizing, 170
nudging drawing objects, 80
number signs (##), in datasheet
    cells, 149
numbered bullets, creating, 44
numbering
    bulleted lists, 44, 50
    notes pages, 171, 172
    See also slide numbers
numbers (in datasheets)
    formatting, 148

as represented by number
    signs, 149

Object Linking and Embedding
    (OLE), 115, 116, 122–25
objects, 64, 84
    adding embossed/engraved
      effects to, 87
    adding hyperlinks to, 184
    adding shadows to, 71,
      86–87
    adding to all slides, 54
    aligning, 92–93
      with the guides, 90
    animating, 210
    arranging, 24–25
    arranging stacks, 94
    coloring, 64, 84, 108–9
    copying, 27
    cutting, 27
    deleting, 27
    deselecting, 26
    distributing across slides,
      92, 93
    dragging, overriding the
      grid/guides, 91
    embedding, 116, 122
    filling, 66–67, 131
    flipping, 82
    getting Help on, 19
    Graph chart objects, 152–53
    grouping, 94
    inserting, 122, 123
    linking, 116, 122, 123
    moving, 27, 80
      with precision, 81, 90–93
    moving through, 95
    pasting, 27, 116, 117
      in a specified format, 117
    placing, 90–91
    recoloring, 108–9

regrouping, 95
resizing, 26, 80, 106
    with precision, 81
    proportionally, 27
rotating, 82–83
selecting, 26, 27, 37, 95
snapping into place, 90
storing, 118
title objects, 53
turning into action buttons,
    184
types, 23
ungrouping, 95
See also drawing objects;
    graphic images
Office Assistant
    animating, 18
    changing the display, 18
    getting Help from, 17
    hiding, 17
    style tips, 49
    turning off, 18
Office Clipboard, 118
    copying/pasting data to/
      from, 118
Office programs, maintenance
    options, 21
Office Server Extensions, 234
Office Update Web page, 196
OK button (in dialog boxes), 15
OLE (Object Linking and
    Embedding), 115, 116,
    122–25
OLE objects, opening during
    slide shows, 125
online broadcasts (of slide
    shows), 216, 226–29
    deleting, 227
    setting up and scheduling,
      226–27
    starting, 228
    viewing, 228, 229
online discussions. *See* Web
    discussions

Nicole Jones Pinard

Nicole Jones Pinard has worked in the publishing industry since 1991. In that time, she has written, edited, or managed the creation of over 300 computer books and CD-ROMs. In 1998 she founded Kaleidoscope Communications and is dedicated to bringing bright ideas to the constantly changing field of computer applications. When Nicole isn't working, she takes advantage of New England's colorful seasons with her husband, Adam, and daughter, Madeleine. They enjoy boating, bicycling, and skiing. Nicole also enjoys cooking, hoping to someday take cooking classes in France.

Author's Acknowledgments

First, I would like to thank David Beskeen and Steve Johnson of Perspection, Inc., for giving me the opportunity to write this book. I have a tremendous amount of respect for their expertise, commitment to quality, and downright good spirit. Next, special thanks to Joan and Patrick Carey – I was lucky to follow in your footsteps. Kudos also to the rest of the developmental team: Lisa Ruffolo, developmental editor, and Jane Pedecini, series editor. Finally, I dedicate this book to Adam and Madeleine, without whom I would not have had the courage or motivation to pursue this new chapter in my life.

The manuscript for this book was prepared and submitted to Microsoft Press in electronic form. Text files were prepared using Microsoft Word 97 for Windows 95. Pages were composed in PageMaker for Windows, with text in Stone Sans and display type in Stone Serif. Composed pages were delivered to the printer as electronic files.

Cover Design
Tim Girvin Design

Graphic Layout
David Beskeen

Compositors
Gary Bellig
Tracy Teyler

Proofreader
Jane Pedicini

Indexer
Michael Brackney
Savage Indexing Service

Stay in the *running* for maximum *productivity.*

The answer books for business users of Microsoft® Office 2000. They are packed with everything from quick, clear instructions for new users to comprehensive answers for power users—the authoritative reference to keep by your computer and use every day. THE RUNNING SERIES—learning solutions made by Microsoft.

- RUNNING MICROSOFT EXCEL 2000
- RUNNING MICROSOFT OFFICE 2000 PREMIUM
- RUNNING MICROSOFT OFFICE 2000 PROFESSIONAL
- RUNNING MICROSOFT OFFICE 2000 SMALL BUSINESS EDITION
- RUNNING MICROSOFT WORD 2000
- RUNNING MICROSOFT POWERPOINT® 2000
- RUNNING MICROSOFT ACCESS 2000
- RUNNING MICROSOFT INTERNET EXPLORER 5.0
- RUNNING MICROSOFT FRONTPAGE®
- RUNNING MICROSOFT OUTLOOK® 2000

mspress.microsoft.com